10,000 DEPOSITIONS LATER

THE PREMIER LITIGATION GUIDE FOR SUPERIOR DEPOSITION PRACTICE

JIM GARRITY

ROSS AND RUBIN PUBLISHERS, LLC

10,000 DEPOSITIONS LATER

Ross and Rubin Publishers, LLC

New York, New York

10,000 Depositions Later: The Premier Litigation Guide for Superior Deposition Practice

While all attempts have been made to verify the information provided in this publication, neither the author nor the publisher assumes any responsibility for errors, omissions or contrary interpretations of the subject matter herein.

The views expressed are the personal views and opinions of the author. The reader is responsible for his or her own actions.

Adherence to all applicable laws and regulations, including international, federal, state and local governing professional licensing, business practices, advertising and all other aspects of doing business in the United States, Canada, or any other jurisdiction relating to the practice of law is the sole responsibility of the purchaser or reader. The reader should be governed by the rules and regulations pertinent to the jurisdictions in which they practice. Neither the author nor the publisher assumes any responsibility or liability whatsoever on the behalf of the purchaser or reader of these materials. Any perceived slight of any individual, organization or culture is purely unintentional.

The crux of strategy is in knowing what to do, but also in what not to do.

— Jim Garrity

Strategy without tactics is the slowest route to victory. Tactics without strategy is the noise before defeat.

— SunTzu

Hope is not a strategy.

— Vince Lombardi

CONTENTS

FOREWORD

I am a retired civil and criminal trial judge. I choose not to use my real name or initials for obvious reasons.

This book is a masterclass in deposition practice, based on Jim Garrity's personal battle-tested expertise in cases *like yours.* His experience in thousands of federal and state cases in a multi-state, high-volume practice, provides him the perfect laboratory for testing deposition tactics and strategies. The fact that he actively practices means his insights are fresh and current.

Speaking as a former trial judge, I say this. Your deposition skills will make or break you as a litigator. It will affect your case strength, your ability to settle cases, and your ability to conduct powerful cross-examinations at trial.

You will not gain expertise reading books devoted to

analyses of celebrity depositions, nor from books by lawyers about other lawyer's work. You achieve mastery by learning the results of a world-class expert's strategies based on *thousands and thousands* of depositions. Jim Garrity is that expert.

L.J., retired Trial Judge

PREFACE

I decided to begin creating a series of advanced guides on deposition skills and techniques after reading studies showing that the civil trial in our judicial system is on the verge of complete extinction.

One legal scholar, Professor Marc Galanter, found that about only about one percent of all federal lawsuits now end in a trial. State court lawsuits have similarly fallen off the cliff. One article in a business publication, citing Professor Galanter's studies, was titled "Will There Be A Next Generation of Trial Lawyers?", underscoring the disappearance of the American court trial.

Without question, depositions are the new trials.

Depositions are for most lawyers the only place any witness will ever testify. This means that in most lawsuits, the outcome is decided by deposition testimony.

There are many books for sale about deposition strategies and tactics. So, what hasn't been written already? The answer is, everything.

The books, treatises, and seminars for sale overwhelmingly address the mechanical aspects of depositions. They tell us to organize documents, to mark exhibits as we use them, and to work from an outline to make sure we don't miss anything. These "tips" are, for the most part, instinctive and need not be taught for an exorbitant price. Indeed, most lawyers learned them in a law school trial practice course.

I began to wonder about the backgrounds of those offering up this kind of advice, so I took a look at their backgrounds.

What I found was disappointing, but not surprising. Most authors and speakers have very little actual experience in depositions. I reached that conclusion by first searching the federal case management/electronic case filing database (CM/ECF) for cases in which they've appeared. The majority of them were identified as counsel in *fewer than fifty cases* in their entire career. Most were not involved in high-volume practices or in fields known for frequent trials. Some practice in areas where documents, not depositions, drive the outcome.

Don't believe me? Think of the most experienced litigator you can think of – someone you know, someone you've seen on TV – and search their name in the Advanced Party Search on PACER.gov. (That field retrieves lawyer appearances as well as actual party names.) Shocked by the result? Don't be. Most lawyers, even the most experienced litigators, just aren't hardcore front-line litigators.

Even in fairly large organizations with substantial numbers of trial lawyers, the skill associated with evaluating the need for, and method of conducting, depositions, is lacking. *E.g., Dalton v. Barrett,* 2019 WL 3069856, at *17 (W.D. Mo. July 12, 2019) (federal consent decree requiring training on depositions imposed where evidence showed no depositions were taken in 97% of criminal cases and lawyers lacked basic knowledge about when and how to take them).

My background is different. If you search the CM/ECF database in the two states where I practice, you'll find that I have appeared as chief counsel in more than a *thousand* federal cases. Over my career, my practice has been roughly divided equally between federal and state courts.

If I conservatively estimate that I have appeared in as many state-court cases as I have in federal cases, you can safely conclude that I have appeared as chief counsel in more than two thousand cases. My practice area is high-volume and involves many depositions. The typical case I handle involves between 10 and 25 depositions. I estimate - based on the number of cases I have handled, and the average number of depositions in each - that I have probably taken or defended in excess of 20,000 depositions over my career. The basic math supports that. I originally chose the title for this series out of sheer modesty (and have kept the reference to 10,000 because the publisher does not want me to change the series title at this point).

My goal was not to add another book to the shelf about the mechanics of taking depositions. It was to discuss strategies and techniques you can't find in the rules. Over the course of thousands and thousands of depositions, I've paid attention to what works and what doesn't and made many changes, sometimes almost imperceptible, in the way I approach the examination of witnesses. Over time I learned that some of those changes routinely led to big payoffs.

Some people say that if you focus on the basics, you'll do just fine. I think the opposite. If you're not looking for opportunities in the corners, where no one else is looking, if you're not looking for the micro-advantages that will make a difference in the close cases, and get you across the goal line, you're missing opportunities.

How big are small advantages? Consider this, from some Wall Street traders that recognize the value of searching out every conceivable advantage. A few years ago, a trading group spent almost half a billion dollars to pay for a relatively short underground cable that would transmit trades about *three milliseconds* faster than the cables currently in place.

Three milliseconds is three one-thousandths of a second.

This uptick in speed is so absurdly small as to be imperceptible. But the traders realized that, in a highly competitive field, every conceivable advantage that can be pursued must be pursued. They scrutinized every component of the trading process and had identified even minuscule changes that could make a difference. They overlooked nothing.

This systematic approach to successful investing is the difference between amateurs and pros. Small changes often result in the biggest gains. Professionals always look in the corners for micro-advantages. Professional athletes, once they establish their basic routines, immediately begin looking for ways to improve them.

They devote enormous resources to finding advantages. It may be a slight adjustment to the way they run, the way they throw, the way they hold the bat, hold the club or kick the ball. Once they make those changes, they begin looking for a way to make that change even better. It never stops. Professionals in every occupation know that continued success demands a constant hunt for improvements.

The practice of law is no different.

Princeton University Professor Daniel Kahneman, a Nobel Prize-winning psychologist and economist, contends that the only real way to develop true expertise is to (a) engage in regular practice, and (b) have swift feedback.

But the problem is that a litigator who takes a limited number of depositions each month, and who rarely tries cases, has neither. It is thus impossible for them to try a range of techniques in heavy practice and quickly see the results. My high-volume practice allows me to engage in frequent experimentation, to see over and over the results of my tactics. I see the results after the depositions, in settlement talks, in mediations, and in trial outcomes.

This advanced guide reveals what I know works. You can use these techniques even if your deposition activity is limited. In other words, you can implement the most advanced strategies without the need to devote thirty years in daily litigation warfare.

Try the techniques in this book, and use them often, making your own adjustments to suit your style. If you are hesitant to implement them on a widespread basis, try them individually. You will see noticeable differences in the effectiveness of your examinations.

Some of these techniques will surely draw criticism or objection from opposing lawyers. Often the opposition will be the result of the lawyer's own inexperience. When my son was two years old, he believed our home, which was two stories, was the tallest building ever built. That's because it was the tallest building *he'd* ever seen.

Opposing lawyers who've never encountered the tactics and strategies in this book suffer from the same myopic thinking: if *they've never seen it, it must not be okay*. But many of your adversaries have astonishingly limited experience, so what they've seen is no gauge of anything. Even lawyers in practice for a decade often lack appreciation for the most elemental notions of deposition practice. They think the rule of sequestration applies to depositions. (It does not.) They think you cannot independently audiotape depositions. (You can.) I could go on and on.

Use these techniques aggressively. Stretch them even further than I have. Stand your ground. That's how you win.

Jim Garrity

1

CHIEF FUNCTIONS OF THE DEPOSITION

Covered in This Chapter:

• §1.01 Knowing Your Goals

ll lawyers have goals in the context of depositions. In the broadest sense, lawyers taking depositions want witnesses to fully and completely answer their questions. Lawyers defending depositions want witnesses to do well and be treated fairly.

New lawyers, in particular, have these very basic goals, but not more. Yet there is so much more to be gained from encounters with witnesses and opposing lawyers. Face-to-face encounters with friendly and hostile participants in a lawsuit are gold mines of information gathering, of information defense, and of psychological evaluation. The goal of this book is to help you squeeze every ounce of value out of your depositions. You will see that I focus not just on the testimony and conduct of opposing lawyers while depositions are in progress, but also the *room* where the deposition is taking place, and what's happening in the *hallways* and the *parking lot* outside. Everything that happens on the day of the deposition is a source of information gathering or, if you are defending, information leakage.

I am not suggesting you overthink it, spending weeks or months developing offensive or defensive plans for witnesses. I am only saying you should give conscious thought to your objectives with each witness. Sometimes five or ten minutes is enough if you already have a general sense for the role each witness is likely to have in the case. Often, more reflection is required.

By example, my goals in conducting a deposition include the following:

- **§1.02 Confirm What Witnesses Know**

If I am taking, I want to know everything material that

the witness knows. The key word is *material.* If I've done my homework, I don't need to review the witness' life history. My depositions of most witnesses run 30 to 45 minutes. My depositions of case-critical witnesses generally run one to two hours. It's rare I go longer. These are much shorter than depositions taken by most lawyers.

But the length of a deposition is rarely an indicator of its quality or effectiveness. Sometimes the opposite is true. Long, ponderous depositions are often a sign the lawyer has not prepared in advance or does not know what they are doing. I begin asking substantive questions as soon as I have finished my preliminary instructions to the witness.

I could probably take even shorter depositions, but I do want to spend some time with witnesses to eyeball them and evaluate how they respond when pressed. I need to know how to approach the witness in front of a jury. (This is one reason why I do not allow other lawyers in my firm to cover depositions for me. My success at trial depends heavily on my ability to use the correct tone and measure of attack in front of the jury. I cannot do that if I have never met the witness.

Many law firms I oppose send junior lawyers to all but the depositions of key witnesses. I never do that. I want pretrial eye-to-eye contact with anyone whose testimony might make a difference.)

Sometimes I defend depositions against lawyers who, by lunchtime, still haven't touched the substance of the case. They've wasted three hours on background, on detritus, on trivia. *Why?* Why didn't they use that time, from the moment the deposition began, to dig deep, to go after the witness? Why spend three hours on information found in the interrogatory answers or in documents that no one disputes? To be safe? To avoid criticism that they didn't drill into minutiae?

The actual risk to you is very different. The risk is that you failed to develop testimony on the critical issues. That's your risk. That's where you lose cases.

- **§1.03 Discover New Information**

Many witnesses know more than I could guess in my wildest dreams. They have talked to people outside their normal circle. They have seen documents they wouldn't normally see. They overheard conversations. Or they are an acquaintance of someone quite unexpected. Quite possibly, they might have even gained unauthorized access to information that would be of use to you.

For all the wonderful qualities of trial lawyers, many are inside-the-box thinkers who do not allow for the extraordinary or the unlikely. Professor Kahneman is fond of saying most people, including professionals like lawyers and doctors, assume they already know the core information. Kahneman describes this mindset as "All I know is all there is." And it is in fact hard for people, even very bright people, to accept that they missed something critical, or made serious errors of judgment. But it happens, and often.[1]

So I make it a habit to ask questions of witnesses that I

would also direct to others who are more likely to know the correct answer. You never know. (Honestly - you don't.)

- **§1.04 Assess Case Strengths**

The acid test for evaluating my case often comes when opposing lawyers examine my clients. Opposing lawyers have the greatest incentive to find, exploit and gain concessions about shortcomings. I count on my opposing number to help me properly evaluate my case and help me shore up weaknesses.

By the end of a deposition I am defending, I will quite likely know much of what the opposing lawyer knows. Their questions reveal a great deal. Their questions will tell me where they think their strengths lie, and where they believe my weaknesses lie. Their questions also tell me what they don't know. This is one reason why I generally allow opposing lawyers to question my client first. Their questions will provide me tremendous guidance in conducting my own examinations and in mapping out my case plan.

- **§1.05 Assess Opposing Lawyers**

Whether taking or defending, depositions allow me to gauge the quality of my adversary. If I am taking, I want to see how the opposing lawyer handles rigorous questions and how well or how poorly they defend the witness. I want to know if the opposing lawyer has a good grasp on deposition procedure and, possibly on trial procedure and evidence.

How do the lawyers respond to aggressive questioning of their witnesses? Do they know what objections to make, and do they make them? Are they paying attention?

If I am defending, I want to see how effective my opposing lawyers are. Do they know how to dig down to specifics? Are they just skimming the surface? Do they know how to get facts from a noncompliant witness? Do they let witnesses run over them? Do they know how to phrase questions in an effective way? Are they skilled in pursuing a witness with respect and dignity, or are they abusive? Is their level of knowledge about the case where it should be at this stage?

- **§1.06 Assess the Witnesses**

Depositions are my chance to preview witness candor, polish, resilience, and probable jury appeal. Sometimes I decide that opposing witnesses are very credible and likable in their presentation, and that informs my judgment about the trial. On the other hand, sometimes opposing witnesses come across as true villains. One of the most critical things I gain from a deposition is a read on the witness. When I take a case to trial, I am like the director and producer of a Broadway play. The actors are the witnesses. The jurors are the critics. They may dislike my client. I need to know that.

And I need to know if opposing witnesses are likable; if they come across as truthful even when they are lying; if they come across as dishonest even when telling the truth. I need to know how strong those witnesses are. This is again why I never farm out depositions to others. I gain invaluable insights in this way.

- **§1.07 Discover Missed Claims or Defenses**

Another objective in taking depositions is to decide whether I have missed potential claims or defenses. I use an extraordinarily thorough screening process when I accept representation, but I realize that I can make errors in evaluation. So I never close the door on the possibility that I have missed something. Depositions are an excellent opportunity to confirm that my assessment is sound. And because I generally try to get depositions scheduled and conducted promptly, I am usually well within governing deadlines for amending my pleadings if necessary.

There are many other functions that depositions can serve. This is just a sampling, but it reinforces the fact that they are the single most important component of your case.

2

TOOLS FOR CAPTURING TESTIMONY

Covered in This Chapter:

- *§2.01 Depositions*
- *¢2.02 Examinations Under Oath (EUOs)*
- *§2.03 Affidavits*
- *§2. 04 Picking the Best Tool for the Job*
- *§2.05 Opting to Pass on a Deposition*

This is a book about depositions specifically. But in broader terms, it is about effectively taking testimony to support your case. For this reason, it is important that you consider the best tool for capturing testimony. In most situations, it will be a deposition.

But there are two other possibilities, and I want to talk about them here. One is a sworn statement, commonly referred to as an examination under oath (EUO). The other is a simple affidavit.

Assuming you know who the likely witnesses are, you should actively think about which tool - deposition, EUO, or affidavit - will best serve your needs. All have pluses and minuses. Let's look at each of these choices and the features of each.

§2.01 Depositions

Depositions are the most formal of the three choices. A deposition is a formal examination of a witness, friendly or unfriendly, in the presence of opposing lawyers, party representatives, and possibly others. They require advance notice, they authorize the use of subpoenas to force witness attendance at a time and place of your choosing, and they are conducted pursuant to well-established rules of court. As a practical matter, this is how you'll gather testimony most of the time.

The chief advantages of using a deposition to capture testimony:

- The governing rules and procedures are well-established
- Most lawyers use this approach (sometimes too often, and without thought on the alternatives) and are comfortable with them
- Your staff is likely familiar with the deposition process

- Depositions work well when you can't talk freely to the deponents because (a) they're openly hostile to you, (b) they're represented by counsel, and (c) they hold a position that prevents direct contact
- Deposition testimony is generally admissible in court if the witness is unavailable
- Depositions expose deponents to the sharpest level of examination, a useful test in deciding whether your witnesses can take the heat, or whether this a case you should settle
- You can learn a great deal about the opponent's case by listening to their examination of each witness, especially your client if you're defending. The questions asked by opposing lawyers will reveal information of considerable value to you. What points are they trying to score? What information do they have that you didn't appreciate? What is their case theme?

The chief disadvantages of depositions include the following:

- They're more costly than other forms of capturing testimony
- It's very easy to run up thousands of dollars in deposition costs. Court reporters generally charge from $3.50 to $6.50 a page. Most also charge an "appearance" fee This can run from a single

charge in the range of $50 simply for the reporter showing up. Some appearance fees are per witness or hour. Appearance fees may be even higher if your depositions continue after hours or on weekends. Reporters may add many other fees and charges for "litigation packages," travel and more. If you're defending the case, your client or insurance adjuster may limit your ability to incur deposition-related expenses. If you represent a plaintiff, deposition costs that eat into and reduce your client's share can make it harder for you to settle

- Deposition testimony can weaken your case prematurely. Compared to EUOs and affidavits, depositions are conducted in the presence of, and often by, opposing lawyers. So weaknesses in your case, specifically in your client's testimony, demeanor or presence, is out in the open for all to see
- They can take longer to set up because of the need to coordinate multiple schedules

§2.02 Examinations Under Oath (EUOs)

An examination under oath, commonly referred by the acronym EUO, is simply a sworn examination in the presence of a court reporter. It *resembles* a deposition, but there are major differences. First, it is not conducted pursuant to rules of court. That means you didn't serve a formal Notice of

Taking Deposition on anyone, and you didn't (and couldn't) use a subpoena to ensure the witness' presence. Second, there are no opposing lawyers or others present. It's just you and the witness.

A chief advantage of EUOs over depositions is that you can question and lock down the sworn testimony of witnesses without interference from opposing lawyers. In some cases, I conduct them to bind most of the witnesses before the first formal deposition is even noticed. They can also be taken before a case is filed. Because witnesses are under oath, they have no room to wiggle on you later.

You will often see the term EUO in the context of insurance claims. Insurers take EUOs of their insureds as part of their assessment whether an incident is covered. But EUOs have widespread value and applicability.

The chief advantages of EUOs include the following:

- You can set them whenever convenient for the witness. There's no need to coordinate with opposing lawyers because they're not going to be there.
- You can use them to swoop in, meet with witnesses, and bind them to their testimony before the opposing lawyers do. The fact that you have no obligation to notify the opposing lawyer means you will likely be the first lawyer to question the witness, a substantial advantage
- The product generated by an EUO - the transcript – carries the same weight and credibility as an

actual deposition transcript. Lawyers and judges are conditioned to see court-reporter generated transcripts as reliable accounts of information. Consider this:

- The EUO is taken before a court reporter who captures every word. There can be no doubt that the testimony is that of the witness. Further, the transcript captures everything you say, so there can be no claim of unfair manipulation or intimidation on your part.
- You will ask witnesses at the outset (a) whether they have been told of the questions in advance, or (b) promised anything for their testimony, or (c) were forced to come. Their "no" answers build on the credibility (and will help prevent the witness from turning on you later).
- Because EUOs are overlooked by many, if not most, lawyers, you will typically have the first shot at witnesses. Compare that to what happens when you choose to depose witnesses. Sometimes, opposing lawyers who receive your Notice of Deposition may approach the deponents before the day of deposition and distort your side of the case, turn the witness against you, or intimidate the deponents. That can cause deponents to become reluctant to share all they know. So the value of an EUO is that you can reach out to the witness early and unilaterally, schedule the statement unilaterally,

and conduct the EUO in an environment free of intimidation.

- EUOs are sworn, and so they are eminently more valuable than merely interviewing the witness with traditional pen and pad.
- They are perfect with cooperating witnesses.
- The friendly, low-stress environment of an EUO enhances the odds of quality testimony, versus the disruptive environment of a deposition, where one or more lawyers may be objecting loudly and often
- Once the EUO is done, it can save you the need to depose the witnesses later
- EUOs, taken out of sight and mind of opposing counsel, can lull adversaries into thinking you've done little to prepare. Some adversaries will craft their needs around what they see you doing. The less they see, the less they do. That's a high-risk way to litigate a case, but it is common. Critical deadlines may pass before your opponents realize just how much work you've done. So a side benefit of EUOs is that your opponents may not have invested the time they needed to defeat you. They were scanning the ocean surface looking for your ships. You were in a submarine passing silently underneath.
- EUOs, because they can be conducted even in the absence of a pending case, can be used to resolve claims without the need or expense of a filed case.

Your adversary will see the transcripts as authoritative even if they don't like the contents. An actual EUO transcript of testimony under oath will produce the same lump in the throat for adversaries as an actual deposition transcript

- EUOs can be used in mediations.[1] There are few things more devastating than for an opposing lawyer to retrieve several transcripts from his or her briefcase - none of which the adversary has seen before - and reading some devastating quotes. Your adversary will see that you are reading from a transcript but may have no idea who you are quoting. That can suck the wind out of the sails of the most ardent opponent. It may also severely undermine the confidence of the opposing party representative and insurers. To the extent you wish to keep the identity of the witness anonymous, you can circulate the actual transcript in mediation, after redacting the witness' identity, court reporter information, and the date and time and location of the statement. Even if you opt not to show the adversaries or the mediator the transcript, the fact that you have an actual transcript will carry great weight.
- The use of an EUO to gather witness testimony, as compared to an affidavit, in particular, can protect you from false claims by witnesses that you forced them to testify in a certain way. I am aware of cases where lawyers drafted affidavits in good

faith and had witnesses, typically unrepresented third parties, sign them under oath. Later, when witnesses began to feel the heat from involvement in adversarial legal proceedings, some claimed the lawyer pressured them to make the statements in the affidavit. This can get lawyers in serious trouble. For those reasons, I never prepare affidavits for witnesses. I use EUO's. Once the statement is under way, I always ask witnesses on the record whether they have been promised anything, provided information in advance, or pressured in any way by anyone. I make sure that I get crystal clear responses. That is my insurance policy against future false claims from witnesses who turn on me. In fact, since I began using EUOs, I have never had a witness subsequently claim that their testimony was the product of anything other than their own free will.

- If otherwise properly disclosed, you can use it as an affidavit or even attach it to an affidavit, just as you might a deposition transcript, such as where your affiant gave testimony in a different case and is submitting an affidavit with that transcript attached and incorporated therein. *See Cont'l Cas. Co., Plaintiff v. Fifth/Third Bank, Defendant.*, 2006 WL 8447690, at *3 (N.D. Ohio Mar. 6, 2006) (quoting Moore's Federal Practice and accepting deposition testimony as part of an affidavit).

The chief disadvantages of EUOs include the following:

- Your transcript might not be admissible in an evidentiary hearing or trial in lieu of live testimony if the witness is unavailable. (You can use them to refresh a recollection or to cross-examine a witness, of course, and you can also use them as you would an affidavit in opposition to motions that require evidentiary submissions.) While the possibility that an EUO will leave you without testimony if the witness is unavailable might strike you as reason enough not to use EUOs, I urge a different view. EUOs, like depositions, serve many purposes. Because most cases do not go to trial, even deposition transcripts are rarely used in court. So, save for the one situation where you opted for an EUO instead of a deposition and the witness is now unavailable – a circumstance you can safely foresee most always - the chief functions of testimonial transcripts are served as well by EUOs as by depositions.

Of course, you can make the EUO admissible if the witnesses are also deposed by showing them the EUO during their deposition and asking (a) if it is a true copy of their prior testimony and (b) if their answers are based on their own personal knowledge.

There should be no hearsay problem if the witnesses

admit on the stand that they made the statement and that it was true, thereby adopting the statement and eliminating a hearsay problem. This makes it their present testimony. Even if it somehow counts as hearsay, it can still come in to rebut an express or implied charge of fabrication, or that the witness is testifying from a recent motive to fabricate. See *Botey v. Green et al*, 2018 WL 5985694 (M.D. Penn. Nov. 14, 2018).

- To the extent it is important, your examination of witnesses in an EUO may not be the best test of the witnesses' performance in front of a jury. In a deposition where the witnesses are subject to cross-examination, you will see who holds their ground and who doesn't.
- Judges vary on the issue when and under what circumstances you must disclose the EUO. If it is attorney-client privileged or protected by the work-product privilege, you may have an obligation to disclose it on a privilege log or, in general terms, on a Rule 26 disclosure if you are in federal court. If disclosure is required, you will need to decide – based on the rules in your jurisdiction - at what point you must disclose it in order to use it. After litigating this issue in front of several federal judges, I now disclose these statements on Rule 26 disclosures or appropriate logs, but all I say is something to the effect of, "Sworn statements taken in June 20XX of

witnesses already disclosed to Defendant in Rule 26 disclosures/interrogatories." I do not specifically identify the witnesses. I do not reveal how many I have taken. And I only reveal the month and year so the judge can determine that they were taken in anticipation of, or subsequent to, litigation. In some cases, opposing lawyers have demanded that I turn over the transcripts as if they are somehow entitled to them, which is inexplicable to me. I have never done so. Nor has any judge ever required me to do so. To the contrary, some federal judges have sharply criticized my adversaries for their lack of diligence in pursuing the same opportunities.

- Opposing lawyers may sometimes falsely portray your EUO as a 'secret deposition. Occasionally, in actual depositions, a witness from whom you took an EUO may get confused when asked if they have ever been deposed before. The witness may point and say you took their deposition. Expect the opponent to explode at that point, but I say ignore it. I have had that happen on several occasions and it is of no moment to me. That is because in every EUO I explain the differences between an EUO and a deposition, and I then ask the witnesses if they understand this is not a deposition. All say yes. If necessary, I will produce those pages to a court to erase any doubt. I explain that an EUO is voluntary and that a deposition is

> not. I explain that an EUO is not pursuant to any rule of court, but that depositions are. I explain that because I am taking an EUO, the witness was not served a subpoena, but that if it were a deposition, they would have been. I explain that the witness did not have to come, can get up and leave at any time, and can refuse to answer any question I ask them. I then ask if they understand the difference between what we are doing and a deposition and that what we are doing is not a deposition. All say yes, on the record. One last pointer: If you did serve EUO witnesses with a deposition subpoena, or ever listed them on a deposition notice, make doubly sure you do not take the EUO on the same day - or close to the same day – of their scheduled deposition. This helps avoid claims that you engaged in a bait-and-switch, by serving witnesses with subpoenas and using that to lure them there for an EEO.

§2.03 Affidavits

An affidavit is a written statement by a witness about specific matters. The statement, once signed by the witness under oath, becomes the witness' sworn testimony.

In litigation, affidavits are almost always crafted by the attorney who needs it. The content of the affidavit is also mostly crafted by the lawyer, with input from the witness. But the drafting attorney has a key role in shaping what the affidavit says and how it says it, and must exercise great caution in that role. Lay witnesses will sign affidavits that only loosely approximate what they actually know, perhaps unaware of the lawyer's objectives and the consequences to the affiant of not paying close attention to what the lawyer has them saying.

Other than depositions, affidavits are the most common tool for documenting testimony. They are easy to draft, fast to produce and cost nothing. Unlike depositions, there is no waiting time between the creation of the content and receipt of the final product. Affidavits are particularly convenient when you are up against a deadline, because you can draft the affidavit and file it all within the space of ten or fifteen minutes.

The chief advantages of an affidavit are that they're fast and deadline-friendly; they cost nothing to prepare; you can get right to the point; you can create as many as you need; and you avoid the hassles of setting depositions.

The chief disadvantages of an affidavit are that everyone knows you drafted them, and judges sometimes hold affidavits to a tougher standard. If the affidavit does not clearly show the affiant has personal knowledge, and if the assertions are technically deficient, it may be stricken and leave a gaping hole in your proof. When I say the affidavit "may not clearly show the affiant has personal knowledge," I do not mean you can satisfy the obligation by typing a sentence that says "The affiant has personal knowledge of all matters herein." That is not enough. The affidavit, the content, must provide enough information for the judge to determine that your affiant was actually in a position to have personal knowledge. This is where many affidavits fail. An ambitious drafter includes a generic statement that the witness has personal knowledge, but then goes on to make broad, sweeping factual representations for which there is no hint elsewhere in the affidavit that the witness was in a position to know those facts.

I routinely have my lawyers comb through affidavits looking for technical deficiencies like that.

Careless preparation of an affidavit can cause other problems. Sometimes the urge to score evidentiary points can lead to the drafting of affidavits that contradict the witness' deposition testimony, rendering the affidavit a nullity. Another common technical flaw is where the affidavit ends with a statement that the information is "to the best of my knowledge and belief." Some courts reject this statement as invalidating the entire affidavit. "To the best of my knowledge and belief" could mean that the affiant knows little or nothing.

I can sign an affidavit that says, to the best of <u>my</u> knowledge and belief, the Australian crocodile has the largest head, but I am not saying this is in fact true. I am only telling you what <u>I</u> think, to the best of <u>my</u> knowledge, is true. That will not suffice in the world of affidavits. Judges want affiants to make unqualified factual statements because (1) the evidence is more likely to be reliable, and (2) and unequivocally false statement of fact allows the judge to hold the affiant liable for the misstatement.

Finally, another key risk in drafting affidavits is that the affiant may turn on you. This typically happens when the witness is confronted during cross-examination about the contents of the affidavit. That is occasionally the first the time witness actually looks at what they signed and begin to appreciate the liberties the drafter took.

At that moment, the witness will likely turn on you if you engaged in such behavior. Sometimes they will do that even if you wrote exactly what they told you, if the witness thinks he or she can avoid responsibility by blaming you. This is an embedded flaw in affidavits because it is always a lawyer who writes or types the words.

Absent safeguards, authorship of an affidavit - of someone else's sworn testimony - leaves the lawyer exposed to claims of coercion or threat.

§2.04 Picking the Best Tool for The Job

All three forms of capturing testimony have value and are useful. Which to choose just depends on the situation.

Here are my general rules of thumb in choosing one form or another, but please remember these are just general rules and circumstances may easily alter them.

I use depositions when the witness is represented by counsel, will not cooperate with me, or is likely to be unavailable at trial.

I use EUOs when the rules allow me to contact the witness directly, when the witness is friendly, and when I want to lock witnesses in without interference from opposing lawyers.

I use affidavits when I need to fill a specific gap in my evidence, or when time is limited, or when I need to address minor points by a nominal witness for whom the formality of a deposition is unnecessary.

§2.05 Opting to Pass On a Deposition

The reflexive and understandable instinct of many trial lawyers is to depose most or all disclosed witnesses.

Certainly, it's a safe path because you're less likely to be second-guessed by your client, your partner, or your adjuster if you depose everyone, compared to a decision to pass on some witnesses and later learn they had bombshell testimony against your client.

The fact is, though, it's rare that a witness will have genuinely shocking testimony that you didn't know or at least suspect before depositions. You usually know who the key witnesses are. You usually know what the witnesses will say. The risk of true, unexpected bombshell testimony from an undeposed witness is minimal. So think carefully about routinely deposing everyone who can be deposed just because you can. A superficial game plan can lead you to develop testimony that hurts you or is a complete waste of time and money.

Need reassurance that depositions aren't always necessary? Here's an order by a federal judge where he points out that depositions *aren't even allowed* in federal criminal cases without court permission. The order rejects a lawyer's argument, in an effort to take untimely depositions in a civil case, that denying them would amount to a "due process violation:"

> Finally, the defendant asserts that denying it the ability to depose the doctors will deny it due process. The assertion is both remarkable and clearly unfounded. For most of the nation's history, a party went to trial without deposing anyone. The Federal Rules of Civil Procedure took effect in 1938 and made depositions available in civil cases. In federal criminal cases, however, depositions still are not available—except that a party may depose a witness in "exceptional circumstances." *See* Fed. R. Crim. P. 15. The federal prisons are full of defendants who were convicted and sentenced without being afforded the right to depose a single witness. Some have been put to death. If, as the defendant asserts, a defendant in a civil case has a due process right to depose every person with knowledge—even if the person will not be called as a witness—then surely a defendant in a criminal case has a due process right to depose the government's actual witnesses. This would mean every person in federal prison, or at least every person who went to trial, was unconstitutionally convicted. Just stating the proposition shows how expansive and clearly unfounded it is. There is no constitutional right to depose witnesses generally. Even more clearly, there is no constitutional right to depose persons who might or might not have relevant knowledge and who will not be called as witnesses. And even more clearly still, there is no constitutional right to depose such

a person after the discovery deadline. The defendant's due-process argument is frivolous. [2]

I make a conscious decision in each case about who to depose and who to skip. I ask myself:

- **Should I depose this witness?** Is this someone whose testimony I need to prove an element of my case? Someone whose story I need to lock down through a formal deposition before summary judgment or trial? Someone whose responses will help settlement? Someone who might be unavailable for trial? Someone whose willingness to testify favorably might fade over time? Someone I need to see in person so I can decide how to handle them at trial?
- **Should I avoid deposing this witness?** Is this someone whose story is already committed on paper? Someone whose deposition will necessarily require me to disclose facts and lines of examination I need to keep close to the vest until summary judgment or trial - such that I might cause the adversary to prepare more robustly against me? Is this someone who will learn from mistakes made in deposition and become more formidable at trial?

If I've learned one thing after taking more than 20,000 depositions, it's that adversaries often misjudge the essence of my case when they only have the individual pieces - the interrogatories, the documents, and other mandatory disclosures. The true shape of my case becomes apparent from my *synthesis* of the pieces through my deposition examinations - the people I choose to question, and the questions I ask them. It's the *synthesis* that reveals my thinking. A box containing a 100-piece jigsaw puzzle contains 100 separate pieces of information, but it means nothing until it's largely assembled.

So it is with interrogatories, documents, and other disclosures. Those are puzzle pieces. They're not the assembled view. I now pass on the deposition of witnesses where I'll gain little and reveal lots. Sometimes I don't need to depose specific witnesses because I know what they'll say and I'd need to reveal too much to opposing lawyers to conduct the deposition properly. So don't be nervous about choosing an EUO or affidavit. Much can be lost from an indiscriminate deposition plan, one where you reflexively depose everyone just because that's what others would do.

~

3

DEPOSITION SCHEDULING ISSUES

Covered in This Chapter:

- *§3.01 Who Goes First?*
- *§3.02 Scheduling Obstruction by Opponents*
- *§3.03 How Much Notice is "Reasonable"?*
- *§3.04 Deposition Locations*
- *§3.05 Timing Your Depositions*
- *§3.06 Before or After Paper Discovery*
- *§3.07 Order of Witnesses*
- *§3.08 After Discovery Ends, For Use At Trial*
- *§3.09 Before Suit is Filed; During An Appeal*
- *§3.10 Exceeding Deposition Numerosity Limits*
- *§3.11 Out-of-Jurisdiction Depositions*
- *§3.12 Never Let Opposing Lawyers Hijack Your Deposition Plan or Needs*

Scheduling depositions should be the least of your worries, at least in theory. But issues do surface, and it is useful to touch on them.

For example, there can be disputes about who goes first, about the physical location where depositions will occur, and about how many you are permitted to take. I do my best to work out disputes like this because judges do not want to get involved.

I have seen orders, and you might have, too, where the judges made their disdain quite clear. In one highly-publicized instance – search online for "rock paper scissors lawyers" – a federal judge forced lawyers who were bickering over the location of upcoming depositions to meet on the steps of the courthouse and play the child's game of rock, paper, scissors. The winner, the judge said, could choose the location.

§3.01 Who Goes First?

In most state-court jurisdictions, depositions can begin as soon as all parties have appeared in the case, either *pro se* or through counsel. In federal court, the rules often forbid depositions before the parties have met, worked out a schedule, and obtained approval once the court issues its scheduling order. Some federal judges now issue an Initial Scheduling Order that immediately authorizes the commencement of discovery.

The federal rules no longer dictate priority in taking

depositions to one side or another. That disappeared from the rules around 1970. Most state courts do not, either, but check the rules in your jurisdiction to make sure. Some - many, most? - lawyers will dig their heels in and insist on going first. But that's a personal preference, an issue for discussion and negotiation, not a rule-based one.

And who goes first isn't even determined by who issues the notice first. I could issue the first notice in January setting depositions for September. But that doesn't limit you from taking depositions before September. Otherwise, the first-noticing lawyer could issue notices for dozens of depositions and delay you forever. So there's no priority and no set order.

On the other hand, if you have a specific reason for taking depositions first, or perhaps for *not* going first, you can reach an agreement with the opposing lawyer, and then seek court intervention if needed. Under the federal rules, specifically Rule 26(d)(3), the court can order that discovery take place in a certain order. But I caution you that before you seek a court ruling on that, you should have an extraordinarily compelling reason for doing so. It's not something for ordinary feuds.

Indeed, most judges will decline to set a priority absent a powerful showing for doing so. *E.g., Eckweiler v. Nisource Inc*, 2018 WL 6011872 (N.D. Indiana Nov. 16, 2018) (declining to set priority). But if the opposing lawyer refuses to cooperate and you have good cause to propose a specific deposition order, by all means, file the appropriate motion and outline your reasons.

§3.02 Scheduling Obstruction by Opponents

When I first began practicing, more experienced lawyers would sometimes tell me they would not agree to any depositions until paper discovery, interrogatories, and document requests had been exchanged. I fell for that. And a few times, I got burned, because deadlines approached (and in one case passed me by) while I sat idly, hoping the opposing lawyer would eventually agree to set them.

- ***The Obligation to Move the Case Is Yours***

You can't do that. Once you identify your discovery needs, you must press ahead. In the situations above where I agreed to wait, judges actually criticized me for allowing deadlines to pass. Their view was that it was my obligation to accomplish my discovery needs, and if an opposing lawyer did not cooperate, I needed to press ahead.

Fortunately, I learned that lesson early in my career, and I never again tolerated delays in scheduling. If an opposing lawyer does not want early depositions, and assuming this does not prejudice my case, I will still insist on setting them, but perhaps a bit further out than I might have otherwise.

But I still set them. And I generally will not move or reset my depositions once they are set. You should do the same. The obligation to protect your client and to accomplish all your discovery needs is yours and yours alone. All of us encounter aggressive or obstructive lawyers on occasion, and when we do, our obligation is to keep our heads down and focus on our needs and the deadlines.

This is true even when the opposing lawyer is asking for delays because of personal convenience.

For example, I have seen situations where a lawyer will, after agreeing to a set number of months for discovery, then serve a notice saying they be unavailable for some extended period for personal vacation. If you have a relatively brief discovery period, that may cause you problems.

Some judges have ruled that unilateral notices of unavailability are not good cause for blocking off unusually long segments of the discovery phase. Those judges inform that such notices do not *ipso facto* halt discovery, including depositions. *E.g., Leitzke v. Nicole,* 2016 WL 1687963 (W. D. Wash. Apr. 27, 2016) (denying plaintiff's motion to bar use of deposition taken after plaintiff served "Notice of Unavailability" for six days in one month and the entirety of the following month; court said reasonable notice is usually at least five days and that "Notices of absence by counsel have no legal significance in the determination of reasonableness.").

I do my best to work with lawyers and to extend professional courtesies. I do not suggest otherwise to you. But if opposing lawyers have agreed on a specific start and end date for discovery, and thereafter serve notice that significant portions of the agreed period are effectively unusable, I am more likely to schedule depositions and insist the lawyer make arrangements for someone to appear on his or her behalf.[1]

- ***Five Requests for Dates is Eminently Reasonable***

When a lawyer is not cooperating in setting depositions, I ask my scheduler to send an email making clear that we are going to ask five more times, and that after the fifth we will set the depositions unilaterally. She is upbeat and professional, but she tells them without equivocation what will happen. We will ask five times, and after the fifth, our depositions will be noticed.

Five isn't a magic number. You could do more, or probably a few less. But it is enough that judges will support my unilateral scheduling. I asked myself, "What number of good-faith efforts would lead a judge to unquestionably rule that the number was good-faith and then some?" Five seemed to meet that test.

You cannot allow time to pass, because the failure to accomplish your discovery belongs to you.

- ***What About Ultra-Inconvenient Dates?***

What if your opponent insists (or unilaterally sets depositions) on especially inconvenient dates? Weekends? Holidays? Or even holiday weekends? The plaintiff corporation in *Cambrian Sci. Corp. v. Cox Comm., Inc.*, 79 F. Supp. 3d 1111, 1119 (C.D. Cal. 2015) did exactly that - set depositions on Saturday, July 6 - smack dab in the middle of the extended July 4 weekend. A federal district judge cited this tactic in an order discussing what the judge said were numerous unreasonable litigation tactics.

If you encounter this kind of scheduling tactic, ask yourself whether (a) there was a legitimate emergency justifying it, (b) whether it was done to avoid great inconvenience by the deponent, or (c) whether it was done because of an imminent critical deadline. If none of these circumstances exist, you're on solid ground for seeking a protective order to force your opponent to choose a new date.

- ***Requests to Reschedule Depositions***

Sometimes your opponent might ask you to reschedule previously-agreed and noticed dates. They may say the witness(es) aren't available. Perhaps the lawyers themselves have a conflict, or have medical needs that prevent them from attending. Maybe the original lawyers have left the firm.

Now what?

Now you need to be professional, courteous, and *careful.* It's important to cooperate in scheduling matters. But it's also important to ensure your discovery needs are met. Ask yourself the following questions:

- Is there enough time left for you to reset and conduct the depositions without adversely affecting your discovery strategy? Do you need to complete these depositions before taking the next round?
- Is the request in good faith? Or is this a tactic?

Does the explanation make sense? How long ago were the depositions noticed? Why now?

- Did the opposing lawyers immediately offer replacement dates? Or are they merely saying they'll do "everything they can" to come up with new dates? When? Why don't they have new dates now?
- Is there a discovery or other key deadline in place? Is there a pending dispositive motion against you?

As a general rule, I do not agree to release existing deposition dates unless and until I have a binding commitment to new dates that meet my needs. That's my only leverage to force opponents to promptly commit to new dates.

§3.03 How Much Notice is "Reasonable"?

I generally schedule depositions months in advance. That gives me time to get other discovery accomplished, to gather information from third parties, and to take EUOs from appropriate witnesses. So I rarely get into disputes over the reasonableness of my scheduling efforts.

But what's the least amount of time you can get away with between issuing the notice (and serving subpoenas if needed) and the actual date of deposition?

My survey of courts, state and federal, around the country suggests that fourteen days is a good *general* rule of thumb for setting depositions quickly, absent other factors. That is likely to keep you out of hot water with most all courts. There are always exceptions - one court held a single day's notice was enough under the circumstances - but that will not fly most of the time.[2]

Why do I recommend fourteen days? Because lesser periods between notice and deposition will put you into a murky zone where some judges will disagree that notice was reasonable. Fourteen is obviously enough in virtually all situations.

The federal judge in *Leitzke,* cited in the section above on refusals to cooperate, said five or more days is reasonable. Another federal judge held that six days was patently insufficient - so insufficient the the recipient could just ignore it. *Parks v. Louisiana-Pacific*, 2019 WL 166559 (W.C. N. Carolina Jan. 10, 2019) (six days held insufficient, particularly where two of those days were not business days). In *Parks* the judge deemed the deposition notice a nullity because six days did not qualify as "proper notice" under FRCP 37(d)(2).

The obvious lesson is that when you submerge into the ten-day-or-less zone, you might just find yourself in dangerous waters. And when navigating in that zone, note that judges will consider whether your five days included weekends or holidays.

There are probably many situations where you can schedule depositions on short notice - less than fourteen days, as I personally define "short notice." The witness may be willing to appear, and the opposing lawyer may be willing to appear. So as with everything else associated with depositions, the correct answer about the minimum notice required in a specific situation is "It depends." But under normal circumstances, I recommend that lawyers allow at least fourteen days between service of the notice and date of the deposition itself.

Of course, if you are noticing a party's deposition *duces tecum,* which requires an opposing party's witness to bring documents, you are required under court rules to allow the party as much time between the notice and the actual deposition as it would have to respond to a request for production. In other words, as to parties, you cannot use a deposition *duces tecum* as a device to shorten the time your adversary has to respond to document requests.

The rules are different for non-party witnesses. You are not required to give them the full thirty days to gather documents. But the notice still has to be "reasonable" under the circumstances. Thus, if you are setting a deposition for non-party witnesses and demanding they bring documents, you should consider the amount of time the witness will reasonably need to gather those documents. It is what's reasonable *under the circumstances.*

§3.04 Deposition Locations

Another common battle between lawyers centers on where the depositions will take place. Your office? Their office? The offices of one of the parties?

[Note: This discussion presumes deponents are in the jurisdiction where the case is pending, which is the norm in

most cases. For an excellent discussion of location when a deponent (particularly a party) is elsewhere, see DeepGulf, Inc. v. Moszkowski, 330 F.R.D. 600, 611 (N.D. Fla. 2019) (cataloguing 32 recognized factors courts consider in resolving location disputes)].

You can waste valuable time and money fighting over location. I generally do not care where depositions take place. I will not tolerate misconduct or intimidation in any deposition, so if the opposing lawyers want to depose my client in their offices, that is fine.

I know this is heresy for many lawyers. I just think it shouldn't matter most of the time. As I mentioned above, judges are intolerant of petty disputes, and disputes over location usually fall into this category.

This assumes there is nothing unusual about the proposed location. Is the adversary proposing somewhere likely to stir specific emotions, such that it would be embarrassing or traumatic? *E.g., Dorkowski v. Pensyl, et. al*, 205 WL 8168071 (M.D. Penn. 2005) (court, considering "appropriate adjustment of the equities," refused to force plaintiffs in wrongful arrest case to depose arresting officers at police station, saying nature of claims and parties' relationship are a factor in choosing deposition location).

Is there something about the proposed location that would otherwise make your client uncomfortable? Is it in a location that might cause you and your client unnecessary expense and inconvenience?[3] One that reasonably poses a threat of one kind or another, or that is otherwise inappropriate for depositions?

Over my career, I have taken depositions in a wide range of locations: factories, hotel conference rooms, in the storage room of a peanut museum, and early one January morning in an ice-cold cocktail lounge that had no electricity. (The dingy, rural motel told us over the phone that we would be in their "conference room." Indeed. I do not doubt that many a discussion had been held right where I sat, but I doubt the participants were under oath, or sober.) But it worked out. Virtually nothing will distract me from the mission at hand.

Other considerations for the deposition location may include the following:

- Is it going to be too hot? Too cold?
- Is it too noisy?
- Are there other activities scheduled near the room of the deposition location that will interfere with the witness? Construction? Foot or vehicle traffic?
- Are there suitable places at the deposition location for conducting private conferences with your witness? Can you trust that those places are secure?
- Is the deposition taking place in a room that has glass walls, such that your witness may be distracted by friends, acquaintances or strangers passing by?

- Is there an appropriate table at which to sit? Does the table place the opposing lawyer and attendees too close to the deponent? Too far from each other?
- Is there Wi-Fi for your computer? Cell service? Are there accessible electrical outlets?

If you are unfamiliar with the proposed location, assume nothing before agreeing to it. Ask specific questions so you are familiar with all facets of the environment. The onus is on you to ensure the location is appropriate. Once you agree, you're likely stuck with it.

If you have legitimate reasons to dispute the location, and cannot reach agreement with the party who set it, you must seek a protective order under Rule 26(c). You cannot just fail to show up.

Rule 37(d)(2) makes plain that failing to appear is not excused unless you have a pending motion for a protective order. *See Bernstein v. BMW of North America,* 2019 WL 3207789 (N.D. Cal. Jul. 16, 2019) (sanctioning defense lawyer for insisting on different location for deposition and for failing to show up). You should also file your motion as soon as practical, in order to avoid claims that you waited until the last minute simply as a stratagem to thwart discovery.

§3.05 Timing Your Depositions

Generally, your depositions should not take place until you have completed other discovery appropriate to your examination preparations. That includes service of, and receipt of responses to, interrogatories, document requests, and request for admissions. You may also want to build in time to allow for court intervention if you believe the discovery responses will be deficient, such as if you know the opposing lawyer always serves responses full of unfounded objections. In a normal case, I will generally schedule depositions three to five months out. This allows me ample time to ask the court to address frivolous objections, protective orders, and other problems. I don't want to take depositions while the fight over deficient discovery responses is still under way.

I may also take depositions in blocks, so that my knowledge and examinations sharpen in subsequent rounds as I gather information.

§3.06 Before or After Paper Discovery

In some cases, I take depositions before I serve paper discovery. This is because I want to catch the witnesses off-guard, before their lawyers have zeroed in on the key issues.

We know that when we serve discovery, it will be the opposing lawyers who review it, meet with the clients, and draft the responses. The service of highly-focused discovery requests may force your opposing numbers to become better versed with the case than they might have otherwise been prior to the depositions. Questions you pose, and the documents you ask for, reveal your thoughts about what is important. That, in turn, will alert your opponent to the need to prepare their witnesses for a specific line of questioning in deposition.

So if I have reason to believe an opponent might not be as well prepared if I've not signaled my views ahead of time, I may take depositions without having served paper discovery.

§3.07 Order of Witnesses

The order in which you take depositions is also a timing-related concern. Should you go after the small fish first, in order to close doors through which bigger fish might try to escape?

Or should you depose the most critical witnesses first, to prevent them from being informed by the testimony of others? Alternatively, is there a reason to schedule specific witnesses later *precisely* so their testimony will be informed by the testimony of prior witnesses or from documents you obtain?

There is rarely a bright-line answer to these questions. It is just something to think about. Many lawyers start with lesser witnesses to develop a framework for examining major players. Deposing the most important witnesses first, in general, may deprive you of that framework. Peripheral witnesses can provide that – the basic details about how things work, who does what, where to find information.

Sometimes you'll need that information to get the most out of your key witnesses. In one reported case, a party opted to take a key witness early in the case. Later, that witness submitted an affidavit that contained much more detail than the witness could provide in deposition. The judge, in deciding whether the affidavit was at odds with the deponent's deposition testimony, held that it was not, simply because his deposition was taken early, before he became aware of the additional facts. *See Munoz v. County of Orange, et. al.* 2008 WL 11422042 (C.D. Cal. Mar. 6, 2008).

I do not have hard and fast rules about who gets deposed in what order. This is something I assess case by case.

§3.08 After Discovery Ends, For Use At Trial

In some jurisdictions and with some judges, you may be allowed to take "trial depositions." These are generally depositions where you plan to read the deposition testimony to the jury in lieu of a live appearance by the witness.

You may have learned, for example, that a particular witness is not available for trial, and that your deposition examination is not suitable for reading to a jury. Or perhaps you held back on your blockbuster cross-examination, hoping to surprise the witness at trial. Maybe the witness is ill or aged and may not live to see the start of the trial.

Some trial or scheduling orders specifically provide for post-discovery trial depositions. If you foresee the need to conduct discovery depositions and then, for specific witnesses, to conduct a formal trial deposition after discovery closes, be sure your scheduling order provides for it. Not all judges will approve such requests.

You must be familiar with the scheduling or trial orders, and familiar with your assigned judge's preferences. If your jurisdiction does not specifically provide for trial depositions after discovery has closed, consider filing an appropriate motion. Under most court rules, many depositions can be read at trial even if taken during the discovery process, so if you are foreclosed from a trial deposition, you are not completely out of luck.

You may see references in some reported decisions to *"de bene esse"* depositions. This is a fancy phrase for a trial deposition – one specifically intended to replace live testimony at trial.

Because of rule amendments, most courts do not use this term anymore and do not treat such depositions differently than any other.

In fact some courts have specifically said that *de bene esse* depositions, like depositions taken for discovery purposes, cannot be conducted after the close of discovery absent extenuating circumstances. *See e.g., Kalitta Air, L.L.C. v. Cent. Texas Airborne Sys., Inc.,* No. C 96-2494 CW, 2004 WL 7339839 (N.D. Cal. Aug. 10, 2004) (noting some jurisdictions allow "trial depositions" after discovery closes, but that rules make no such distinction and courts allowing it do so as matter of discretion in managing discovery); *Broker Genius, Inc. v. Seat Scouts LLC, et al.,* No. 17CV08627SHSSN, 2018 WL 6242226 (S.D.N.Y. Nov. 29, 2018).

§3.09 Before Suit is Filed; During an Appeal

There will be situations where you must depose a witness before a lawsuit has been filed. You might be the plaintiff's counsel and have concluded you are not quite ready to file. Or you might be the defendant's counsel and you know a lawsuit is coming. You also know there are important witnesses who might not be around when the action is commenced. They may be in poor health, moving to another country, or about to be deployed to combat.

And there will be situations where a lawsuit was filed but dismissed by the court before depositions were taken. The plaintiff is now appealing. So both sides know that the case may be revived, and the absence of key witnesses is a major concern.

The rules provide for the possibility of taking depositions in both situations.

In federal court, the basis for doing so can be found in Rule 27, titled Depositions to Perpetuate Testimony. Subsection (a) applies to situations before a lawsuit has been filed. Subsection (b) governs requests for depositions while a matter is on appeal.

If you find yourself in one of these situations, the justifications you will assert to gain court approval are similar, and they will typically involve probable witness unavailability or the loss/destruction of evidence. Those are the grounds to assert.

It is essential, in filing your papers, to provide the court with as much information as possible. This includes detailed explanations of the circumstances, of the roles of the witnesses, and of your proposed examination topics. You should not assume a ruling in your favor is a lock. You should assume the opposite. Courts are leery about allowing lawyers to compel others to appear for examination under oath when there is presently no basis for doing so.

Even if you are allowed to conduct limited depositions, be mindful that the judge might not allow you the same leeway as you have during discovery in a pending case. At least one court has specifically held that depositions under Rule 27 are more limited than a Rule 30 deposition. Its theory was that Rule 30 depositions operate under the broad and general language of Rule 26(b)(1) ("Parties may obtain discovery regarding any matter ... which is relevant to the subject matter involved in the pending action.") *Ash v. Cort*, 512 F.2d 909, 911 (3d Cir. 1975).

Rule 27 depositions do not. So you may be restricted in what you can ask in a perpetuation deposition. This is why it is critical that you outline the circumstances and the role of the witness. You should consider submitting an affidavit, as counsel, and you should also consider affidavits from others who can attest from personal knowledge the role of the witnesses you seek to depose under Rule 27.

Rule 27 outlines the procedures to follow, including the filing of a petition in the appropriate district court and jurisdiction.

§3.10 Exceeding Deposition Numerosity Limits

Federal procedural rules impose a limit of ten depositions per party. Your jurisdiction may impose similar limits. But what if you need more, or substantially more?

There are a few ways to persuade a judge to allow more than the default number.

Argue the obvious: there are more than ten relevant

witnesses. Show the court that there are legitimately more than ten relevant witnesses, and that the default limitation will hamper prosecution of your case.

Critical to this showing, however, is that your first ten depositions were well-chosen. Any motion you file asking a court for more depositions *must* include a discussion of the depositions thus far, and why each of those was necessary. Judges are less likely to approve a request to exceed the ceiling if you wasted the slots you were originally allowed.

Argue newly-discovered evidence. Show that you have newly-discovered evidence that justifies more depositions, or the redeposition of a prior deponent.

Point out that you made use of a Rule 30(b)(6) deposition first to gather as much information as possible before choosing your remaining nine depositions. Taking the deposition of a corporate representative first often helps clarify who knows what, and can make your remaining deposition choices obvious. I have successfully argued for additional depositions by showing that my first step was to proceed under Rule 30(b)(6), to make sure that my remaining witness selections were as precise as possible. This helped avoid criticism that I wasted some slots by deposing the wrong people, even if I'd had a good-faith reason for choosing them.

Argue that your adversary's disclosures or discovery responses forced you to waste prior deposition slots. Still another argument may be that Rule 26 disclosures (or interrogatory answers or document responses) served by your opponents were deceptive or poorly drafted, causing you to waste deposition slots on unnecessary witnesses. Courts have been receptive to this argument. *E.g., Milam v. Ranger Ins. Co.*, 2006 WL 8436494 (W. D. Okla. 2006)

Argue that you need them to authenticate documents or other evidence. The need to authenticate documents is recognized as a basis for additional depositions. This is particularly true where there are multiple entities producing documents in your case, and where there is no agreement on authenticity between the parties. *E.g., A. Farber and Partners, Inc., v. Garber*, 2006 WL 8439939 (C.D. Calif. Mar. 22, 2006)

If experts are involved, argue that expert witnesses are outside the ten-deposition limit. Some courts have said experts should not count toward the default limit. This seems to make sense, but it is not explicitly addressed or resolved by the rule. *Safeco Ins. Co. of Am. v. City of Jacksonville, Fla.*, No. 3:08-CV-338-J-25JRK, 2011 WL 13176635, at *1 (M.D. Fla. Apr. 20, 2011). For a nice motion summarizing the argument in favor of deeming experts outside ten-deposition limit, *see Narushka v. R.J. Reynolds Tobacco Co.*, 2012 WL 1930780 (M.D. Fla. Apr. 9, 2012); *see also Royal Bahamian Ass'n Inc v. QBE Ins. Corp.*, 2010 WL 3003914 (S.D. Fla. July 29, 2010) (declining to address issue but finding movant showed its use of the ten prior depositions was prudent and that additional depositions were justified).

§3.11 Out-of-Jurisdiction Depositions

Scheduling, noticing and taking depositions in other jurisdictions, as well as serving associated subpoenas, requires a bit more work, although it is not as complicated as some think. It's just different.

- ***In U.S. Federal and State Courts***

The specifics about whether and precisely how to take depositions, and to serve subpoenas, outside your jurisdiction beyond the scope of this material. The chief reason is that there are almost a dozen federal circuits, almost one hundred federal court districts, and hundreds of state and intra-state court jurisdictions. The best I can do is to provide an overview to get you started.

First, scheduling depositions and serving document subpoenas is a simple process if you are in federal court and seek to take depositions and obtain documents within the United States. Rules 30 and 45 both have well-established procedures. Rule 4, which deals with service, may come into play as well. With that three-pack of rules, you should be able to determine your needs quickly.

If you are in state court and wish to take depositions outside your state, the procedures may be different. There are uniform acts which should help speed the process and with which you will need to become familiar. These include the Uniform Foreign Deposition Act (UFDA) and the Uniform Interstate Depositions and Discovery Act (UIDDA). Your jurisdiction has likely adopted one of these two uniform acts.

You should be able to determine the correct procedure with a few Internet searches and a careful review of governing statutes in the jurisdiction where you plan to take depositions, as well as in your own jurisdiction to determine whether there are procedures that your legislature adopted in coordination with a uniform act.

For additional information, there are additional resources at no cost online. *See Out-of-State Subpoenas: Compelling an Out-of-State Non-Party Witness to Give Testimony or Produce Records at A Deposition* (available free online), by the Interstate Deposition Subpoena Service, Inc. (2015); *What Is A Commission to Take An Out of State Deposition*, www.CompellingDiscovery.com (Nov. 3, 2016); *Tips For Taking An Out-Of-State Deposition* (free online), American Bar Association Young Lawyers Division, The 101 Practice Series: Breaking Down The Basics, www.abanet.org/yld/101 (2007); *Deposing Nonparties In States Other Than Where Your Case Is Pending*, by Adam Reich, American Bar Association Section Of Litigation, Fall 2014, Vol. 5, No. 1 (free online).

- ***Outside the United States***

While the thought of learning how to conduct depositions and serve document requests outside your own country, wherever you may be, may trigger a bout of brain fog, there are uniform acts adopted by most countries that streamline the process for countries where you are most likely to be taking foreign depositions.

Again, the number of variations here are endless. Further, there are regular changes to the procedures in each country, so anything I write beyond this overview is likely to be out of date by the time this book hits the shelves.

But I can provide some basic starting points.

First, check to see whether the country where your depositions will take place is a signatory to the Hague Convention, more formally known as the Hague Convention on the Service Abroad of Judicial and Extrajudicial Documents. The United States and roughly fifty countries are parties to this agreement. If the country where you seek to conduct discovery is a signatory under the Hague Convention, that pact provides the exclusive method through which service of process can be effected on a deponent residing within that nation.

There are a few other sources you should know about and evaluate. First on your list will be an international treaty known as the Hague Evidence Convention. Further, review Rule 4, which outlines the service of documents outside the United States. Finally, be sure to review Rule 28, which addresses the deposition of witnesses outside the United States. For more resources in general, *see Discovery in Other States and Countries*, Meenu Sasser, The Florida Bar, Business Litigation CLE Series (available on Westlaw) (9th Ed. 2017); *Interstate Discovery Chart* (available on Westlaw), Practical Law Litigation USA & Federal (2018).

- ***Tips for Depositions in Other Jurisdictions***

Apart from rules and procedures governing depositions and document requests (including subpoenas) in other jurisdictions, there are ways to minimize the inconvenience and delays associated with such efforts.

- ***Easiest: Seek Consent from the Participants***

First seek consent of the parties, of the deponents, and of persons or entities from whom you seek documents. Simple consent avoids virtually every obstacle and process that will otherwise get in your way.

- ***Next Best: Plan Long in Advance***

If you can't get consent, plan ahead. *Far ahead.* There are a number of hoops to jump through. And you may have substantial opposition from the court, from opposing parties, from the target of your deposition or document efforts, or from government officials in the jurisdiction where you seek to conduct discovery. So if you don't have consent, start the process as soon as discovery opens, certainly as soon as you have an inkling that you must do so.

This is just a matter of bulletproofing your discovery plan, by planning ahead and by having several alternatives. In this setting, the backup plan for your backup plan needs a backup plan. If the chosen path does not work, you must be able to switch quickly to an alternative, and continue working through alternatives until you achieve your objective.

All litigation is at best an unpredictable science. You should build resilience and robustness into all critical phases of your case, but particularly those phases that require you to operate under someone else's rules.

If there is a local governmental authority where you'll be taking depositions, such as a local judicial office, call them for insight and guidance. Many clerks' offices will say they cannot give legal advice, but once you assure them that isn't what you seek, they will usually share invaluable insights that cut through obstacles.

§3.12 Never Let Opposing Lawyers Hijack Your Deposition Plan or Needs

One last thought about setting depositions, and it's this: Never let opposing lawyers commandeer your deposition plan or schedule. Some will try.

One lawyer I ran into early in my career routinely sent emails, once I identified the witnesses I planned to depose, saying that "we" could set his depositions for X date, that "we" would set mine the next day, that my depositions of his witnesses needed to be set in a particular order (for one reason or another) - on and on.

At first I thought he was just being efficient and helpful. After another case or two, I started to believe he was just very busy and trying to pin things down. After four or five cases, I realized he was simply hijacking the entire deposition process for his benefit. First, he was setting a very tight schedule so I couldn't serve discovery to capitalize on what I'd learned after his depositions, because my depositions were the very next day. Second, he was pushing a particular order so his key witnesses would know what others said before they were deposed. It prevented me from using surprise to my advantage.

If you're going to maximize the value of your depositions, it's important to develop your own plan, independent of your adversaries. You don't need to be disrespectful. When your opposition tells you "the plan" for depositions, you can respectfully say you'll make sure the depositions they need get set, but that you haven't worked through your needs yet and so yours will be set separately. Leave it at that.

This kind of issue also arises when your opposing counsels are from other cities or states. They naturally want to group all the depositions together, both for strategic reasons and for (their) convenience as well. Again, while I take pains to be cooperative and to extend professional courtesies whenever possible, I will not agree to a deposition plan that puts me at a disadvantage. If my client's best interests require opposing counsels to travel twice, so be it. Certainly, parties appreciate that hiring lawyers far removed from the jurisdiction is likely to negatively impact matters of cost and convenience. My clients certainly do, when I am hired to represent them in distant jurisdictions, and I expect that I may not be able to negotiate a schedule entirely favorable to me.

So be respectful, courteous and professional, as long as it does not compromise your client's needs.

4

SUBPOENAS

Covered in This Chapter:

Subpoenas are a critical tool in conducting discovery. They have the force of a court order, and sanctions generally follow a violation of their terms.

But because they have such power, there are consequences to you and your case if you misuse them.

In one case, a federal judge barred the use of a deposition

that was facilitated by the lawyer's improper use of a subpoena. The court said that the lawyer knowingly issued an invalid subpoena, compelled a non-party witness to travel further than the rules allow, and subpoenaed documents without first providing the opposing lawyer with a copy of the subpoena.

As among these violations, the judge seemed particularly incensed that the issuing lawyer exaggerated the non-party witness' obligations to persuade the witness to comply with the subpoena. *See DirectTV, LLC v. Spina*, 2016 WL 11458295 (S.D. Indiana Mar. 13, 2016) (ECF Doc. 57).

§4.01 Subpoenas to Parties

The rules governing the issuance of subpoenas to another party are fairly straightforward, and I see little confusion among lawyers about their use. But I will offer two practical observations.

First, you cannot use subpoenas to shorten the time a party would otherwise have to respond to discovery requests. In other words, if the opposing party has thirty days to respond to your document request, you cannot serve a subpoena, with or without a deposition, and demand production in less time.

Second, consider subpoenaing opposing party witnesses even if the adversary agrees to produce them. This simple step can eliminate a lot of nonsense. Why? Because if you have properly served a subpoena, the witness cannot avoid attendance without seeking court intervention.

I grew weary of lawyers who promised they would produce all of the currently-employed defense witnesses, only to hear on the eve of depositions that one witness or another "is on sabbatical," "is at a conference," or has some other excuse preventing them from attending. If you didn't subpoena the witness, you will likely need to reschedule.

Serving a subpoena on deposition witnesses, including current employees of a party, puts the heavy burden of avoiding the deposition on the witness. Otherwise, the burden and mess of their non-attendance fall on you. My experience is that judges don't particularly care if an opposing lawyer has promised to produce a witness and did not. Lawyers can come up with great excuses why the witness just could not come. In the absence of a subpoena, you lose a lot of leverage in these fights.

Another reason I subpoena witnesses is to provide them protection in jurisdictions that offer anti-retaliation protection to subpoenaed witnesses.

In such jurisdictions, the deponents will have their own cause of action if their employer punishes them for their deposition testimony. To illustrate, in one of the states where I practice, the subpoenaed witness statute reads as follows:

> "*Termination of employment of witness prohibited.*—A person who testifies in a judicial proceeding in response to a subpoena may not be dismissed from employment because of the nature of the person's testimony or because of absences from employment resulting from compliance with the subpoena. In any civil action arising out of a

> violation of this section, the court may award attorney's fees and punitive damages to the person unlawfully dismissed, in addition to actual damages suffered by such person."

Even if you do not generally subpoena witnesses under the control of the opposing party, you should consider it if you have witnesses you know (a) are inclined to testify for you, and (b) are likely to face retaliation for the testimony. Your subpoena could provide an extra layer of protection for them.

Lawyers representing organizations will sometimes strenuously, and oddly, insist on producing their client's witnesses voluntarily. If your jurisdiction provides anti-retaliation protections for subpoenaed witnesses, this insistence may be specifically driven by a desire to strip such witnesses of protections under such statutes.

So be mindful of that, and determine whether your jurisdiction has an anti-retaliation statute for subpoenaed witnesses. I am not suggesting you must subpoena all witnesses for every deposition. That could be costly. I am saying instead that you should be aware of the additional rights afforded witnesses if you subpoena them, and mindful of the motives of opposing lawyers who insist that you let them voluntarily produce your deponents.

§4.02 Subpoenas to Non-Parties

Rule 45, or your jurisdiction's equivalent, is the source of your authority for issuing subpoenas to non-party witnesses. As one court put it, "Rule 45 serves to facilitate access outside the deposition procedure provided by Rule 30 to documents and other information in the possession of persons who are not parties." *Juno Therapeutics, Inc. v. Kite Pharma, Inc.*, 2019 WL 3069009 (C.D. Calif. Apr. 29, 2019).

It lays out the process for serving non-parties, in your jurisdiction or in others, in detail. On your own, it's useful to thoroughly read and understand Rule 45. You will use it or its equivalents often. It is not complicated, but there are nuances. The last thing you want is to get hit with fees and costs because you didn't comply with the rule. And you sure don't want to fly cross-country only to learn that you didn't properly subpoena witnesses and, as a result, you have none.

There are two common and serious mistakes lawyers make in attempting to depose or obtain documents from non-parties. Let's start by covering them. But let me note before we begin this discussion that you can subpoena documents from a non-party using Rule 45 without requiring (or characterizing it as) a deposition. *E.g. Powell v. CUNA Mut. Grp.*, No. 06-5061-KES, 2007 WL 9773465, at *1 (D.S.D. Feb. 13, 2007) ("In amending Rule 45 in 1991, the advisory committee noted, "[Rule 45](a)(1) authorizes the issuance of a subpoena to compel a non-party to produce evidence independent of any deposition. This revision spares the necessity of a deposition of the custodian of evidentiary material required to be produced." Fed. R. Civ. P. 45 advisory committee's note.").

Certainly, you may want to depose the non-party about their documents and other matters. But it isn't required.

1. You Cannot Obligate a Non-Party to Appear Without a Subpoena

You cannot compel a non-party to appear for a deposition or produce documents without a subpoena. Serving a deposition notice on a non-party without a subpoena is the equivalent of doing nothing. *Mayla v. Campos,* 2013 WL 12387156, at *1 (S.D. Tex. Apr. 18, 2013) (deposition notice without subpoena is not proper procedure to depose a non-party).

2. You Cannot Obligate a Non-Party to Appear Without a Check

Rule 45(b)(1) requires you to tender – deliver a check for - fees for attendance and mileage. Some courts hold that if your subpoena requires the tender of payment at the time of delivery and you did not do so, the deponent need not attend. *Truck Pro Holding Corp. v. Garner*, 2009 U.S. Dist. LEXIS 98555, *1-2, 2009 WL 3425673 (S.D. Ala. Oct. 22, 2009) ("Service of a subpoena pursuant to Rule 45 requires both "delivery" of the subpoena to the individual commanded to appear and, if the person's attendance is required, tender of the witness fee. Fed.R.Civ.P. 45(b)(1). Failure to meet both of these requirements results in ineffectiveness of service, citing

In the Matter of Dennis, 330 F.3d 696, 704 (5th Cir. 2003) ("The plain meaning of Rule 45[(b)(1)] requires simultaneous tendering of witness fees and the reasonably estimated mileage allowed by law with service of a subpoena."); *Schildkraut v. Bally's Casino New Orleans, L.L.C.*, 2004 U.S. Dist. LEXIS 12917 (E.D. La. July 9, 2004)."

§4.03 The Basics of Rule 45

Let's start with the obvious. Through the issuance of a proper subpoena, you can command a nonparty to do the same things on (mostly) the same terms and conditions as a party:

1. Attend and testify at deposition
2. Require witnesses to attend a deposition within 100 miles of where they reside, 100 miles of where they work, or 100 miles of where they regularly transact business in person
3. Command the production of documents from witnesses without requiring them to appear for deposition. The production will be on the same terms as a deposition, *e.g.*, within the same 100-mile limits
4. Command both appearance at a deposition for testimony and the simultaneous production of documents at the deposition under Rule 45(a)(1)(C) (by noticing the deposition as a *duces tecum* – "bring with you" – deposition)

§4.04 Rules About Issuing Subpoenas

There are two chief mistakes lawyers make in the process of drafting and serving subpoenas. Both are easily avoidable.

- **Use the Case Style of Your Pending Action to Issue the Subpoena**

The procedure for issuing a subpoena is outlined in Rule 45(a)(2). It provides that the subpoena must issue from the court where the action is pending. This simply means the subpoena itself must contain the case style of the court where your case is filed. So, to give an example, if you are in the Southern District of New York, your subpoena must bear the case style of the action in that court.

As you will see, however, disputes relating to subpoenas usually occur in the jurisdiction where the witness must appear and/or produce documents.

So if you subpoena a non-party deponent to appear in San Francisco and the deponent opts to contest it, you or the deponent may initiate an ancillary proceeding in the Northern District of California. (An ancillary proceeding is one secondary to the main case. Ancillary jurisdiction allows a court that could not hear the main claim to hear an offshoot issue over which they do have jurisdiction. So in our example, a San Francisco court could not normally preside over a New York lawsuit, but it can address things like subpoena disputes that arose out of the New York proceeding but that call for action in San Francisco.)

- **Provide Advance Notice to Other Parties of Your Intent to Issue Subpoenas to Non-Parties**

If you intend to issue a Rule 45 subpoena to a non-party for a testimonial deposition, you will draft and serve a Notice of Taking Deposition after agreeing on dates with the other parties. You will then serve your Notice, subpoena and witness fee on the non-party. Actual testimonial depositions rarely take place without the knowledge of all the parties. Few lawyers would dare conduct a deposition without providing proper notice.

On the other hand, some lawyers serve Rule 45 subpoenas for the production of documents by non-parties without even pausing to wonder whether they must first notify other parties of their plan to do so. Rule 45 allows the use of subpoenas to compel document productions from non-parties without requiring the recipient to sit for a deposition. So where lawyers wish to obtain documents from third parties, but do not need an actual deposition, their subpoena simply instructs the non-party to show up at a designated location - at a date and time certain - and produce the listed documents for copying. Rule 45(a)(1)(C), (D); (d)(2)(A).

No deposition. No testimony. And, sometimes, no notice to other parties, who are entitled to advance notice and an opportunity to object.

Under Rule 45(a)(4), before you serve a Rule 45 document subpoena on a non-party, you *must* serve a notice of your intent to do so and you *must* provide a copy of the proposed subpoena to the other parties in your action. This gives other parties time to review your subpoena and object – preventing production, or providing for production on specific terms - if they have standing to do so.

This requirement is chiefly to prevent parties from abusing their subpoena power to surreptitiously obtain documents from others, including documents they are not entitle to receive (*e.g.*, medical records, phone logs and similar information).

§4.05 Objections by Non-Party Recipients

Just as parties can oppose discovery subpoenas, non-party witnesses can, too. In fact, they have several options. Keep in mind when dealing with objections from third parties that many courts require a stronger showing of need. *Pullman Arms, Inc. v. Healey*, No. CV 16-40136-TSH, 2019 WL 3802526, at *2 (D. Mass. Aug. 13, 2019) (non-parties have different expectations about releasing personal information; accordingly, concern for the unwanted burden thrust upon non-parties is a factor entitled to special weight).

- ***They Can Serve Objections***

If you are only seeking documents without a deposition, the recipients can serve objections under Rule 45(d). Those objections must be served before the *earlier* of the time specified for compliance or fourteen days after the subpoena is served. The burden is then on you to move to compel compliance if you choose to do so. You must generally file your papers in the district where compliance is required.

The local court can, pursuant to Rule 45(f), transfer your motion to the court from which you issued your subpoena. A judge will occasionally do that if he or she feels resolution of the subpoena dispute is better handled by the judge overseeing the actual litigation.

In most cases, however, expect the local judge to take charge and resolve the dispute. Judges like to control matters within their own jurisdiction and do not generally farm them out to distant courts.

Note that non-party witness objections are held to the same standard as if they were a litigant responding to a Rule 34 request for production. Thus, the objections must be specific, tailored, and free of boilerplate. So the non-party recipients of your subpoenas get no special treatment when obstructing legitimate discovery requests. Bogus objections made by a non-party subpoena recipient will be rejected as quickly as any other.

- ***They Can Move to Quash Your Subpoena***

A non-party recipient can also move to quash the subpoena on various grounds. Thus, if you are seeking their deposition, for example, they may also file a motion to quash or modify the subpoena. But the deadline applicable to subpoenas seeking documents without testimony does *not* apply where you are seeking actual deposition testimony. In that case, your recipient must only "timely" file their motion to quash, meaning, in most cases, before the deposition is to take place.

The rules are clear that a court will take whatever action is needed to protect the recipient of the subpoena from abuse.

You should expect objections and court intervention if your subpoena purports to obligate the non-party to do more than Rule 45 requires, such as requiring recipients to travel more than 100 miles from their place of residence or work, for example.

Similarly, you should expect consequences if you demand non-party witnesses produce documents that are clearly inappropriate. This is a recurring problem. Some lawyers assume that because non-party subpoena recipients may not have counsel, they can get away with more than with a represented or savvy litigant. But judges save special ire for lawyers that pull fast ones on lay witnesses. The requirement that you provide advance notice to opposing counsel - if your subpoena requires the production of documents - is another hedge against playing fast and loose with non-party witnesses.

§4.06 Dealing with Non-Party Objections

Let's assume that the non-party recipient of your subpoena does not wish to comply. How will that play out? There are several possible responses, and several ways for dealing with opposition and obstruction.

- ***The Recipient Just Ignores You***

First, the recipient might just ignore you. This happens. People in distant places, unfamiliar with the legal system, may assume that throwing the subpoena in the wastebasket is the most efficient response.

If your recipient fails to honor the terms of your subpoena, move to compel compliance and contempt in the district where attendance or production was required.[1] (That is sometimes referred to as the "compliance court," whereas your subpoena will be issued from the "issuing court," which is where your original action is pending.)

The easiest way to deal with this is to call the clerk's office in the district where compliance is required. Often, the court will have an option for something sometimes referred to as an "ancillary action."

Think of this as "Odds and Ends Proceedings." It doesn't mean you'll be filing an entirely new lawsuit. Often, you can simply file your motion to compel, or a motion to hold the non-party in contempt. The cost is about $50.00. The clerk will will assign a case number and assign the matter to a district judge or magistrate judge. The assigned judge will immediately consider the motion as he or she would if it were part of a pending case in that district.

By example, I recently filed a motion to compel enforcement of a non-party subpoena in another federal district. I filed the motion itself and paid a filing fee of $47.00. It could not have been easier.

So if your impression is that a remote dispute over a

subpoena will bog you down in costs, filings and travel, let me assure you: It's as easy as filing a motion in your pending action. And that's how it should be. Resolution of disputes arising from your service of Rule 45 subpoenas in other federal jurisdictions is straightforward. Federal judges want these matters off their desk. So the procedure is easy. The cost is cheap.

- ***The Recipient Serves Objections***

Non-party recipients of Rule 45 subpoenas who opt to challenge them can serve objections. If they do, the onus is on you to seek an order compelling production, appearance or other compliance. As discussed above, that means filing in the compliance court. So again, even though your underlying lawsuit may be in the Southern District of New York, if the production of documents from the nonparty, or if the deposition of the nonparty, is going to take place in the Northern District of California, your motion will be filed there and classed as an ancillary proceeding.

- ***The Recipient Seeks a Protective Order***

Non-parties can move for a protective order, just as a party can do so. If recipients opt to seek court protection, they will follow the same procedure you would, by filing in the court where compliance would take place. You can then file a response and the court will take it from there.

§4.07 Standards for Resolving Subpoena Disputes

District courts will resolve non-party subpoena disputes just as they do discovery disputes between parties. And they will use the same standards. Rules 26 and 45 make clear that the scope of permissible discovery against a third-party is not broader than that permitted against a party. *See Metro PCS v. Frazin* 2018 WL 2933673 (N.D. Texas 2018).[2]

Note that Rule 45 governs your ability to seek relief against the *non-party* recipient. Rule 37 applies to *parties* you may have subpoenaed. Rule 26 may have applicability in *both* situations. The key consideration will always be whether the recipient of the subpoena is a party or non-party. Which rule you chiefly rely upon depends on your situation, but you should review all three.

~

5

AUDIOTAPING AND VIDEOTAPING

Covered in This Chapter:

- *§5.01 Audiotaping Depositions*
- *§5.02 Practical Tips for Audiotaping*
- *§5.03 Utilizing Audio After the Deposition*
- *§5.04 Editing Audio Is a Breeze*
- *§5.05 Playing Audio in Mediation or at Trial*
- *§5.06 Other Uses for Your Deposition Audio*
- *§5.07 Using Transcription Software*
- *§5.08 Audio and the Rule of Completeness*
- *§5.09 Using Audio To Verify Transcript Accuracy*
- *§5.10 Overcoming Objections to Audiotaping*
- *§5.11 Videotaping Depositions*
- *§5.12 Defending Videotaped Depositions*
- *§5.13 Learning from Visual Imagery Experts*

- *§5.14 Videotaping Parts of Depositions*
- *§5.15 Additional Practice Pointers*

The federal rules expressly allow you to audiotape and videotape depositions with proper notice. In contrast, most state court rules specifically allow videotaping, but do not address audiotaping (or approach it ambiguously, by requiring court approval for any method other than those specified). I am a strong advocate for both under the right circumstances. Few lawyers independently audiotape depositions, and are uncomfortable at the mere thought of it. I will address that first.

§5.01 Audiotaping Depositions

As with much of this book, I speak to issues chiefly from the perspective of the federal rules. That is easiest because they are uniform across the country and largely inform how state-court rules are adopted.

Rule 30(b)(3)(A) and (B) provide the authority for audiotaping. Those provisions simply require, if you are the party noticing the deposition, that you specifically state in your notice the method you intend to use for recording the testimony. Subsection (A) says "...Testimony may be recorded by audio, audiovisual, or stenographic means." In other words, you may capture the testimony purely with an audio recording, purely with a videotape that captures sound as well, and/or through a transcription service.

Subsection (B) authorizes parties who are not the noticing party to capture the testimony in additional ways – other than those declared by the noticing party.

Let's assume you are defending the deposition and that the plaintiff has noticed your client. Under subsections (A) and (B), the plaintiff serves notice advising that it plans to record the testimony by stenographic means. As a party to the case, you can now provide notice under subsection (B) that you will also recording the testimony, and that you plan to do so by different means. That would allow you to video record or audio record the deposition, apart from the stenographic method noticed by the plaintiff. Put another way, you have the right to capture the testimony in ways not chosen by the plaintiff/noticing party.

So there may be situations where your adversary does not want a video of the deposition. Perhaps the witness through demeanor and tone is clearly being deceptive and, knowing this, your opponent opted to capture nothing but words through stenographic recording. You, on the other hand, want the jury or trier of fact to see the witness, especially in case the witness is not available to testify live at trial. Under these rules, you are not bound by the adversary's choice of recording. With proper notice, you can both audiotape and videotape the deposition.

The availability of multiple recording options for each party is an implicit acknowledgment of two important principles.

First, it is an acknowledgment that credibility judgments

are informed not just by words but by demeanor, tone of voice, even pauses.

Second, and attendant to the first principle, it is recognition that by allowing multiple options for capturing deposition testimony, wily litigants whose cases are built on the words of unsavory characters might smartly choose the recording method that best camouflages their insincerity.

A jury can easily judge credibility if all witnesses testify live. But if your adversary is allowed by rule or consent to read stenographically-recorded deposition testimony into the record, the jury will lack important cues about its reliability.

So the rules provide you the ability to capture all three streams of information: the verbiage used, the pacing, tone and pauses as the witness speaks, and the witness' visually-observable demeanor.

Note that under subsection (B), you must provide notice not only to the parties but to the deponent as well. If the deponent is a party or employed by a party, notice to the party's counsel is enough. (Frankly, few lawyers appear to read my notices, because they usually claim surprise when I set up my audio recorder. But notice to the party's counsel is sufficient whether the lawyer bothers to catch it.)

On the other, if the deponent is a non-party witness not under the control of anyone, you must provide specific notice to both all parties and to the deponent specifically. So if another party has noticed that deposition and does not provide for audiotaping or videotaping, you must independently serve notice on the witness of your intention to do so under subsection (B). Otherwise, you are not in compliance with the federal rule for audiotaping.

§5.02 Practical Tips for Audiotaping

I recommend a high-quality digital recorder to capture testimony. I use a Zoom H5 four-track digital recorder, but there are others similar to it. Mine ran about $250 online. It comes with a hard-shell case so I can throw it into my briefcase without worrying. I have had it for several years and it has never failed me. It runs on two AA batteries and I have only had to replace them a few times.

It is essential to invest in the highest-quality recorder you can afford. You have undoubtedly seen small, inexpensive recorders used by court reporters. I'm not sure you've heard how terrible their recordings sound. Remember that reporters use the recordings as a backup. It is not for use in a large courtroom, or anywhere else, for that matter. And most reporters will put up a ferocious if you ever ask for a copy of their audio. Typically they say it is for their private use and is not part of the record.

And that's true. If you want audio (or some method beyond what the noticing party is using), you must capture it yourself, and you must provide proper notice to the deponent and parties. That the reporter is capturing audio as a backup does not alleviate you from the obligation of independent action and notice.

In rare cases, a judge may compel a reporter to release the audio, but that will most likely be in the context of a claim that the transcript is inaccurate, or an accusation of misconduct for which the audio is instructive. Otherwise, a judge will not allow you to obtain a stenographer's audio for your use as an adversarial tool.

Back to my device. The Zoom H5 is a studio-quality, professional recorder. Professional musicians use it; professional broadcasters use it for interviews. The sound quality is unbelievable. And when you play it back, either in mediation, at trial, or somewhere else, you will fully appreciate the depth and quality of the sound.

The H5 is about 5 ½ inches tall. You can lay on the table between the examiner and the deponent or you can place it on a small tripod. I carry a small tripod in my briefcase and attach the H5 to it so that it is above the table surface. I've never laid the H5 on the table because I assume it will capture extraneous sounds from people picking up or putting down pencils, bumping into the table, and so on.

I start the recording just before the reporter swears the witness in. It is essential to capture every moment that will appear in the transcript. I stop the recording on breaks (which many court reporters do not do with their own recorder, by the way) in order to avoid capturing ordinary or confidential conversations that are not part of the deposition. I start it again as soon as we are ready to begin testimony. The H5 is super simple to operate.

§5.03 Utilizing Audio After the Deposition

The H5, and most high-quality recorders like it, use an SD card. Once you're back at the office, you can plug the included cable into the recorder and your computer and upload the entire recording. I recommend that you first save the entire unedited recording in at least two places. Preservation of a complete unaltered version will protect you later in the event of claims the audio was manipulated. So keep a clean original file in at least two locations as a backup.

§5.04 Editing Audio is a Breeze

I edit audio the same way I edit video. I use iMovie, a free Apple product, and Adobe Audition, a professional sound-editing program. Both are easy to use and require no particular training. My audio editing chiefly consists of creating individual sound bites for use at mediation or trial, and using noise reduction features to remove generic background sound. The result is movie-theater-quality audio.

If you're not accustomed to editing audio files, it's worth giving it a shot. Eliminating background noise, for example, is as complicated as clicking the "Reduce Background Noise" button. That step alone makes for near-flawless audio if you've used a high-quality recorder.

§5.05 Playing Audio in Mediation or at Trial

There is nothing more compelling than audio or video of damaging testimony by an adversary. You can read aloud from depositions yourself, of course, but that doesn't compete with the actual voice of the witness.

I like audio clips in particular because they are very easy to edit, and they consume far less space on drives than video.

In mediation you can play one clip after another. What did Amy Moore say about her investigation? Let's hear Amy. [Press play.] And did Mr. Cohn admit that he sent a copy of the source code to himself? Here's what he says. [Press play.]

It's an absolute riot to use this technique.

Even when played on a laptop, sound quality from a high-end recorder is spectacular. It has a deep, crystal-clear resonance. And you can cut testimony up into dozens of clips. Done right, your opponents in mediation will be squirming.

The same is true at trial. Audio clips played over the court speakers, or over your own speakers brought to the courtroom, are extremely powerful. Because they are smaller digital files than video, they are easier to use in whatever order you decide at the last minute and tend not to hang up or lag, as video clips tend to do.

I have never seen another lawyer independently audiotape a deposition, or present audio at a mediation or trial. Lawyers as a group, respectfully speaking, aren't always the most tech-savvy professionals. But recording, editing and presenting audio doesn't require advanced technical knowledge. And if you are considering videotaping the deposition, you should actively consider audiotaping as an alternative or as a secondary method.

§5.06 Other Uses for Your Deposition Audio

Even if you don't use the audio at mediation or trial, it still has tremendous value. You can play it for your staff. You can have an expert, or other witnesses, listen to the audio. The audio track can tell your witnesses and experts a great deal about the truthfulness of the witness, what is causing the witness anxiety, and where the witness might be dissembling. The audio might help persuade another witness to open up more candidly about an important issue, to the extent, for example, a witness listens and believes the deponent was deceitful.

Just as in mediation and at trial, your own account of what was said, or your own reading of the testimony, doesn't compare to the words in the witness' own voice.

§5.07 Using Transcription Software

You can also use software like Dragon NaturallySpeaking to create a written version of the testimony, although it won't put it into transcript-style pages unless you have someone edit it. You can upload a digital audio file and it will transcribe every word, usually within a few minutes. I once dictated a lengthy speech of about 10,000 words while I was in the car. When I got back to the office, I uploaded the file.

The program transcribed the entire thing in about two minutes. It needed some modest editing, but it was spectacular. Obviously, testimony is a little different than a speech. You would need to have someone go in and break it into individual lines by speaker. But it's an alternative.

§5.08 Audio and the Rule of Completeness

If you do use audio at trial, remember Rule 106, Remainder of or Related Writings or Recorded Statements. Most lawyers refer to this as the "rule of completeness." The rule provides that:

> If a party introduces all or part of a writing or recorded statement, an adverse party may require the introduction, at that time, of any other part — or any other writing or recorded statement — that in fairness ought to be considered at the same time.

So, as with videotape and plain old paper transcripts, it remains the right of your adversaries to insist that the jury hear other pieces of the testimony to put your clips in context. Unless they also have the audio ready, that likely means they'll ask you to read additional specific passages from the transcript.

§5.09 Using Audio to Verify Transcript Accuracy

In some cases, you may encounter a court reporter who you suspect might not produce a perfect transcript. It happens. In such situations, the ready availability of an audio recording will allow your staff to review the transcript before the errata-sheet deadline runs and verify that the reporter accurately captured every spoken word.

That's something to think about.

We all take the accuracy of transcripts for granted, but even the best reporters sometimes get it wrong. Remember – that's why <u>*they*</u> audio-record the deposition. You may never get reporters to release their audio, but that won't be an issue if you have your own.

§5.10 Overcoming Objections to Audiotaping

Nassim Taleb, the author of *The Black Swan: The Impact of the Highly Improbable*, defines a "Black Swan" as an unpredictable, rare event that invalidates long-held beliefs and has great impact. Such so-called Black Swans are outliers, he says because they ". . . [are] outside the realm of regular expectations."

Audio recording a deposition is an example of a legal Black Swan. As I mentioned previously, I have never seen another lawyer audio record a deposition. This means that when you begin setting up your recorder, you are likely to be immediately set upon by opposing lawyers. "What are you doing?" "You can't do that." "I don't consent." "We're not going to proceed unless you agree to put the recorder away." "I'm going to call the judge."

What do I do? If I have properly noticed the deposition, and given proper notice to the witness if needed separately, I ignore the lawyer. I will point to the federal rule on depositions and to the language in the notice that I served. But I absolutely will not refrain from audio recording.

On one occasion, and only one occasion, I had a lawyer stop the deposition and file a motion with a federal judge asking that I be barred from audiotaping. The judge issued a one-paragraph, dismissive order saying I had fully complied with the rule and denying the motion. It was a non-event.

Lawyers are creatures of habit. Some are startled to see your recorder, because nothing in their past of ordinary depositions with ordinary lawyers doing ordinary things would lead them to see this even as a possibility. And, quite likely, they will immediately appreciate that your independent capture of testimony on audio may give you unexpected and extraordinary options.

So expect objections. And ignore them.

§5.11 Videotaping Depositions

The same rules that apply to audiotaping also apply to videotaping. If you are noticing the deposition, the notice must clearly state that you will videotape the event. If you are defending the deposition and plan to capture the testimony by video whereas the examining lawyer is not, you must likewise provide notice to other parties and to the deponents if they are not represented.

When to videotape? Some obvious situations:

- You have a surprise bombshell to drop on the witness and want to capture the reaction
- The opposing lawyer is obstructive, and you believe the fact of having an audiovisual record will minimize misconduct
- You expect the witness to be unusually deceptive, and you want to capture the pauses and facial gestures for the jury to see
- You have an expert who cannot attend the deposition but who wants to observe the deponent while testifying
- The witness is going to be unavailable at trial and you plan to use the videotape deposition testimony in place of live testimony

These are the chief reasons, but there are many more. Pictures are truly worth a thousand words and your circumstances may warrant the use of video images

- *Mechanics of Videotaping*

It is important to give careful thought to how the videotaping will be conducted. This is true whether you are the noticing lawyer or the defending lawyer. Some points to consider:

- **Tips When Taking**

- Check the camera set-up and the framing. The video must capture witnesses closely enough so that when displayed in the courtroom, the jury has a genuine close-up shot. Nothing is more boring than a video of a person talking at a distance. As a rule of thumb, I suggest that the video capture the deponent from roughly mid-chest to about a foot above the head of the witness, with about a foot of space on each side. If you're not entirely sure about the proper imaging, watch a news network before the deposition and see how close the networks capture the anchor or a talk show host. See how they capture guests that are appearing remotely - a circumstance similar to your video deposition - or when an opinion journalist is speaking about an intense issue.
- If you expect the witness to be dishonest, aggressive or unlikable, you may want a slightly tighter shot - in other words, show the witness up close.
- If the witnesses are likely to be distraught over a tragic event, you may also want a tighter shot so that the jury can feel their emotions. Remember the screen on which the jury views your video might be on a small screen in front of each juror, or it might be across the brightly-lit courtroom on a hard-to-see screen. The test isn't how it looks on

the videographer's display screen. It's how it will look to a juror in your courtroom. If you expect to have extended video testimony, go to the courthouse and check out the video capabilities in the courtrooms where your trial will likely take place. Some courtrooms where I try cases have outstanding setups. Some have equipment decades old. Some have none. That is important to know as well. If your courthouse does not have this capability, or has ver poor capabilities, find a video production company from whom you can rent equipment and a large screen. These details can derail your trial presentation if you haven't thought them through.

- If the deponent is a peripheral witness covering routine matters, or perhaps authenticating records, you may want the cameraman to zoom out slightly, to send a visual cue to the jury that this witness is not as important as the others. A very tight shot tells the viewer this is an important moment. More mundane witnesses should be the subject of wider or longer shots. The mechanics of your visuals can send messages. This is something to be managed, and not left to chance or the whims of whoever shows up with a camera.
- If the witness tends to be animated or will be demonstrating gestures or movements, ask the camera operator to use a wider shot.
- Make sure the camera lens is at eye level to the

witness. It must not look down on the witnesses, or up at them. The jury will be at eye level to live witnesses. They should have the same view perspective of witnesses appearing by video. Camera operators most often aim down at the witness, which is inappropriate. High or low angles are something you see daily on your friends' social media posts - looking up into their nostrils, or down at their forehead - but that you never see in professionally-run video productions. Deponents on video should appear as they would if they were sitting across a small table from you. Close, personal, eye level.

- Listen to the sound. Have someone speak for a few minutes before the actual deposition begins. Not just "Testing, testing, testing," but actual conversation. Variants in tone or pace might warrant a different sound volume. Videographers usually have headphones you can use to listen. Don't overlook this. Poor sound quality can destroy the value of the video deposition. Post-editing can fix some of that, but not always.
- Look carefully at the lighting as captured through the lens of the camera. Does it cast unusual shadows on the witness? Is there something about the particular witness that makes the lighting unexpectedly unpleasant? If this is a potential issue, check out the location before the day of the deposition.

- Pay attention to the background behind the deponent. In some reporters' offices, there are decorations in the background that are inappropriate to the moment. Some have candy jars, pictures of race cars, Lladro ballerina or clown sculptures, or other tchotchkes. They will distract the jury. They may even prove more interesting than the testimony. A clown sculpture in the background may send more of a message about the witness or your case that you intend. After one trial, I had a juror tell me that they noticed a framed display box of various knots used by boaters, and that some of the jurors got into a heated debate about whether one of the knots was a bowline or a double bowline.
- Pay close attention to where every participant in the room is seated. Is there someone within the line of sight of the deponent, but offscreen, in a position to convey (helpful or insulting) nonverbal signals to the witness? When I am concerned about that, I will ask the witness at the start of the deposition to identify each person in the room and to look at each such person as they identify them. That way, the jury will know who the witness is looking at if they see the witness looking offscreen.
- If you expect your witness to look at important documents, consider a wider shot so the jury can see what the witness is looking at. Even if the jury

cannot read the documents themselves, this will keep their attention if they see the stack of documents in front of the witness. It is uninteresting to watch a video of someone looking and talking about something offscreen.

- If there is something critical about the documents, including specific sections within them, consider using a second, overhead camera. That will capture the witness pointing at various provisions. The more your jurors are active participants in the action, the better you will be. So the overhead camera, which could, of course, be somewhat off to the side, as it doesn't need to capture the top of the witness' head, helps the jurors see exactly what the witness sees. That makes juries follow along. You may be able to arrange for two cameras - one showing the witness and one showing the document - and later create a split screen showing the witness looking at the document and showing the content of the document itself. That is not difficult to do.[1]
- Decide whether you want the witness chiefly looking toward the camera or toward you. The video camera does not have to be at the opposite end of the table. It can be behind you, off to one side, directly facing the witness.

§5.12 Defending Videotaped Depositions

Most of the same considerations apply if you are defending a video deposition. Make sure your witnesses are properly situated and the lighting and camera angles are appropriate. Speak up immediately if you sense a problem. Carefully check the sound as well.

- *Deponent Apparel*

Inform your witnesses to dress appropriately for the occasion. CEOs should look like CEOs. Others should look their part. It is fine if some of your witnesses are a little better dressed than they might be for their jobs. Jurors expect that. A truck driver can wear business casual with a blazer and that is fine. But if all of your witnesses are dressed conspicuously above or below their positions or status, the jury will see your presentations as orchestrated and phony. Give thought to your case theme, and make sure the visual message each witness conveys meshes with your theme.

Do not allow key witnesses to show up for a video deposition wearing whatever they randomly chose. Manage this piece of your case. Your clients and witnesses will not appreciate the impact of their appearance on your jury. You will not offend them if you explain with appropriate deference the way that clothing can send positive or unexpected messages.

You don't know who will be on the jury yet. Apparel must

allow for a wide range of perceptions, judgments and stereotyping by those who will decide the outcome.

§5.13 Learning from Visual Imagery Experts

I have spent considerable time reading books meant for motion picture and Broadway producers and directors. A trial is just as much a production and many of the dynamics are the same. If the visuals do not match the story, you have a problem.

There are many excellent books available, if you're so inclined, on producing and directing in particular. There are also books available on character development and wardrobe. All of them have crossover messages for trial lawyers. The more you learn from professionals in the art of storytelling and story presentation, the better you will be at spotting the opportunities for reinforcing your message. Videotaped depositions are a part of that and deserve thought.

§5.14 Videotaping Parts of Depositions

Don't hesitate to videotape later portions of a deposition if things go haywire and you now realize that videotape of the witness will be important. Some courts have held that there are legitimate reasons why a party might not consider videotaping the deposition at the outset but then determine the need exists.

In *Riley v. Murdock*, 156 F.R.D. 130, Case No 92-442-CIV-5-

BR (E.D. N.C. July 6, 1994), the plaintiffs decided the defendant's witness had been so evasive and mechanical in his answers that they scheduled the balance of the deposition to be captured on video. The defense objected.

In rejecting the defendant's motion for protective order seeking to block the partial videotaping of their witness, the judge said he found "...nothing in [Fed. R. Civ. P. 30(b)(2)] or elsewhere in the law to prevent the deposing party from switching to a different medium for the subsequent portion of a continued deposition." He also pointed out that video captures testimonial elements that a transcript cannot, such as pauses, facial gestures, and tones of voice. Since the plaintiffs believed the witness was being less than candid, the judge reasoned, and because fact-finders must make credibility determinations, the use of videotape, even for just part of a deposition, made sense.

Consider this the next time you face a cagey witness and are wondering whether you missed a valuable chance to videotape the witness. You haven't. If circumstances permit continuing the deposition to a later date, do so and simply notice it as a video deposition.

§5.15 Additional Practice Pointers

I offer these additional tips for you on the subject of videotaped depositions. These are in no particular order.

- Determine in advance whether you plan to use a videographer associated with your court reporter, an independent videographer, a professional camera operator, or whether you plan to videotape it yourself. That is completely proper in most jurisdictions. *See* Memorandum Decision and Order, ECF Doc. 23, *Maranville v. Utah Valley University,* Case No. 2:11-cv-958 (D. Utah Apr. 27, 2012) (order allowing lawyer to videotape deposition rather than using independent person or entity).

- If the case is a high-value one, and if the witness is particularly critical, you may want to retain a professional camera operator with high-end equipment. Camera operators are highly skilled and can adjust the framing as needed during the course of the deposition. The rules do not require a static or fixed image during the entirety of the deposition. They only require a faithful and fair portrayal of the witness. Many court reporters hire a friend or family member to serve as their "videographer," and while their equipment may appear better than what you have at home, they are usually amateurs who lack the skill to produce a polished product. They press play when needed, stop when needed, and you get the result. There is so much more to a high-quality video operation.[2]
- You may be deemed the custodian of the video recording (or audio) if you independently capture testimony in that manner. Take caution to preserve the originals.

- The rules do not require you to rely on the videographer hired by the opposing party. I have attended depositions where multiple parties hired videographers for various reasons. Do not hesitate to do so if you deem it appropriate. For example, you may decide to do so if the specified videographer is closely associated with your adversary, is an employee of your opposing counsel's firm, or is the opposing counsel.
- Related to the point above, it pays to ask your opposing counsels who they are using to videotape the deposition. Don't assume the adversary is aiming for high quality. The answer might be "Well, I'm going to do it myself." That may lead you to retain your own videographer.
- If you are videotaping the deposition but are not attending the deposition in person, you must take as many of the same steps as possible to ensure a polished final product. For example, you can ask the videographer to frame the image of the witness and then to text you a photo showing the framing and lighting. That is very simple to do. If needed, ask the videographer to pan the room at the start of each segment showing where everyone is seated and what they have in front of them.
- Be prepared to advocate for use of the videotape deposition in the event the witness disappears suddenly before trial. In one 2018 case, a judge

allowed the use of a videotaped deposition at trial because the opposing lawyer caused the witness to leave the courthouse just before he was to be called to testify. *See Botey v. Green et al*, 2018 WL 5985694 (M.D. Penn. Nov. 14, 2018).

- Be sure your deposition notice is crystal clear that the witness may be videotaped or audiotaped. It will avoid unnecessary carping by your opponent. See *Jones v. Natural Essentials, Inc.*, 2018 WL 6622908 (Ct. App. Ohio Dec. 17, 2018) (deponent walked out of deposition because notice said testimony would be recorded "stenographically and/or on video;" deponent, who was sanctioned, considered notice ambiguous).

~

6

COURT REPORTERS

Covered in This Chapter:

- *§6.01 Best Practice for Finding Reporters*
- *§6.02 Verify the Transcription Method*
- *§6.03 Verify Wi-Fi and Power Availability*
- *§6.04 Use The Same Reporter for Multi-Day Events*
- *§6.05 Secure Confirmation from the Reporter*
- *§6.06 Price-Shop Your Reporters*
- *§6.07 Negotiate Reporter Fees and Costs*
- *§6.08 Don't Hesitate to Change Agencies*
- *§6.09 Don't Hesitate to Change Locations*
- *§6.10 Remember: Reporters Need Breaks, Too*
- *§6.11 Asking the Reporter to Change Seats*
- *§6.12 Asking the Reporter to Move Gear*
- *§6.13 Removing Distracting Objects*
- *§6.14 Arrive Early for Prime Seating Options*

We tend to see court reporters as benign folks selling a commodity product - a transcript that is identical from reporter to reporter. The fact is that there can be wide variations between reporters, both in how they do their job and the product they create. So if you don't have an existing, regular relationship with an excellent reporter, or if you are taking depositions in other cities or states, consider the following points.

§6.01 Best Practices for Finding Reporters

In this next section I share tips and strategies for finding court reporters, for spotting possible problems, and for solving them.

- *Check Online Reviews*

Run searches using at least three different search engines.

Take both overly positive and overly negative reviews with a grain of salt. By ignoring the fringes, you'll get a more accurate read.

If you'll need spacious facilities and multiple rooms for depositions or private conferences, run their street address through Google Street View and see what the place looks like. Does the reporter or agency have a traditional office, or is it someone's house? Is the location convenient to restaurants, office supply stores, and gas stations? If you travel often, you will run into a wide range of reporting agencies and physical locations. A poor location and reporter can ruin your depositions. Check ahead.

- *Ask Other Lawyers About Reporter Accuracy*

While all reporters are in theory generating the identical product, it doesn't work that way. Some are just not as diligent as they should be. The result is a transcript filled with errors, misspellings, punctuation mistakes and less-than-faithful renderings of what witnesses and lawyers said. The result is maddening. A transcript with errors require great effort by witnesses and counsel to correct them. And if you did not independently audiotape the deposition, you may not be able to fully correct the transcript.

Litigators in the area where your depositions will occur are likely to be willing to share their thoughts. All it takes is an email.

§6.02 Verify the Transcription Method

If you have not traveled to remote or rural locations for depositions, you might not have encountered "mask reporters" or "pen writers." While traditional reporters use stenographic machines, essentially computers with specialized keyboards, in some areas, they may be in short supply. So you may end up with a reporter who either transcribes the testimony using shorthand with a pen and pad, or who wears a mask covering their mouth, repeating the testimony into a digital recorder wired to the mask.

§6.03 Verify Wi-Fi and Power Availability

Continuing the theme that you can't take anything for granted when taking depositions on the road, be sure to verify the existence of Wi-Fi and sufficient working power outlets. I have taken depositions in many locations that lacked both, and it affected the flow of the depositions. I rely heavily on web access during depositions. Power and a good signal is essential. One chart I saw in 2019 said about 16 million people in the US have no access to internet. I did not see a current chart showing where they live, but that number is high enough to necessitate your advance planning.

§6.04 Use The Same Reporter for Multi-Day Events

Unless you ask, the reporting agency will decide who appears each day for your depositions. In multi-day depositions, it's good to have the same reporter. After the first day, the reporter will know your preferences and style, and will have spellings and other unique information memorized.

Otherwise, you effectively start over with these issues every day.

§6.05 Secure Confirmation from the Reporter

Written confirmation is important. You may arrive to find that the reporter never received your notices, and they may not have reporters available to fill in, either. Small details, big consequences.

§6.06 Price-Shop Your Reporters

Reporting agencies vary widely in per-page prices and in the cost of add-ons. The variation can be shocking. I took eleven brief depositions in a major city and the final invoice was almost $10,000.00. The agency had very high per-page rates, and charged a high appearance fee for every hour of deposition, even if it was the same witness. It added a host of other fees we never expected or requested: setup fees, after-hours fees, delivery fees and "litigation support package" fees. The "litigation support package" was basically the transcript in seven different file formats, six of which I did not need or ask for. But that is how they sell it.[1]

They charged more if you did not order the transcript immediately. They charged higher per-page rates for EUOs than they did for depositions. They charged exorbitant fees for copying and attaching exhibits to the depositions. They charged more when at least one lawyer was on the phone.

Like many lawyers, I sometimes learn the hard way. We

now maintain a notebook of price sheets for reporters in every city and state where we practice. And we ask for updated price sheets before we book with a reporter. Price gouging by court reporters is growing worse with the consolidation of the industry by a handful of major national companies.

§6.07 Negotiate Reporter Fees and Costs

One of my career mentor's favorite sayings was, "No price is ever fixed." He would negotiate everything. I do, too. And I pay lower fees for court reporters than any lawyer I know. I don't think many folks ask for lower rates. There's no reason not to. You can save a small fortune if you have an active litigation practice.

It doesn't matter whether you have a regular book of business with an agency or not. Ask for discounts. Demand them. I can save hundreds of dollars per deposition because I negotiate deals. If you aren't comfortable demanding lower rates, at least clarify what you want and what you don't.

And change agencies if prices are too high. There is no reason to be shy about switching reporters if you learn their rates are too high. For the most part, agencies offer a commodity service you can find elsewhere at better prices. Even though court reporting bills are pass-through costs, you will save your clients a fortune by getting better deals on reporting services.

§6.08 Don't Hesitate to Change Agencies

If the first day's reporter or agency is not satisfactory, is not respectful, or is charging too much, you should not hesitate to substitute another reporter for the balance of your depositions.

With national booking services and agencies, you may not know who is coming to your deposition or even what the charges will be. Most of the national services do not tell you who the reporter is and do not allow you a voice in who comes. You can ask, of course, but because they rely on a large pool of local agencies and freelancers, even they may not know. I've had depositions where a reporter drove three hours, from another state, for a single very short deposition.

You are not bound to use the same reporter or agency from day to day or deposition to deposition. If you are unhappy with the choice that was made for you, make your own for the balance of your depositions.

§6.09 Don't Hesitate to Change Locations

It is a fact of life that you are going to encounter court reporters whose offices are inappropriate for depositions.

I have traveled to locations that turned out to be the court reporter's home, and I had to conduct depositions at their kitchen table. I've taken depositions in very small offices where it looked like the tables were from from a bar supply or picnic store. On several occasions, I conducted depositions at "conference tables" so small that the witness and I were literally breathing in each other's faces.

I understand why some do this. Minimum investment, maximum gains. Even so, I do not want to conduct depositions in any environment that is unsuited for the purpose.

- ***Ask for Photos of the Proposed Deposition Rooms***

This is useful when you are unfamiliar with the agency or suspect it may not have adequate facilities. I have done this many times. And on occasion, I opted to change locations because the rooms were not appropriate. You must manage every facet of the deposition process. You should not assume that, because a court reporter has an office, it will be suitable. Sometimes it just isn't.

- ***Consider Alternatives to Agency Offices***

We all default to the reporters' offices on occasion, but there are often other facilities that are far more pleasant and convenient, and even cost less.

Hotels rent their conference rooms at surprisingly low rates. Those rooms often sit empty and you can strike excellent deals to use them. Depositions are low-capacity, low-impact uses. Managers will love you for booking them. Hotel conference rooms are spacious and comfortable. They are often near other rooms you can slip into for confidential discussions on breaks. And you are likely to be close to the hotel restaurant and snack areas.

So think creatively if your reporters' offices just don't cut it. I have been pleasantly surprised at how inexpensive and accommodating many hotel chains are.

There are now also many daily-use office spaces through companies like Regus and WeWork, that are available for very reasonable rates.

§6.10 Remember: Reporters Need Breaks, Too

Some lawyers seem to pay no attention to the fact that court reporters need a break to rest their hands and have lunch. Always include the reporter when asking around to see who need a rest or meal break.

§6.11 Asking the Reporter to Change Seats

On one occasion, in a cramped room, the reporter set up at the end corner and had the witness sit at the very end, on her left. That meant the reporter would be seated between me and the witness. Further, by the time I arrived, the opposing lawyer was seated across from the reporter, meaning that if I did not speak up, I would be two people away from the witness.

I cannot have that. I cannot have anyone, or anything, functioning as a barrier that separates me from the deponent. I politely explained the situation and asked the reporter to swap places so I could sit next to the witness. She did (and was very nice about it).

I suspect she didn't think about it one way or the other.

For most reporters, a deposition is a deposition. For me and you, it's high science. Nothing can be left to chance. Nothing can be left to someone for whom strategy does not matter. Don't be shy about asking reporters to move if they take a spot that interferes with the dynamics of your examination.

(If you're worried about saying something because the reporter needs to next to the witness, that just isn't so. Reporters in different proceedings sometimes sit 30-50 feet away from a witness, particularly in many courtrooms. They just need a clear line of sight.)

§6.12 Asking the Reporter to Move Gear

I arrived at a deposition in a small office that had an even smaller table. The reporter was already set up. Unfortunately, her equipment and cords stretched directly across in front of me, and it was a bundle.

If left as is, I could not easily pass documents across the table to the deponent. Further, the equipment functioned as a barrier between the witness and me, and, as I have said, that is not acceptable. Just as law enforcement interrogators ensure that there is nothing between them and the suspect, I insist when examining witnesses that there be nothing between us, either. Barriers give witnesses psychological comfort. They protect the witness. This is so even if the barrier is a modest one.

I respectfully asked the reporter to pull up a small table in the corner of the room and put her equipment on that. She did so. I did not explain the reason for my request, but I achieved my objective. The bottom line here? You must not let others, even those who mean well, configure the room in a way that interferes with your deposition environment.

§6.13 Removing Distracting Objects

There are occasions where you'll walk into a deposition room and find candy jars, tissue boxes, coasters, jars full of pens, note pads with the court reporter's logo, staplers and paper clips laying about. It's a combination office supply store and living room.

This is not acceptable. All are capable of distracting the witness and interrupting the flow. I generally arrive thirty to sixty minutes before the first scheduled deposition of the day to inspect the room and make adjustments as needed. Sometimes this means removing everything on the table.

§6.14 Arrive Early for Prime Seating Options

Do you want to be near the exit? Do you want a view out the window, so the witness isn't distracted? Or do you want the witness to have the window view, to feel more relaxed? Do you have a preferred side of the table for opposing parties to sit? Seating choice affects deposition dynamics in many ways. Unfortunately, deposition rooms don't yet have reserved seating, but you can get there early and accomplish the same thing.

§6.15 Don't Let Reporters Snap at Your Witness

When a reporter gets frustrated about multiple people talking at the same time, they will often turn to the witnesses - likely because they perceive them to be the least powerful people in the room - and sternly remind them not to talk over everyone because it makes transcription impossible.

It is clear the reporter's comments are aimed at everyone. But the reporter directs them to the witnesses. I suppose this is to avoid offending those paying the bill. But abrupt commands from the reporter can startle deponents and cause them to withdraw and become more submissive.

Bear in mind that lay witnesses are often fearful of the entire deposition experience. They see the reporter as an authority figure, perhaps even connected to the judge.

To be sure, reporters are important, but they have no business injecting themselves into the deposition in a way that affects the testimony. So if a reporter continues to express frustration and does so only to the witness, I will speak up. I will remind the reporter that it isn't just the witness who is talking over others and that the reporter needs to direct his or her comments to everyone. I do not want reporters to become a factor in the outcome of my case. They're neutrals. They need to act like it.

§6.16 Don't Let Reporters Give Instructions

One reporter who occasionally covered my depositions would give lengthy explanations to deponents about the process, about answering audibly, about not talking over others, and so on. The reporter covered all the basic instructions that are the province of the examining lawyer.

And it was all done off the record.

I have very specific instructions for witnesses, and I do not delegate that task to others, including reporters. I use this opening moment in depositions to develop a rapport with witnesses, and I have preferences for explaining the process in a particular way.

Perhaps that reporter got tired of lawyers who skipped the preliminary instructions. I don't know. But it was inappropriate and it prevented me from building early rapport. It also created a modest problem because the preliminary instructions did not appear in the transcript. Again, I politely took the reporter aside, explained my reasons for needing to cover those topics on the record, and respectfully asked him to refrain from doing so in my depositions. He was absolutely fine, and I never had a problem again.

§6.17 If No Reporter Shows Up, Do This

On a few occasions in my career, the court reporter failed to appear. Once, the reporter was in a bad accident on her way to the deposition. Another time, the reporter became ill the night before. I had to find a reporter who could transcribe the deposition by phone.

But that left me with no one present who could administer the oath.

Oaths must generally be administered to the deponent in

person. For purposes of Rule 28(a), 37(a)(2), 30(b)(4) and 37(b)(1), a deposition takes place where the deponent answers the questions. So a telephonic deposition is deemed to occur at the location of the testifying witness, and the witness must be sworn before an officer authorized to administer the appropriate oath. To do otherwise is procedurally flawed and typically unusable.

But there are workaround solutions.

One option is to find someone who can swear the witness in, even if the officer administering the oath is in a remote location. At least one court approved this and allowed the testimony because the way it was handled bore "indicia of reliability." A lawyer adverse to the witness was present with the witness and knew there was no coaching. *Akins v. Mason*, No. 3:06-CV-248, 2008 WL 4646142 (E.D. Tenn. Oct. 17, 2008).

That case contains a useful discussion of the circumstances and will provide you helpful guidance if you face that situation. So don't abandon the deposition just because the reporter and officer administering the oath will be elsewhere. Make the process as similar to, and as reliable as, a deposition. Consider even using your phone to videotape the deposition so the court can see the witness isn't looking around for signals from lawyers who might be coaching them. Further consider photographing the room where the deponent is testifying, so the court (and others) can see the witness had nothing in front of him or her and that the room was appropriate for testimony.

If it turns out you have neither a reporter nor someone to

administer the oath, I still recommend you find a workaround.

In this situation, I will propose agreement with the opposing counsel (a) that the witness, even if unsworn, will voluntarily agree to the penalties of perjury just as if they had been sworn, (b) that the testimony will be admissible as if a court reporter had sworn the witness and was transcribing the deposition, (c) that we will state for the record who was present in the room and confirm that the witnesses had nothing in front of them, and (d) that we will audio-record the entire examination and all share the unedited recording. I will also propose that we have the recording transcribed and share the cost.

With this, I will use my Zoom H5 portable digital recorder to record the entire examination. I will also make sure everyone carefully identifies themselves so the eventual transcriptionist can properly identify the speakers by voice. With the intelligent cooperation of counsel for the parties, this allows us to accomplish the same thing as if the reporter had been present.

It is not ideal, but if you have to choose between something closely resembling a deposition by the book and nothing at all, the choice is an easy one. This is another reason I advocate taking a high-quality digital recorder to all depositions. Failing that, a cellphone with video or audio recording capabilities should work just fine.

§6.18 Objections About the Room Or Reporter

Some objections may be directed not to questions but to the reporter or to the environment. These kinds of objections, found in Rule 30(c)(2), must be made while the deposition is in progress or they are lost forever.

In this category are objections to "...to a party's conduct, to the officer's qualifications, to the manner of taking the deposition, or to any other aspect of the deposition..." These must be noted on the record, but the examination will still proceed, with the testimony taken subject to the objections.

This includes any concerns you have about the court reporter, about the room, about the seating, about noise, about distractions or intimidating circumstances, about the manner or substance of the oath administered by the reporter, and about the manner in which the reporter is behaving or is transcribing the testimony.

It also includes objections to the mandatory announcements the rules require but which most reporters skip, such as identifying the location of the deposition and the names of everyone present.

Going further, it includes methods of recording the deposition that were not properly noticed, such as audio or video taping. And it includes other seemingly minor housekeeping matters, such as whether the court reporter announced the moment the deposition ended (which is required under the federal rules) and announcements about who will receive the original transcript and who will maintain the exhibits.

These are things many lawyers don't think about until a

problem surfaces later. But the rules are unforgiving. If you did not voice objection to these while the deposition was in progress, you have no standing to complain later.

§6.19 Reporters' Bias

Remember that reporters are people, too. They have friends, acquaintances, and enemies. Be sensitive to indications the reporter is favoring the opposing counsel - in scheduling, in taking breaks, in how he or she treats witnesses. Reporters can be called as witnesses if something goes haywire, and so it's important to be mindful of actual or perceived favoritism that might lead to problems. *Brooks v. SAC Wireless, LLC,* 2019 WL 3996594 (N.D. Ill. Aug, 23 2019 (order dismissing case for deposition misconduct by plaintiff, based in part on affidavits from two court reporters).

§6.20 Obtaining the Reporter's Backup Audio

What if there's a dispute about the accuracy of the transcript? What if a lawyer or witness was shouting and you'd like to provide the court reporter's backup audio recording to the court to support a motion for protective order?

As a rule of thumb, assume you're out of luck unless the reporter voluntarily agrees to provide a copy. Courts have generally shown an unwillingness to compel reporters to provide their backup recordings, concluding that the backup audio is not an official record and its the reporter's personal property.[2] On the other hand, at least one court allowed the parties to listen to the reporter's backup audio, while at the same time quashing a subpoena to force production of the actual audio. *Antonacci v. Seyfarth Shaw, LLP*, 2015 IL App (1st) 142372, ¶ 40, 39 N.E.3d 225, 240. In one other reported filing - a post-trial motion - the motion asserts that a court reporter who transcribed a trial was subpoenaed for deposition and required to bring (and did bring) the backup audio of the trial. *Moria and Echevarria v. State Farm Fire & Casualty*, 2012 WL 11893947 (Fla.Cir.Ct. Miami Jan. 24, 2012)).

This kind of problem is easily avoided. Where permitted by rule or order, you should independently audio-tape the deposition or proceeding. Court reporters do make mistakes, as you undoubtedly know. But the transcript is the official record and absent an audio account, you may be stuck.

~

7

WITNESS CAPACITY & CHARACTERISTICS

Covered in This Chapter:

- *§7.01 The Rule on Witness Capacity*
- *§7.02 The Presumption: Everyone is Competent*
- *§7.03 Witness Types and Competency Issues*
- *§7.04 Age - The Immature and the Advanced*
- *§7.05 Mental Disorders*
- *§7.06 Drug Use Prior to Deposition*
- *§7.07 Stress from Life Events*
- *§7.08 Exhaustion*
- *§7.09 Illnesses*
- *§7.10 Language Barriers*
- *§7.11 Doctors, Lawyers, CPAs*
- *§7.12 Clergy*
- *§7.13 Spouses*
- *§7.14 Common Interest/Joint Defense*

- ***§7.15 Mediators***
- ***§7.16 Opposing Lawyers***
- ***§7.17 Fifth Amendment Witnesses***
- ***§7.18 Apex Witnesses***
- ***§7.19 Witnesses in Other Countries***
- ***§7.20 Active-Duty Military***
- ***§7.21 Prisoners***
- ***§7.22 Witnesses With Outstanding Warrants***
- ***§7.23 Hearing & Speech-Impaired Witnesses***
- ***§7.24 Blind & Low-Vision Deponents***
- ***§7.25 Witnesses with Confidentiality Agreements***

For the most part, deponents are fully capable of giving accurate, complete testimony. But there are occasions where a witness lacks the capacity to do so.

This section identifies some of those witnesses by category and provides practical guidance on dealing with the situation.

§7.01 The Rule on Witness Capacity

Rule 601, Competency to Testify in General, is short and sweet:

> Every person is competent to be a witness unless these rules provide otherwise. But in a civil case, state law governs the witness's competency regarding a claim or defense for which state law supplies the rule of decision.

This rule swept away a host of rules and principles from the past that deemed certain witnesses incompetent to testify. They were known as Dead Man's Laws, or Dead Man's Statutes. They held that an interested party cannot testify – indeed, is legally presumed *incompetent* to testify - about conversations with a deceased person, where the testimony is adverse to the deceased. This principle is designed to minimize false testimony for the benefit of the testifying party, since the deceased obviously cannot contradict what is being said. [1]

§7.02 The Presumption: Everyone is Competent

Your starting principle is that all witnesses are presumed competent unless circumstances suggest otherwise, or unless there is a governing state law that deems the witness, by virtue of position or status, unable to testify about a particular matter. For this reason, most judges will allow witnesses to testify, and leave it to the lawyers to impeach the witness if appropriate. Witnesses that are utterly incompetent are rare.

There is no single bright-line rule for determining whether a witness is competent. Typically, the witnesses' qualifications to give testimony will depend on your ability to evaluate truthfulness based on their answers.

The administration of an oath at the beginning of every witness' testimony is there as a reminder. Rule 603 provides:

> Before testifying, a witness must give an oath or

affirmation to testify truthfully. It must be in a form designed to impress that duty on the witness's conscience.

And while we're on the subject, Rule 603 is written specifically to allow flexibility in how the oath is administered. Some witnesses do not want to "swear" to the truth. Some prefer to "affirm." You should be fine as long as the witness has promised in some fashion to tell the truth before the testimony starts.

§7.03 Witness Types and Competency Issues

Let's talk about witness competency in the context of specific types of witnesses. The fact is that witnesses come to the deposition room with varying levels of education, intelligence, language skills and mental capacity.

§7.04 Age - The Immature & the Advanced

As a rule of thumb, I may have concerns about age as a capacity issue if the witness is under ten or over the age of eighty. Most children ten and older understand what telling the truth means. And most adults through age eighty retain the capacity to understand questions and to answer fully and completely.

So age is typically an issue at the extremes. Where a witness is nine or younger, or over the age of eighty, I will typically conduct a respectful inquiry on the record to establish capacity. This is not based on science. In fact, it is largely based on my own concern about the fact that a jury may stereotype a witness as lacking capacity.

So even where I believe a witness above the age of eighty is competent, I may still conduct an inquiry to document the witness' competent state of mind at the time of testimony. (And that is the only moment when competency matters - at the time of testimony.) Witnesses of advanced age may not survive the delays leading up to trial, so the transcript should establish the deponent's sound mind to the satisfaction of your jury, in the event that is all you have to present to the jury from that witness.

If you suspect there is an age-related capacity issue, you should first review the rules and statutes governing your jurisdiction. I doubt there will be anything specific, but it is important to check.

Here are some things you can do to ease the anxiety of youthful and elderly witnesses, and to evaluate and confirm their capacity to testify truthfully:

*** Pick a Comfortable Location**

It could be their home, a clinic, an assisted living facility where they reside or some other environment where the surroundings are familiar and will not contribute to difficulties your witness may have.

Limit the Number of Participants

The presence of unfamiliar spectators makes witnesses of

all ages uncomfortable, particularly those who are very young or of advanced age.

Ask Questions to Establish Competency

If you have concerns about competency, begin by asking basic questions about the witness' family, home, school or life history, to show the deponent understands your questions and is answering truthfully about familiar matters.

A key question for very young children is to ask if they understand what it means to be truthful and what it means to tell a lie. Ask them to explain the difference and why telling a lie is bad. Judges and juries want to see that the witness – young or old - clearly understands the difference between right and wrong, and between telling the truth and being dishonest.

You can use simple tests such as asking the witness if you would be telling the truth or a lie if you said that you are wearing a red shirt when in fact you are wearing a white shirt. There are lots of questions in this category you can use.

Seek Court Guidance if Necessary or Helpful

If for some reason there is an issue about how to approach a youthful or elderly witness, seek court guidance.

Consider Sealing the Transcripts

This can give witnesses additional comfort about testifying freely, especially if the topics are sensitive matters. Judges are amenable to sealing transcripts under the right circumstances, and you should not encounter opposition from other lawyers. This can give both deponents and their caregivers the kind of comfort they need to help you achieve your objectives.

Use Initials When Referring to Underage Children

This is common in depositions where children are witnesses or victims. Not only does this allow the transcript to be filed without excessive, time-wasting redactions, but it might also give the witness and his or her family a greater degree of comfort from the layer of confidentiality this provides.

Consider Videotaping the Deposition

Doing so could avoid the possibility of further traumatizing the witness, and could be a substitute for live trial testimony.

Evaluate Whether A Facilitator Might Help

Consider whether this is a situation where you might want a facilitator to help in conducting the examination. Is there someone who has the unquestioned trust of the child? Someone who can pose your questions to the child?

Have A Parent or Caregiver Attend

For the very young and for those who are advanced in age, the presence of a familiar face can provide the kind of comfort and sense of protection the deponent needs to speak freely.

Consider Depositions Upon Written Questions

Rule 31 allows for depositions by written questions. That is rarely an effective tool for depositions, and mostly used where a witness has limited specific knowledge, such as a record custodian.

But it could be effective for use with a child in some situations. It is at least worth consideration. Even where a child witness might suffer trauma from live examination, though, some judges may still permit it because of the need for lawyers to evaluate the child as a witness. *See Estate of Chen v. Lingting Ye*, 208 A. 3d 1168 (S. Ct. R.I. 2019) (reversing order limiting plaintiffs in drowning negligence action to deposition by written questions of ten-year old girl who was sole witness; held, claims of likely trauma too vague to outweigh benefit from live deposition, where counsel could make critical assessments of credibility and demeanor, and further citing to risk that likely counsel involvement in crafting answers will generate additional discovery disputes).

But Don't Forego Your Case Needs

Once you establish witness competency, proceed with your planned examination. There is nothing improper about thoroughly deposing children and the elderly. They will garner great sympathy with a jury, so you must press ahead to fully vet their knowledge and to explore apparent inconsistencies.

I recently defended a deposition where the deponent was a very soft-spoken nine-year old female. She was about 4'11', wide-eyed, and absolutely adorable. Her mother and father sat in on the deposition as well. The opposing lawyers took turns questioning her but their examination was exceedingly brief. The first lawyer, with eleven years' experience, questioned her for about six minutes. The second lawyer, with 43 years' experience, opted not to ask any questions. I sensed that both felt the child should be questioned gently, and that both were sensitive to the parents' presence.

I could appreciate their decisions, but they left a great deal on the table. The young girl was the key witness. Most of what she knew did not surface. They could not depose her again, and they wound up paying a heavy price for their deference. Don't make that mistake.

§7.05 Mental Disorders

In many cases, you will know before the date of deposition whether the deponent suffers from mental disorders. And you will have done your homework on the impact of such diagnoses on the ability to give testimony.

Except in rare cases, most mental disorders will not affect

the quality of testimony. I have represented and deposed many who suffered from depression, bipolar disorder, anxiety, and ADD/ADHD, and have never encountered a situation where it rendered them incompetent to testify.

You should inquire of witnesses, of course, whether they suffer from any condition they believe will affect their ability to understand questions or to answer truthfully. You should also ask, apart from the witness' own belief, whether they have been informed by a healthcare provider that their ability to understand, to remember, and to tell the truth are affected by any conditions or medications.

§7.06 Drug Use Prior to Deposition

You should ask about drug use, prescription or otherwise, that the witness has ingested in the week prior to the deposition. It may further be appropriate to inquire about drugs ingested as much as six months prior to the deposition. While most prescription medications wear off after a few days, some – Prozac and many antidepressants, for example - can take months to leave the system. There is no way to know whether the deponent continues to experience the effects of those or other drugs, legal or otherwise.

The only solution is to ask.

§7.07 Stress from Life Events

Stress is a common testimonial impediment. Many witnesses are under considerable stress when being deposed. That is true of plaintiffs, who appreciate the consequences of a bad performance, and of defense witnesses, who similarly appreciate the possible impact of their testimony on their career.

And you never know what other stressors are affecting your deponents. Perhaps they just came from home after a terrible argument with their partner. Perhaps they're being hounded by the IRS and just got another threatening letter. Perhaps the deponent has engaged in case-related misconduct that has not yet been discovered and is suffering anxiety out of fear that you are about to discover it. There is no end to the list of malignant spirits that may be hounding your witness. We all have something going on in our lives that is consuming valuable headspace.

So it's good to ask witnesses generally if there is something affecting them at the moment that would make giving testimony unwise. Better to find out now than at trial, when the witness is trying to weasel out of their deposition testimony.

§7.08 Exhaustion

On many occasions, I have begun my examination of witnesses only to learn that they worked the overnight shift and are sitting across from me without having slept for the last thirty hours.

That puts me in a difficult spot. Regardless of the answer I get about exhaustion, the testimony may simply be unreliable. Even the answer to my question "Are you too exhausted to proceed?" may be unreliable. If the witness is truly mentally exhausted, how would he or she know how the exhaustion is affecting them?

In this situation, it is a judgment call. If I get the sense that the witness is too tired to testify, I will reschedule them. But I will make sure the record is clear about their condition: When did you last sleep? What were you doing in the twenty-four hours prior to this deposition? It is important to make sure the record supports your decision to terminate the deposition. But I will not depose a witness that I feel is genuinely exhausted. I can't afford to leave that escape hatch for the witness and for the opposing party down the road or at trial.

If you absolutely must proceed with the deposition of an exhausted witness for reasons unique to your case, I recommend that you conduct an exhaustion inquiry at the beginning of the deposition and at various points throughout, so the record shows you gave the witness multiple opportunities to tell you he or she was tired.

With a sufficient number of denials, a judge and jury are not likely to let the witness off the hook later.

In one deposition, I neglected to ask about exhaustion and medications at the beginning of the examination. The deposition went well until the end, when the deponent and his lawyer took an extended break after I concluded. When they came back in, the lawyer asked as a follow-up question whether the witness felt competent to testify, and the answer, of course, was "No." The witness said he was on medications that he felt affected his ability to understand the questions, and that his testimony was not reliable.

Lesson learned.

§7.09 Illnesses

On occasion, you will encounter a witness who is ill or recovering from a serious illness. One or two questions should be sufficient to address any concerns you have.

§7.10 Language Barriers

Another common impediment to quality testimony is a language barrier. Depending on where you practice and your particular practice area, you may commonly encounter witnesses for whom English is not their native tongue. The problem arises not when the witness speaks no English at all, but when the witness speaks marginal English. You will know in advance when witnesses clearly need an interpreter, but perhaps not if the witness speaks some but very poor English, particularly if they are not represented by counsel.

What then?

In these situations, you should directly ask witnesses if they feel sufficiently fluent in English to understand questions. It is the same approach you would use with exhausted witnesses. If the witnesses say no, then you should halt the deposition and reset it once you have lined up an interpreter.

If witnesses say yes, then you should proceed, but continue to exercise caution, and ask multiple times throughout the deposition to confirm they are understanding your questions. You should also remind the witness, throughout the deposition, to ask for clarification if he or she does not feel a question is clear. With this kind of repetitive, but respectful, inquiry, you should be immune from efforts by the witness or counsel to backtrack on the testimony as unreliable.

In one federal case, a party attempted to use the deponent's language difficulties as justification for an affidavit in opposition to summary judgment that contained material contradictions to the witness' deposition testimony. *CSX Transportation, Inc. v. Five Star Enterprise of Illinois, Inc.*, Case No. 1:16-CV-09833 (N.D. Ill. Dec. 23, 2018).

The court was having none of it, saying that the witness had specifically testified he was sufficiently fluent to understand questions and that the examining counsel gave multiple opportunities for clarification. The affidavit was rejected.

§7.11 Doctors, Lawyers, CPAs

There are several considerations in deposing professionals. Among them are (a) scheduling problems, (b) privileges that may be asserted, and (c) fees demanded for the witness' attendance. The thorniest of these problems is likely to be the assertion of privilege, either to the deposition as a whole or to individual questions.

Scheduling Considerations

You should obtain available dates for professionals as

soon as you determine their depositions will be necessary. Courts are protective of other professionals and may issue protective orders if your scheduling is improvident. Precisely how far in advance you should book them will depend on your case. I try to allow two or three months between issuance of the notice and the date of the deposition. But that is fluid. Some situations do not require this kind of waiting period. Others might. The goal is to choose a date that will require as little disruption as possible to the professionals' existing schedule.

Privilege Assertions, in Whole or In Part

You will almost always encounter privilege objections when deposing professionals whose work is normally protected by a statutory or common-law privilege. Objections typically come in two forms. First, the professional may object to giving any testimony whatsoever. Second, the professional may, with the assistance of counsel, attend the deposition but opt to assert the privilege on a question-by-question basis.

There are splits of authority as to whether a witness can assert a blanket privilege to giving testimony, absent an extraordinary showing that harm will result if the witness answers even a single question.

In one recent decision, a trial judge refused to allow a criminal defendant charged with murder to take *any* deposition of a woman whose family members may have ordered the killing.

In that case, the victim was a law professor locked in a bitter custody battle with his ex-wife. The police suspected that the ex-wife's family may have had a role in having the ex-husband killed. The alleged intermediary between the family and the hitmen - Katherine Magbanua - is one of several people charged in connection with the killing. Magnabua sought to depose the ex-wife during pretrial discovery. The trial judge said no. *Magbanua v. State of Florida*, Case No. 1D19-1875 (Fla. 1st DCA May 31, 2019) (dismissing petition for writ of certiorari). The appeals court declined to jump into the fray at that point, saying Magbanua could raise the issue on appeal if she is convicted. But it clearly signaled its belief that the trial judge was wrong in refusing to allow any deposition whatsoever.

The better approach is to allow witnesses who assert the privilege to be deposed and let them assert it on a question by question basis. And it makes sense. There are few witnesses whose testimony is such that liability could obtain from every answer they give. Allowing privilege-bearing witnesses to be deposed permits the trial judge to review the transcript and determine with specificity what questions should be answered.

If you encounter a blanket assertion of privilege, you will need to seek an order compelling the testimony. It is crucial that you be thoroughly versed in the governing law of your jurisdiction. It is also wise to outline the subject areas of your planned examination in your motion, so the court has as much information as possible before ruling. Judges can be very skittish about allowing you free reign to question a privilege-bearing witness. The more information you can provide to show that your examination is within permissible bounds, the better.

Fees for Appearances

The issue of fees - the payment a witness wants to appear for deposition - most commonly arises with physicians. Some doctors see requests for testimony as a severe intrusion into their practice, and demand exorbitant fees. At that point, their thinking goes, you will either give up or make their day a very profitable one.

What you actually wind up paying may depend on whether the doctor is the treating physician or has been hired as an expert.

If the physician has been hired as an expert, expect to pay substantially more, although the proposed fee must bear some relation to the expert's credentials and role in the case.

Payment of fees for an expert's deposition is governed by Rule 26(b)(4)(C), which provides that: "[u]nless manifest injustice would result, the court must require that the party seeking discovery [ ] ... pay the expert a reasonable fee for time spent in responding to discovery."

In evaluating the reasonableness of an expert's fee demand, courts consider a range of factors. See *Fraser v. AOL LLC, No. 3:06-cv-954-J-20TEM, 2008 WL 312670, at *1 (M.D. Fla. Feb. 4, 2008) (citing Adams v. Mem'l Sloan Kettering Cancer Ctr., No. 00 Civ. 9377(SHS), 2002 WL 1401979, at *1 (S.D.N.Y. June 28, 2002).*

The factors can include:

- The witness' area of expertise;
- The education and training required to provide the desired expert insight;
- The prevailing rates for other comparably-respected available experts
- The nature, quality, and complexity of the discovery sought;
- The cost of living in a particular geographic area;
- The fee being charged by the expert to the retaining party;
- The fee traditionally charged by the expert on related matters; and
- Any other factor likely to be of assistance in balancing the parties' interests

There is little guidance in the decisions about what is a "reasonable" fee for an expert. There is no single governing principle. Judges use their own best thinking to set an amount they deem reasonable. In theory, Rule 26(b)(4)(C) seeks to calibrate the fee so that plaintiffs will not be hampered in efforts to hire quality experts, while defendants will not be burdened by unfairly high fees preventing feasible discovery (and resulting in windfalls to the expert).

Another obvious goal of Rule 26(b)(4)(C) - but not often stated - is to prevent one party from unfairly obtaining the benefit of the opposing party's expert work free from cost. If I am forced to hire multiple costly experts to defend against your claims, you should not be able to depose my experts for the benefit of your case at a nominal cost. Rather, uou should be forced to bear some of the expense of the expert. The way courts ensure this is to require adversaries to pay hefty fees to depose those experts.[2]

Now, if the physician is a treating doctor and was not privately retained as an expert, the hourly charges should be in line with a reasonable hourly rate for the doctor. Courts say there is a clear difference between what is reasonable for a treating physician and for a hired gun. See *Hose v. Chicago & N.W. Trans. Co., 154 F.R.D. 222, 225-26 (S.D. La. 1994)* (noting that a treating physician "assumes the obligation born by all citizens to give relevant testimony" by virtue of knowledge gained in the doctor-patient relationship; fee reduced to $400 per hour).

§7.12 Clergy

Some jurisdictions - less than ten - recognize a clergy-parishioner privilege. If your case involves a religious figure as a potential witness, your first step will be to determine whether you are in one of the handfuls of jurisdictions that recognize this privilege.

Assuming you are, you will want to evaluate this the same way you might the application of other privileges. Who qualifies as a pastor, minister, priest or clergy? Who holds and can assert the privilege? What qualifies as a communication protected by the privilege?

Religious figures can be a valuable source of information

because their guidance is often sought in times of great conflict or stress. *See Depositions: Testimonial Privileges Checklist*, by Practical Law Litigation (2018) (available on Westlaw).

§7.13 Spouses

Most if not all states, and the federal court system, recognize some form of marital or spousal privilege. Therefore, you must check the governing law in your jurisdiction and in the court system where your action is pending.

There are nuances to spousal or marital privileges, which you will want to master before you depose a witness who may assert it.

Issues to evaluate include whether the marriage or relationship is one that qualifies for the privilege, whether the communication took place before or after the marriage (which may render the privilege inapplicable), and whether one spouse may bar another from testifying even if the other spouse is willing to do so.

Further, the substance of the communication may render the privilege inapplicable. For example, communications for the purpose of committing a crime may be outside the scope of any applicable privilege.

§7.14 Common Interest/Joint Defense

In cases involving multiple plaintiffs or multiple defendants, you may find them asserting a privilege to prevent you from inquiring about communications between the parties in the presence of their counsel. This doctrine travels under several names but is most commonly known as the common interest or joint-defense privilege.

It is at its core an extension of attorney-client privilege that protects the compelled disclosure of communications between two or more parties and/or their lawyers when the parties have a common legal interest.

If this privilege is asserted, you should determine through discovery whether there is a written agreement documenting the arrangement. That will be useful in outlining the scope of your examination. The absence of such an agreement might raise questions about whether your opponents are simply trying to prevent legitimate lines of inquiry.

Courts will typically enforce such agreements once signed, but may still allow discovery prior to the date the agreement was signed and, further, may allow discovery of anything outside the scope of the agreement regardless of time period. *E.g., City of Spokane v. Monsanto Company, et al.,* No. 2:15-CV-00201-SMJ, 2019 WL 3246503 (E.D. Wash. July 19, 2019)

§7.15 Mediators

You generally cannot depose mediators. But, like everything else, there are exceptions. The first step in your inquiry is whether your jurisdiction recognizes a mediation privilege. Also helpful is determining whether your jurisdiction has adopted the Uniform Mediation Act.

Mediation serves a valuable purpose, but it is not without flaws. You may be able to depose the mediator or, at minimum, force the mediator to testify at an evidentiary hearing if the mediator, opposing party or other attendees engaged in civil or criminal misconduct. You may also be able to depose the mediator if there is a dispute about whether agreement was reached and, if so, on what terms.

Finally, it may make a difference in your situation if the mediation was voluntary and not court ordered. Some courts hold voluntary mediations to a different standard in many respects. For example, if the mediation was presuit and not expressly conducted as part of a pending proceeding, the litigation mediation privileges may have no applicability.

§7.16 Opposing Lawyers

There is no hard and fast rule that prevents you from deposing an opposing lawyer in litigation. It may raise the proverbial judicial eyebrow, but it is not categorically forbidden. This includes both current and former lawyers retained or employed by the adversary.

A federal magistrate put it thusly in her 2019 order allowing the deposition of a defendant's former in-house counsel, in the case *Abington Emerson Capital, LLC v. Landash Corporation,* Case No. 2:17-CV-143, 2019 WL 3779779, at *1 (S.D. Ohio Aug. 12, 2019) :

> To start, lawyers are not immune from deposition. *See Shelton v. Am. Motors Corp., 805 F.2d 1323, 1327 (8th Cir. 1986).*

> While a party may move, under Rule 26(c)(1) for a protective order limiting or preventing a lawyer's deposition, it is rare for a court to prohibit a deposition in its entirety...
>
> ***
>
> Relevant here, courts do not automatically apply [a balancing test] each time a party seeks to depose a lawyer. To the contrary, "the Federal Rules of Civil Procedure create no special presumptions or exceptions for lawyers, or anyone else[.]" *United States v. Philip Morris Inc.*, 209 F.R.D. 13, 19 (D.D.C. 2002) This is because "the Federal Rules presume openness in discovery[.]" *Id.* To allow otherwise, "the presumption of discoverability in the Federal Rules would be turned upside down," and it would allow a party "to immunize themselves from discovery on key issues, by knowingly and strategically placing persons who happen to be attorneys in positions where they perform critical [functions]." *Id.*

The test is a balancing one, weighing the value of discovery against the oppressive nature of burdening the opposing side through the deposition of its counsel. You should assume a court will view with at least some skepticism your request to depose a current or former lawyer.

Factors courts consider include the role of the attorney to be deposed, the risk of encountering privilege and work-product issues, the likelihood that relevant and admissible testimony will be obtained, and the availability of alternative methods – including other sources of the same information, and other forms of discovery, such as written questions rather than a live deposition. *See Abington, infra* (applying three-pronged test for deposition of former counsel, namely that (1) no other means exist to obtain the information; (2) the information sought is relevant and nonprivileged; and (3) the information is crucial to the preparation of the case); *Johnson v. City of New York*, 2018 WL 6727329 (E.D.N.Y. Dec. 21, 2018) (allowing deposition of lawyer, but on written questions only); *In re Subpoena Issued to Dennis Friedman*, 350 F.3d 65 (2d. Cir. 2003) (appeal dismissed as moot, but opinion issued for guidance noting that lawyer status does not automatically insulate counsel from depositions).

Another case in point is *Schiller v. Schiller*, 2018 WL 6815178 (Ct. App. Mich. Dec. 27, 2018). There, during a custody battle, the wife's lawyer talked to the couple's children directly, in apparent violation of a court order, and then relayed that information to child protective services, which further led to police involvement. The husband's attorney sought permission to question the wife's attorney, with the inquiry to be limited solely to the conversation the opposing lawyer had with the children. He did not seek to inquire about privileged communications between the lawyer and the wife. The court allowed the deposition.

Your odds of deposing a current or former opposing lawyer improve when you can show a legitimate need, genuine non-privileged involvement by the attorney, and a willingness to confine the scope of the questions to pertinent matters.

§7.17 Fifth Amendment Witnesses

In civil cases, the Fifth Amendment does not provide an all-encompassing right of refusal to respond to discovery requests. The privilege must generally be asserted in response to a specific question, and the matter submitted to a court to determine validity. A good overview of the privilege can be found in *Construction Industry v. Wellington Concrete*, 2018 WL 2717909 (E.D. Missouri 2018). See also *District Title v. Warren*, 2019 WL 8798745 (D.C. Aug. 1, 2018) (lawyer allegedly involved in hiding assets required to attend deposition and assert Fifth Amendment and attorney-client privileges on a question by question basis).

As I noted elsewhere in this book, some courts take a different view. Some see the risk of self-incrimination as so grave that a blanket assertion of the Fifth Amendment can be made to block all questions.

Beware of baseless assertions of this privilege. There must be a real threat of self-incrimination. The threat must be a substantial and real hazard of incrimination, and the witness must have reasonable cause to apprehend danger from a direct answer.

A court will determine in context whether a responsive answer might result in an injurious disclosure. But courts must have context. In situations where a witness refuses to answer any question whatsoever, the trial judge has no way to evaluate the validity of the privilege. That can lead to a finding that the witness can be questioned because there is no basis for any other ruling.

Some courts have held that failing to appear at a deposition, and appearing but refusing to answer, are one and the same. *E.I. DuPont de Nemours & Co, Inc. v. Thompson,* 29 Ohio App.3d 272, 276, 504 N.E. 1195 (8th Dist. 1986). So where a witness refuses to answer any questions at all, the court is more likely to find that the witness has not established a real danger of incrimination, and has not established a basis to assert the privilege.

Bear in mind that in a civil setting, the Fifth Amendment privilege protects individuals from both compelled testimony and from the compelled production of personal papers and effects. So just as witnesses cannot be forced to place themselves in legal jeopardy, they cannot be forced to turn over tangible items that would have the same effect. In the context of civil litigation, then, it is unlikely you can achieve an end run by asking the witness to produce incriminating non-testimonial evidence.

A few other twists and turns are pertinent to the assertion of the Fifth Amendment privilege. First, it only applies to natural individuals. Corporations cannot generally assert the privilege against self-incrimination. *Brazwell v. US*, 487 US 99, 102 (artificial entities are not protected by the Fifth Amendment).

Second, an individual who holds corporate records "in a representative capacity" cannot invoke the Fifth Amendment to avoid producing them even if the records personally incriminate the individual.

This is because companies can only act through their agents. Thus the records custodian's assumption of a representative capacity imposes certain obligations, including the obligation to produce corporate records on proper demand.

§7.18 Apex Witnesses

The term "apex deposition" refers to one where the proposed deponent is a high government official. The deponent, or your adversary, may object to the deposition on the grounds that forcing the witness to prepare for and attend a deposition will disrupt operations of the witness' organization, and that you can gather the same information from alternative sources. The doctrine likely has its genesis in *United States v. Morgan*, 313 U.S. 409, 422 (1941), where the Supreme Court refused to allow the deposition of the Secretary of Labor, saying that "top executive department officials should not, absent extraordinary circumstances, be called to testify regarding their reasons for taking official actions."

While I use the term "apex deposition," you should when researching cases also search using the phrase "high government official." Many cases use that phrase without referencing the word "apex."

- *Understanding the Apex Doctrine*

Why do "apex" individuals enjoy protection?

Because of the fact that litigants sometimes use depositions to disrupt the adversary. Depositions of senior officials are particularly distracting to the organization they help run.

Add to that the fact that apex depositions are routinely a waste of time. They often seek testimony from someone who was a mere figurehead, who was not really involved in the action, and who may have signed off on a matter long after the actual decisions were made. In such situations, others can testify with better specificity. So courts will protect an apex witness to avoid harassment or unnecessary inconvenience

Except for truly senior-most officials in a government organization, there is no bright-line rule for deciding who is sufficiently "high-ranking" to enjoy the benefits of the doctrine. So don't accept as gospel the mere claim that a given witness enjoys apex protection. Research your jurisdiction to determine the parameters of the doctrine in your arena.

Further, not all courts treat this doctrine with equal respect. Some treat the rank and role of the witness as just another factor in evaluating the reasonableness of discovery under Rule 26. *Tierra Blanca Ranch High Country Youth Program v. Gonzales*, 2019 WL 133270 (D. New Mexico Jan. 8, 2019). Others treat it as creating a rebuttable presumption that depositions of apex officials are an undue burden. *See Tomaszewski v. City of Philadelphia*, 2018 WL 6590826 (E.D. Penn. Dec. 14, 2018) (discussing standards and noting that courts for "good cause" can issue protective order against apex depositions).

- ***Forcing and Opposing An Apex Deposition***

How to avoid (or assure) an apex deposition? Some practical pointers:

- Focus on the *actual* involvement of the proposed deponent
- Focus on the *importance* of the deponent's role in the decision
- Whether the deponent is currently in a high-ranking position or has left and is no longer overseeing the entity
- Whether the deponent is a named party, in an individual or official capacity
- Focus on whether the deponent did, or did not, have *firsthand material knowledge*
- Focus on whether the deponent's knowledge is remote, limited, or duplicative
- Use documents or affidavits to flesh out what the witness can or cannot add
- Propose a time limit on the deposition, if you seek to take an apex deposition, commensurate with the scope of the official's role and knowledge
- Look for the *absence* of an affidavit from the proposed deponent; in other words, is the opposition based on evidence, or mere unsworn representations of counsel[3]
- *Identify other witnesses* who have superior knowledge
- Address the *size of the organization, and the day-to-day duties of the purported apex witness,* to evaluate

> whether this person is truly a senior official - notwithstanding his or her job title - or someone operationally involved on a day-to-day basis.

Your judge will want to know whether the apex witness has, or lacks, truly meaningful personal knowledge. The judge will also want to know whether the witness made key recommendations pertinent to the case. Another factor is whether the proposed deponent currently holds the "high-ranking" position. *Byrd v. D.C.*, 259 F.R.D. 1, 8 (D.D.C. 2009) ("[I]t is the current position, and not any former position, that is evaluated").

The factors cited above are driven by common sense. The court does not want parties wasting the time of senior officials. Nor do you. *See Tomaszewski v. City of Philadelphia*, 2018 WL 6590826 (E.D. Penn. Dec. 14, 2018) (Mayor of Philadelphia protected from deposition); *Tierra Blanca Ranch High Country Youth Program v. Gonzales*, 2019 WL 133270 (D. New Mexico Jan. 8, 2019) (governor, agency secretary and judge protected from depositions); *Gesualdi v. D. Gangi Contracting Corp.*, No. 18-CV-3773-FB-SJB, 2019 WL 3821221, at *1 (E.D.N.Y. Aug. 7, 2019) (rejecting demand to depose corporate owner where corporate 30(b)(6) deposition appeared sufficient). *Beaulieu v. Board of Trustees of University of West Florida*, No. 3:07CV30/RV/EMT, 2007 WL 9734885, at *4 (N.D. Fla. July 18, 2007) (order declining to allow deposition of university president); *Greater Birmingham Ministries v. Merrill*, 321 F.R.D. 406 (N.D. Ala. 2017) (allowing deposition of Alabama Secretary of State).

- *Examples: Who's "High," Who's Not*

To illustrate the concept, courts have held the following to be generally immune to depositions:

- Secretaries of federal and state agencies, *Morgan, supra*
- Governors, *Gonzales, supra*
- Board of Directors of FDIC, *Beaulieu, supra*
- State and federal cabinet members
- University presidents, *Beaulieu, supra*
- Mayors of large cities, *Tomaszewski , supra*
- Attorneys generals, Senators and Members of Congress, *Byrd v. D.C.*, 259 F.R.D. 1, 7 (D.D.C. 2009)
- Corporate presidents, *Thomas v. Int'l Bus. Machines*, 48 F.3d 478, 483 (10th Cir. 1995)

I say "generally" because the odds of a deposition of such officials appreciably increases if the official in fact has material personal knowledge and the deposition will not cause meaningful interference. *Friedlander v. Roberts*, No. 98 CIV. 1684 (RMB), 2000 WL 1471566, at *2 (S.D.N.Y. Sept. 28, 2000), aff'd, No. 98 CIV. 1684 RMB JCF, 2000 WL 1772611 (S.D.N.Y. Nov. 21, 2000) ("A deposition of a high government official will be permitted if '(1) the deposition is necessary in order to obtain relevant information that cannot be obtained from any other source and (2) the deposition would not significantly interfere with the ability of the official to perform his governmental duties').

In contrast, courts have held the following to be outside the notion of an "apex witness" or "high-government official":

- Police chiefs, *Detoy v. City & Cty. of San Francisco*, 196 F.R.D. 362, 368 (N.D. Cal. 2000)
- Deputy mayors, and general counsels of sub-departments within a city, *Byrd, supra*
- Human Resource officials
- Working owners or "corporate presidents" of small businesses

- ***Extension of Doctrine to Private Sector***

Even assuming a party has a legitimate basis to oppose the deposition of a high-ranking official, the doctrine may not extend to private-sector entities and officers. Florida, for example, has recognized the doctrine as applicable only to high-ranking *government* officials, not to private-sector entities. *See Suzuki Motor Corp. v. Winckler,* No. 1D18-4815, 2019 WL 4062353, at *2 (Fla. 1st DCA. Aug. 29, 2019) (affirming effort to depose Osamu Suzuki, chairman of the Suzuki Motor Corporation, saying the "[d]octrine is only clearly established in Florida in the government context, with respect to high-ranking government officials"). Judges in other states take a different approach. *Pizzuti v. Nashville Hospitality Capital LLC*, 2018 WL 5303061 (S.D. Ohio Oct. 25, 2018) (founder, CEO and Chairman of real estate empire authored a total of 15 emails on complex project, and most of those were irrelevant)

- ***Rule 26(c) As Alternative To Block Depositions of High-Ranking Officials***

If you are seeking to prevent the deposition of a high-ranking government or corporate official, note that even if your jurisdiction does not recognize the doctrine, or is unwilling to label your deponent as "high ranking," you may still argue Rule 26(c) as a basis for thwarting the deposition. That rule provides judges broad authority to curb unnecessary or disruptive discovery. Some courts have relied on it in lieu of, or in addition to, the apex doctrine to bar depositions of senior officials. *E.g., Thomas v. Int'l Bus. Machines*, 48 F.3d 478, 483 (10th Cir. 1995).

§7.19 Witnesses in Other Countries

Deposing witnesses in other countries requires considerable advance planning and thought. In terms of the procedures and rules governing such depositions, I have covered that in other sections in this book.

But there are other issues to address as well. Whether you are doing them remotely or in person, you will need to consider your technology needs, the impact of time zones, the possibility of language difficulties, and limitations imposed by foreign governments. In some circumstances you can compel a citizen of the United States to return to the country to testify in either a civil or criminal proceeding- through the use of a Walsh Act subpoena - but this section deals with depositions in other countries. Still, the ability to compel a witness' return to the U.S. for deposition is something to be aware of. *See Teller v. Helbrans*, No. 19-CV-3172-SJB, 2019 WL 3779863, at *1 (E.D.N.Y. Aug. 12, 2019) (discussing Walsh Act and its use in conjunction with Rule 45 subpoenas to compel a citizen's return to the U.S.; declining to compel return); *SEC v. Sabhlok,* No. C 08-4238 CRB (JL), 2009 WL 3561523 (N.D. Cal. Oct. 30, 2009) (allowing issuance of subpoena to compel witness' return from Hong Kong for civil deposition).

Let's walk through these.

- ***Technology***

If you are conducting the deposition from the United States, you will need to arrange for audio or video connections with the witness. That can pose more of a problem than you might expect. Many countries do not have reliable phone service. This means you might have trouble connecting and staying connected.

The same is true of Internet service, if you choose to use a web-based connection. I know lawyers who waited until the last minute to depose overseas witnesses and simply could not complete the depositions because of technology problems. This is something your staff must begin researching the moment you realize such depositions will be needed. Multiple technical practice runs from your location to the deposition location are wise.

If you are appearing in person, you must ensure that devices requiring electrical current can be used in the foreign country and have the appropriate plugs.

Keep in mind as well that you will need to supply any equipment you need that the stenographer does not provide. This includes videotaping equipment. You should not assume that the local stenographer has such equipment or, if it does, that it works properly.

- *Time Zones*

The title of this subsection tells you everything you need to know. Be sure to check the time difference between your location and the deposition location. And it's smart, if you're forced to choose between starting the deposition at a time convenient for you or convenient for witnesses, to choose the latter. Start late if you must so witnesses are deposed during ordinary business hours in their country. You will find witnesses, court reporters and others who must participate are much more cooperative this way.

- *Language Difficulties*

As with technology issues, assume nothing when it comes to potential language complications. Research whether any of the participants - deponents, schedulers, attendees, stenographers, videographers, security, whatever - speak English and/or the language of the other participants.

- ***Foreign Government Rules and Regulations***

Many foreign governments impose strict restrictions on the conduct of court proceedings, including depositions. Even countries friendly to the United States impose restrictions that cannot be varied by you, by the US government, or by US courts.

For example, Japan has advised the United States that it does not permit purely telephonic depositions. And if you wish to take a deposition by *video* conferencing, you must make a special request to the Ministry of Foreign Affairs. Expect a long delay between your request and their response.

For a nice example of the efforts taken by a party to depose witnesses in another country, and the incredible obstacles they faced, take a peek at *Khan v. United States*, No. 18-12629, 2019 WL 2865298, at *12 (11th Cir. July 3, 2019).

In some countries, you are only permitted to conduct depositions at a US Embassy or US consulate office. Those offices likewise impose strict restrictions on visitors, including lawyers.

Further, there are severe limitations on what you can take into the embassy, for obvious security reasons, and most embassies and consulates will not store prohibited items for you while you conduct your deposition inside.

There are also limits on the hours during which you may conduct such depositions.

You should begin researching the requirements for conducting depositions in your target countries the moment the need becomes apparent. That includes travel concerns (passport, visas, letters of authorization if required) and the limitations imposed by the host country. Internet searches about conducting depositions in a specific country will bear valuable fruit.

Finally, if your judge imposes discovery deadlines, you should build in considerable delay for discovery and subsequent activities to account for overseas discovery needs. Even routine approvals for depositions in countries like Japan can take many months and can consume nearly your entire discovery period.

§7.20 Active-Duty Military

Active-duty military members who live off base within the United States can be served with deposition subpoenas just as any private citizen. If they live on base, you must generally follow the procedures laid out in the federal Code of Federal Regulations for each branch of the service. Base commanders will generally help facilitate service, however.

§7.21 Prisoners

Deposing those in custody, in either state or federal institutions, is a fairly straightforward process. Typically, the rules governing depositions in general will provide all you need. In some situations, you may need an order from the trial court authorizing the deposition and, if needed, directing the correctional institution to produce the inmate for examination. *See Rule 30(a)(2)(B)* (party must obtain leave of court to depose confined prisoner). You may also need to secure approval from administrators for the prison system.

You should assume that if you are visiting a correctional institution, officers will search you and your briefcases or bags, and may search your vehicle. Vehicle searches are unusual, but you should nonetheless assume it is a possibility.

For these reasons, you should leave behind anything that you do not want a law enforcement officer or police dog to find. Better safe than sorry. You will certainly be required to pass through a metal detector, and anything you are carrying will certainly be searched.

I have known lawyers that had properly-licensed concealed weapons who forgot to remove them before passing through the metal detectors. They were promptly arrested. It was an oversight, but an inexcusable one.

Be mindful, too, when deposing inmates, that correctional facilities have restrictions on apparel. Visitors cannot wear inappropriate clothing. This includes revealing apparel, shirts or pants that contain offensive messages, jewelry and anything that could be used as a weapon. And if you are wearing excessive amounts of perfume or cologne, expect to be turned back.

Some facilities require you to alert the inmate's assigned

counselor as well. This is a person inside the facility assigned to act as the intermediary between the inmates and those in the outside world. It is wise, even if you have a court order authorizing the deposition, to reach out to the facility and ask about their local procedures for entering the prison and for meeting with and questioning inmates.

I have never met a correctional officer who cared about my deadlines. They care about one thing: institutional security. Know the rules before you arrive.

§7.22 Witnesses with Outstanding Warrants

In some cases, your deponents may have outstanding warrants. It is understandable that they may not want to be deposed, or appear at a predetermined place and time, for fear of being set up for arrest.

But courts take the position that those with outstanding warrants or other "wanted" statuses are not entitled to special treatment. Thus you need not agree to depose such a witness under unusual conditions, such as at a location determined by the deponent at the last moment, or only by telephone. *See American Modern Select Insurance Company v. Gardner,* 2015 WL 13740737 Ill. 2015).

§7.23 Hearing & Speech-Impaired Witnesses

In most cases, you will know in advance if the witness is unable to conduct an ordinary conversation because of hearing or speech limitations. In these situations, you should inquire about the assistive technological devices that the witness normally uses to hear or speak. That can include interpreters and TTY or TTD devices.

If the witness can hear and speak but has substantial difficulty doing so, consider the following tips:

- Give the deponent your full attention. Do not interrupt or finish their sentences. Listen patiently and carefully.
- Do not assume a deponent with a speech impairment cannot understand you. A speech impediment is not a hearing impediment. Witnesses with speech impediments may think you are trying to embarrass them, or that you see them as stupid, if you talk in an unusual, slow or exaggerated manner.
- If you have trouble understanding the individual, do not hesitate to ask the person to repeat the statement. If, after trying, you still cannot understand, ask the person if writing it down would be easier or suggest another way of facilitating communication. Don't pretend to understand the person. They will know what you are doing, as would I or anyone else.
- If you are not certain what the witness has said in response to a specific question, it is fine to repeat your understanding of his or her answer to verify what was said.

- Provide a quiet environment to make communication easier.

If you do need an interpreter for a deponent who is deaf, choose carefully. There are organizations that certify interpreters and require rigorous proof of competency. But there are also many individuals offering translation and interpretation services who should not be doing so.

And if another party has hired the interpreter, be sure to throughly vet the interpreter's qualifications. I've provided a list of questions to ask to ensure you're not being misled or are relying on an interpreter who is unqualified to perform the task. You have probably seen videos online of individuals shamefully pretending to have signing skills. One that comes to mind stood next to a law enforcement officer who was making an important announcement about a serious crime. The interpreter stood next to him making bogus hand gestures as if she were in a dance contest. (She was their newly-hired official interpreter and no one had yet discovered she was a fraud.)

Whether hiring or challenging the hiring of an interpreter, I recommend you verify that the interpreter is certified and that you question the interpreter rigorously to ensure he or she can provide verbatim translations. You should not use or agree to use a friend of the deponent, a colleague, or someone recommended by your adversary.

The following are sample questions for sign-language interpreter candidates. Do not be shy about asking them. The quality of your testimony, and possibly the outcome of your case, depend on it. Consider conducting an on the record examination if appropriate. The record can then be used to mount a challenge to the interpreter and deposition if needed:

- Tell us your name and address
- Where are you employed?
- What is your educational background?
- How long have you known sign language?
- Where did you learn American Sign Language?
- Can you communicate fluently in ASL?
- Are you certified? By whom? What is your certification called?
- What formal interpreter training have you undertaken?
- What formal *legal* interpreter training have you undertaken?
- What knowledge and skill areas did you study?
- How many times have you interpreted in court and in what kinds of situations have you interpreted?
- Please explain the difference between interpreting and transliterating, and between interpreting and translation.
- Are you familiar with the RID?
- What is meant by minimal language skills?
- How do you find out the specific language used by a deaf person?
- Have you met the deponent here?

- Were you able to establish communication?
- How did you determine that you were being understood and that communication was established?
- What language does the person use?
- How long does it take you to determine the language the person uses?
- Would you consider this person to be ASL-English bilingual?
- Is it possible to sign in ASL at the same time you are speaking in English?
- Will the interpretation you provide today be verbatim?
- What process will you use to inform the Court of errors in your interpretation?
- Can you explain the difference between simultaneous and consecutive interpretation?

§7.24 Blind or Low-Vision Deponents

The term "vision impairment" generally applies to a person whose vision cannot be corrected to a normal level. But this can mean all kinds of things. Most everyone suffers vision impairment of one kind or another.

Unless the deponent has no usable vision, you may simply need to proceed at a slower pace than you do with other witnesses. If the witness indicates he or she does have a genuine low-vision issue, inquire respectfully and gently about the nature and scope of the limitation, so that you can conduct an examination consistent with the needs of the witness.

§7.25 Witnesses with Confidentiality Agreements

You may occasionally encounter deponents who have signed a severance or settlement agreement that forbids them from speaking about their employment, the agreement, or about specific topics in general. They usually allow the witness to speak if subpoenaed, but not always.

Most courts will allow you to depose such witnesses after properly serving subpoenas and scheduling them for deposition. Parties to these agreements cannot use them to obstruct legitimate discovery demands. You might encounter a witness or lawyer who contends the agreement prevents you from deposing the person, but that is simply wrong. For the most part, those agreements are enforceable on this point only to the extent they forbid the witness from talking outside the context of a deposition or other court proceeding.

The best approach is to subpoena such witnesses and properly notice them for deposition. That will either trigger their appearance, the filing of a motion for protective order by somebody, *e.g.*, the witness or the other parties to the agreement, or your filing of a motion to compel the witness to attend.

If you must seek an order, your motion must make clear that the witness has relevant information, has been identified in discovery or mentioned by other witnesses (if that is the case), and is a person likely to testify. The witness or other party seeking to block testimony must then show good cause to prevent your deposition.

Opposition to your motion will be based on one of the same grounds argued as a basis for avoiding discovery in general - harassment, oppression, relevance, undue burden or expense, or annoyance or embarrassment.

The proponent of the confidentiality agreement must show a particular and specific injury, as opposed to stereotyped and conclusory statements that some vague harm will result.

A successful showing sufficient to block your deposition will be a tough sell to most courts, assuming your proposed deponent is a legitimate witness. Courts are understandably averse to efforts by organizations to buy the silence of witnesses who have relevant knowledge. *See Williams v. Nex-Tech Wireless LLC* 2016 WL 11468885 (D. Kan. 2016); *Kalinauskas v. Wong*, 151 FRD 363, 365 (D. Nev. 1993); *Davis v. The GEO Group* 2011 WL 2941291 at *1 (D. Colo. 2011); *Gulf Oil v. Bernard* 452 US 89, 102 n. 6 (1981); *but see Phillips ex rel Estates of Byrd* 307 F.3d 1206, 1212 (9th Cir. 2002); *see also* Richard L. Marcus, *The Discovery Confidentiality Controversy*, 1991 U. Ill. Rev. 457, 502 and 504.

~

8

THE DAY OF DEPOSITIONS

Covered in This Chapter

- *§8.01 Outside the Deposition Room*
- *§8.02 Who's Arriving with Who?*
- *§8.03 Are Arriving Vehicles Relevant to the Case?*
- *§8.04 Who's Interacting with or Comforting Whom?*
- *§8.05 Inside the Deposition Room*
- *§8.06 Attendees: Specific Considerations*
- *§8.07 Sequestration Rules Do Not Apply*
- *§8.08 But Ask for Sequestration if Appropriate*
- *§8.09 Excluding an Actual Party*
- *§8.10 Sequestering Transcripts from Review*

There is often a lot more going on in and around the deposition room on the day of depositions than you might imagine. In this section, I share thoughts about various events and opportunities.

§8.01 Outside the Deposition Room

The opportunity to observe and collect evidence on the day of depositions goes beyond what is being said in the room.

I and my staff pay close attention as witnesses and attendees arrive and depart. We also pay close attention during breaks, to see who is talking to who and the demeanor of those involved in the conversations. You don't have to hear a word to draw conclusions from such events.

§8.02 Who's Arriving with Who?

In terms of arrivals and departures, I like to know who arrived with who. I also like to know who drove the deponent. Were those who rode with the deponent chosen to send a message? Did your witness arrive in the same car as their boss and the HR chief?

In other words was the ride an especially chilly one? Laden with an unspoken but unmistakable message about the consequences of unflattering testimony? Would the witness appreciate that the ride back would be a very unpleasant one, depending on what's said?

Can we tell, by who rode with who, which witnesses

probably align with the adversary? Are there multiple deponents in the same car? Are they not only aligning with the positions of your opponent but further making sure their testimony matches each others'?

Are some witnesses arriving as a group while others arrive alone? Put another way, have some been isolated because of their expected testimony? Or are they arriving separately because they intend to support you and do not want to feel pressured?

Even seemingly innocuous things like transportation arrangements can be powerful cues. If you are not paying attention, these cues are lost. But if you know and appreciate them, you'll better understand what words mean when witnesses testify.

It is quite understandable that a witness seems reluctant to testify where the witness arrived with, and will leave with, people who can fire them the moment the car door opens back at the office or plant.

§8.03 Are Arriving Vehicles Relevant to the Case?

The vehicles your deponents arrive in might be relevant as well.

Does your case involve vehicles the opposing party owns and operates? In multiple cases, I have seen witnesses arrive in vehicles that had some bearing on the issues. In one case that involved the transportation of a large and valuable animal, the witness - *unbelievably* - drove the exact truck that housed the animal when it was killed.

I had a paralegal discreetly photograph the vehicle on the outside, and I then asked the witness during the deposition if she minded us photographing the interior cage where the animal was transported. She freely agreed, and we managed to capture some fantastic visual evidence relevant to the issues.

Everyone participating in the deposition walked outside and used their smartphones to photograph the truck. It was bonus evidence for everyone. But if we hadn't developed a habit of broad deposition-day awareness, we would have missed an incredible opportunity.

In another case involving a disabled plaintiff, several current employees of the defendant arrived in the precise types of vehicles the employer refused to let our client drive. Again, I had an investigator discreetly photograph the vehicles, which were parked on public streets, from every conceivable angle.

The investigator was also able to use measuring tapes to measure the length of various devices on the trucks that our client would have used on the job, as well as labels identifying the exact makes and models of the equipment. That allowed us to immediately go to the manufacturer's websites and obtain data about the equipment, weight, and capabilities. I then used online images of the equipment - which, obviously, was the exact type used by drivers - during the remaining depositions. Can you otherwise imagine the motions, court hearings, rulings and, possibly, appeals, we would have had to endure to get the same information the company had literally delivered to us on a silver platter?

Obviously, if you are observing and capturing visual evidence of arriving vehicles, or of the occupants of arriving vehicles, you must do so discreetly and in a way that does not expose you to claims of witness intimidation. But what happens on public streets is public, and enjoys no privacy protections. You should take full appropriate advantage.

Just as obviously, if you are defending claims, you should give equal thought to the show going on in the parking lot as your witnesses arrive and depart. You may not want an observant adversary photographing specific vehicles, and you may not want conclusions to be drawn about who arrives with who. Everything matters. Everything needs to be managed.

§8.04 Who's Interacting with or Comforting Who?

Of equal import are the individuals' activities and conversations taking place in the parking lot, in hallways, and in conference rooms before, during and after depositions.

On breaks, what's happening? Who's talking to who? Who's *not* talking to who? Who's going off to talk separately and confidentially to who? Anyone look angry? Anyone being given the thumbs up, in the presence of other witnesses who've not yet testified?

Who's sitting with who in the lobby, and what are they saying? Are witnesses being intimidated in some way just before they testify? Pay close attention. You must never inappropriately listen in on conversations, nor ever make witnesses uncomfortable, and you must avoid going anywhere near privileged conversations.

But you can pay attention to how the witnesses line up, who they talk to, and the general demeanor of those talking and those listening.

§8.05 Inside the Deposition Room

Now let's talk for a moment about the interior of the room where the deposition is taking place.

Pay attention to the seating and to the general room environment. Seating considerations include an assessment of where you should sit vis-à-vis the deponent and where friendly and hostile forces will sit. And take note of other seating that might allow an opponent or others to situate in a position to stare down or intimidate deponents.

Pertinent to the room environment, pay attention to the temperature, to the availability of confidential break rooms, to food and water, to potential dangers to you and the deponents, to the availability of Wi-Fi, and to distractions and situations exposing witnesses to embarrassment by others passing by.

§8.06 Attendees: Specific Considerations

A key issue to address relates to those in attendance. For the most part, litigators give little advance thought to the guest list, so to speak, at depositions. That is understandable. Typically, but depending on your type of practice, depositions are attended by one lawyer for each party, one deponent at a time, and the court reporter. This configuration is so common that we don't think about others who might show up. As a result, we often take no steps to inquire about who's coming, and to determine whether we should seek court intervention.

There may be occasions where an adversary arrives with attendees specifically chosen to intimidate deponents. The intimidation could be threatening or it could even be sympathetic, *i.e.,* intended to trigger feelings of loyalty by the witness.

It could be someone the witness is fearful of, or someone the witness has a crush on. It could be a harasser or an assailant. It could be someone who has the ability to cause your client psychological, business or career damage, or the ability to give your client raises, promotions or other favorable assignments, offices or perks.

I give active thought in every case to the potential attendees. I speak to my clients about the deposition process and make sure they realize that most anyone associated with the case might be in the deposition room. I then ask whether there is anyone whose presence might materially affect their focus, mindset or testimony. If so, I will then inquire of the opposing parties. If the answers are not satisfactory, I may seek a court order under Rule 26, among others, asking that the court preclude certain actors from appearing at deposition.

The Basics

§8.07 Sequestration Rules Do Not Apply

Who can sit in on a federal deposition? Most anyone except by agreement or court order.

Rule 30(c)(1) says the trial sequestration rule (FRE 615) does not apply to depositions. So lawyers cannot simply demand, at the start of a deposition, that others leave the room. The 1993 amendments to Rule 30(c) make that clear:

> "...[O]ther witnesses are not automatically excluded from a deposition simply by the request of a party."

You may run across older cases that say otherwise, but they are pre-1993 amendment rulings. *E.g., Lumpkin v. BI-LO*, 117 F.R.D. 451 (M.D. Ga. 1987).

Indeed, one federal judge deemed frivolous a lawyer's claim that exclusion of witnesses at deposition was required by FRE 615. In *Panama City Beach Condos, Ltd. v. Adjusters Int'l Colorado, Inc.*, 2009 WL 10674351 (N.D. Fla. Feb. 3, 2009), a lawyer stopped the deposition and called the court after the opponent refused to honor his demand that certain people in the deposition room leave. The judge made short work of the lawyer's position, and then fined him for even making the argument.

For more on that, read the order of US District Judge Robert Hinkle in the *Panama City Beach Condos* case, cited above, and a similar order in *Lopez v. Gibson*, Case No. 6:17-CV-327-ORL-40-GJK (M.D. Fla. filed March 12, 2018). That order is ECF document 23. *See also In re Stratosphere Corp. Sec.*

Litig., 182 F.R.D. 614, 620 (D. Nev. 1998) ("The basis and reasons for this decision begin with Rule 30(c) in which the first sentence reads: "Examination and cross-examination of witnesses may proceed as permitted at the trial under the provisions of the Federal Rules of Evidence except Rules 103 and 615." In other words, a deposition should be conducted just as though the witness were testifying at trial, with the exception that there is no judge there to rule on objections or admissibility and others may not be precluded from sitting in on the deposition.")

§8.08 But Ask for Sequestration if Appropriate

While the rule of sequestration cannot be invoked unilaterally at the deposition, the 1993 Note to Rule 30 says a party can make application for imposition of the rule:

> "Exclusion, however, can be ordered under Rule 26(c)(5) when appropriate; and, if exclusion is ordered, consideration should be given as to whether the excluded witnesses likewise should be precluded from reading, or being otherwise informed about, the testimony given in the earlier depositions. The revision addresses only the matter of attendance by potential deponents, and does not attempt to resolve issues concerning attendance by others, such as members of the public or press."

So if you wish to exclude one or more individuals, or even everyone but the deponent and lawyers, you must do so in advance by seeking a protective order under Rule 26(c), not under FRE 615 and not under Rule 30. You can, of course, call the judge while at the depositions, but think twice about waiting until then, unless the situation is particularly egregious. Otherwise, if the situation at hand was predictable, you risk being fined and criticized for not seeking relief beforehand. The bottom line is that the law has long allowed you to seek an order preventing a specific person from attending a deposition, upon good cause shown. *E.g., Cornell v. A & K Energy Conservation, Inc.*, No. 8:10-CV-393-T-30TBM, 2011 WL 13257551, at *2 (M.D. Fla. Feb. 2, 2011) (excluding multiple fact witnesses because of possibility witnesses were attending to coordinate their future testimony).

§8.09 Excluding an Actual Party

Since 1970 it has been possible under Rule 26(c)(1)(E) to even exclude a party. If a deponent is likely to be severely traumatized by the presence of the opposing party's owner, corporate representative or key witness, seek a protective order under Rule 26(c)(1)(E) to exclude them.

This may be important where, for example, the deponent was the victim of emotional or physical trauma and the adversary wants to park the harasser or attacker across the table.

Exclusion of a party is a more extreme ask, but if good cause exists, you are more likely to get serious consideration than in the past. This is largely because of technological advances.

Now, if the exclusion is as to physical presence but not as to the testimony itself, those excluded still have the option of watching using video conferencing software. They can also communicate with their counsel by text or instant messaging. So the party isn't prevented from aiding their counsel during the deposition.

If you need to seek this kind of relief, look at the January 19, 2017 Opinion issued by Robin L. Rosenberg in *Doe v. Lynn University*, 2017 US DIST LEXIS 7528, Case No. 9-16-CV-80850 (S.D. Fla. Jan. 19, 2017). She approved the magistrate's exclusion of an assailant on these exact grounds and cited the use of technology as a reasonable alternative way for the person to participate. Similarly, a New York federal judge excluded two individual party defendants that had allegedly severely harassed the plaintiff. *Ameduri v. The Village of Frankfort*, No. 611CV0050MADDEP, 2012 WL 13172920, at *4 (N.D.N.Y. July 17, 2012).

Also, check out the court's order in a case involving 1,600 plaintiffs, *Alphonso Mitchell, et al., v. Osceola Farms Co.*, No. 05-80825-CIV, 2006 WL 8433692 (S.D. Fla. May 8, 2006). There the judge approved the defense request for exclusion of other plaintiffs as each plaintiff testified because of a fear the plaintiffs were colluding with each other to keep their stories consistent.

But remember that an order limiting attendance at deposition does not by itself prevent witnesses from reading others' transcripts later. So let's talk about that.

§8.10 Sequestering Transcripts from Review

Apart from having people physically excluded from the deposition room, you can also ask the court to bar them from learning what witnesses said. To do so, you simply include a request in your sequestration motion to bar the witness from obtaining transcripts and to bar others from otherwise informing the excluded about what witnesses said. This is the other piece of the puzzle. Absent an order in place by your court, there is nothing to stop witnesses from reading each others' deposition transcripts after the depositions but before trial. *See Naismith v. Prof'l Golfers Ass'n*, 85 F.R.D. 552, 567 (N.D. Ga. 1979); *Thun v. Maine*, No. 09-cv-85, 2009 WL 2366052, at *15 (D. Me. July 28, 2009); *Lumpkin v. Bi-Lo, Inc.*, 117 F.R.D. 451, 453 (M.D. Ga. 1987).

As an aside, you should routinely consider whether to restrict distribution of deposition transcripts once they are produced. Deposition testimony sometimes resembles the Wild West. We've all encountered deponents who traffic in the juiciest of gossip and speculation.

But absent agreement or a confidentiality/protective order, your client might suffer harmful and potentially irreversible consequences from an inadvertent, or malicious, release of transcripts. Reputations could be ruined. Businesses could be destroyed because of unfounded claims of improper business practices. Marriages and familial relationships can be forever broken.

An Ohio appeals court issued an opinion in 2017 touching on the traditional confidentiality of discovery, and it reminded me of the value of proactively thinking about agreements (or orders) protecting clients from gratuitous disclosures of otherwise private information. In *Speece v. Speece*, Case No. 2016-G-0100, Ct. App. Ohio, 11th Dist. (Sept. 29, 2017) , the court reflected on the traditional limitations of pretrial information gathering:

> First, "[d]iscovery has historically never been open to the public. Indeed, noting that discovery proceedings were not open to the public at common law, the United States Supreme Court has held that 'pretrial depositions are not public components of a civil trial.'" *Adams v. Metallica, Inc.*, 143 Ohio App.3d 482, 487 (1st Dist. 2001), quoting *Seattle Times Co. v. Rhinehart,* 467 U.S. 20, 33 (1984). Jurisdictions that require filing of discovery materials customarily provide that trial courts may order materials not be filed or that they be filed under seal.'" Id., quoting *Seattle Times, supra*, at 33, fn. 19. 2017 WL 4335536.

Some courts have long recognized that the general public's right of access to the judicial system does not include the discovery stage, including depositions. Deposition testimony, in particular, may be highly-invasive, may reveal trade secrets, or may cause emotional trauma if revealed.

This is one reason why many courts do not require the routine filing of discovery materials. Federal courts generally forbid it. And state courts often only require the filing of notices that discovery has been served or is scheduled, not the discovery information itself.

The Eleventh Circuit Court of Appeals appeared to actually invite parties to seek limitations on access to discovery where appropriate, in *Romero v. Drummond Co.*, 480 F. 3d 1234, 1245 (11th Cir. 2007)

> The right of access does not apply to discovery and, where it does apply, may be overcome by a showing of good cause……."[t]he prospect of all discovery material being presumptively subject to the right of access would likely lead to an increased resistance to discovery requests," and "...discovery is "essentially a private process ... the sole purpose [of which] is to assist trial preparation" *citing United States v. Anderson*, 799 F. 2d 1438, 1441 (11th Cir.1986).

The takeaway? Consider making the confidentiality of deposition testimony part of your new-case checklist. If other information in your case justifies an order restricting disclosure - medical records, trade secrets, customer lists, business records, personnel files and the like - then testimony about them may also warrant restrictions on access and dissemination.

You can do this easily by including deposition proceedings and transcripts as documents subject to confidentiality in your case management plan. If your court does not require such a plan at the outset, file a motion and request an order that does the same thing. You can also provide for deposition sequestration in the same plan or motion.

9

TAKING DEPOSITIONS

Covered in This Section:

- *§9.01 Vary Your Opening Examination Routine*
- *§9.02 Maintain Eye Contact with Deponents*
- *§9.03 Choose Psychologically-Powerful Seating*
- *§9.04 Discuss the Oath with the Witness*
- *§9.05 Let Other Lawyers Take Depositions First*
- *§9.06 Use Spreadsheets for Methodical Notes*
- *§9.07 Memorialize Inappropriate Nonverbal Conduct*
- *§9.08 In Phone Depositions, Memorialize the Room*
- *§9.09 Protect Clients from Exhaustion*
- *§9.10 Use Your Smartphone Proactively*
- *§9.11 (Mostly) Ignore Evidentiary Objections*
- *§9.12 Bring Observers Who Make a Difference*
- *§9.13 Consider Deposing Your Own Client*
- *§9.14 Use the Internet to Sharpen Your Examination*

- *§9.15 No Confidential Talks in the Deposition Room*
- *§9.16 Location, Shmocation*
- *§9.17 Have a Deposition Misconduct Kit Ready*
- *§9.18 Take EUOs Whenever Possible*
- *§9.19 Don't Be Shy About Calling the Judge*
- *§9.20 Play the Phone Game When Using Exhibits*
- *§9.21 Never Take a Non-Answer for An Answer*
- *§9.22 Use Witness-Centric Hypotheticals*
- *§9.23 Pursue Selective Memory Failures*
- *§9.24 Explore the Selectively Perfect Memory*
- *§9.25 Your Appearance Affects the Testimony*
- *§9.26 Create Powerful Exhibits for Depositions*
- *§9.27 Maintain a Neutral Affect*
- *§9.28 Never Go Off the Record for Discussions*
- *§9.29 Scale Your Examination to the Witness*
- *§9.30 Summarize and Cap Witness Testimony*
- *§9.31 Don't Hold Back Bombshells*
- *§9.32 "The Usual Stipulations?" Huh?*
- *§9.33 Insist Documents Be Marked as Exhibits*
- *§9.34 Address Deponent Misconduct*
- *§9.35 Remove Unnecessary Deponents From Your Notice as Soon as Feasible*
- *§9.36 Strategic Deposition Cancellations*
- *§9.37 Be Wary of Making Judicial Admissions*
- *§9.38 Telling Deponents About Other Testimony*
- *§9.39 Cross Far Beyond the Scope of Direct*
- *§9.40 Making Unsworn Document Sworn*
- *§9.41 Jury Instructions as a Deposition Tool*
- *§9.42 Phrase Questions to Match Trial Themes*

In this section, updated and expanded from the original book, *10,000 Depositions Later: 33 Tips for Taking Superior Depositions*, I outline tactic and strategic approaches to taking depositions. In some sections, I have updated my commentary and included additional case law.

§9.01 Vary Your Opening Examination Routine

Vary your opening deposition routines to regularly include - as one of your approaches - the *immediate* inquiry into the most critical case issues. Varying the speed of your takeoffs and landings, so to speak, can increase your effectiveness against lawyers who are well-prepared for your style of examination because you always follow the same routine. "Sometimes a hang glider, sometimes a rocket" is a good rule of thumb for altering the order in which you address deposition topics.

This particularly applies to the opening segment, but variation in your routine has value in later segments as well.

Most witnesses, even seasoned experts, are anxious during the first round of examination questions. It is similar to the nervousness seen in the opening minutes of play in the Super Bowl or World Series. The best players in those sports are on the field, and yet those opening moments are filled with players' mistakes.

There is an expression for it in military conflicts: "No battle plan ever survives contact with the enemy." When strategies for conflict meet the real world, the real world wins. Nothing goes as planned. Errors pile up. Mistaken suppositions have costly consequences.

But if your opening topics always follow the same order, your depositions will be easier to defend. Imagine a football coach who always uses the same play. Or a general whose battle plan always calls for troops to come from the left. How effective is repetition in adversarial conflicts?

Some lawyers waste opportunities in the first rounds by predictably asking about topics such as address, phone number, current employment, family members, and educational history. This allows witnesses to settle down, to gauge you, to develop an accurate sense for what they can get away with. Once this anxiety disappears, the witnesses will be comfortable with even the most difficult questions.

So the first segment is a critical opportunity for you. If you use the same approach all the time, the opposing lawyer has told the witness the first round will be your warmup act, the second will be topics D, E and F, and so on. The batters all know what pitches you're throwing long before you throw them.

How do they use this? They prepare deponents for your opening segment, and give them a heads up on what's coming after. During the first break, the lawyer will get the witness ready for your next topics. They can efficiently use every break to sharpen the witness for the next, predictable package of topics.

Don't waste this invaluable opportunity. Start with a pitch/topic you've never opened with before, and mix it up. The same is true of subsequent segments as well. There is value in altering the order in which you address topics in your substantive field of practice.

Good lawyers can easily predict the order of topics you cover, and use that knowledge to prepare their witnesses in stages. This works only if you remain predictable.

§9.02 Maintain Eye Contact with Deponents

It is wise to maintain eye contact as much and for as long as you possibly can when questioning witnesses. The deponent's eyes and facial gestures are without question the most valuable clues you'll have to the truthfulness and completeness of the testimony.

In Western cultures, some say, the eyes are the windows to the soul. They reveal critical information about a person's emotion, state of mind and truthfulness. They provide much more information than the witness' words alone. Some forensic psychologists believe the flow of information from the eyes is so voluminous that processing all the information can be difficult.

The avoidance of eye contact is also a valuable clue. Some avoid eye contact in an effort to mask true feelings or thoughts. Avoidance can be an admission or a sign of guilt. Standardized psychiatric diagnostic tests have long used eye contact, or the avoidance thereof, as a marker in diagnosing possible disorders.

Of course, you must be sensitive to different cultural norms. In some cultures, prolonged eye contact may be inappropriate. But on balance, there is no substitute for eye contact for determining whether a witness is being truthful or complete.

I see even very experienced lawyers conducting examinations with their head down, poring through twenty-five or thirty pages of printed questions they prepared. These lawyers rarely look up as they work through their checklist. Sometimes it seems they never do make eye contact with the witness.

This wastes an unbelievable opportunity. Lawyers who work excessively from checklists miss two golden opportunities.

First, their limited eye contact with witnesses results in the loss of feedback coming from the witness' expressions. That's a critical failure for an interrogator.

Second, such lawyers become so invested in the process of mechanically moving from one question to another that they miss much of what the witness is really saying.

Sometimes just looking at the witness, talking to them, allows you to see what's really being said. Reading between the lines is possible only if you are both looking and listening.

So make eye contact. Listen to their tone of voice. Take note when the witness avoids eye contact. Pay attention when the witness sometimes answers quickly and sometimes answers with great pause. Their eyes and facial gestures will help you understand these variations in style of response as well as the full meaning of the responses themselves. If you need to use a checklist, fine. But spend most of your time looking at the witness, and really listening to what they're saying.

§9.03 Choose Psychologically-Power Seating

Consider sitting as close to the witness as you can, ideally with the witness at the end/head of the table and you on one side in the chair closest to the witness. This spot, known as the "corner position" in psychological research, places you diagonally to the witnesses, not across from them. "Corner position" seating has been shown to be the most effective configuration for a cooperative and productive examination.

The other lawyer will sit across the table from you, also diagonally to the witness. Court reporters can sit wherever they feel comfortable, as long as it is not between you and the witness.

It may surprise you to learn that considerable research has been done on seat location as a variant both as to the environment of a meeting and the dynamics of interaction between seated participants. Robert Summer, a leading psychologist from the University of California, conducted the first major study.

His research, and more done by others, shows that, even across cultures and socioeconomic status, seat locations are driven by the relationships and roles of the seated participants. Your own behavior in choosing where to set vis-à-vis another person at the same table probably follows the models studied by Dr. Sommer.

For example, where would you sit if you were meeting a first date at a restaurant, and the table was square? Likely in the corner position. What about if you were reviewing documents on a laptop computer, in your office conference room, with a colleague? Corner position. Now, where would you sit if you were (a) playing chess against someone, (b) participating in an interview in a small friendly company, or (c) if you were trying to avoid interactions with others at a long public table in a library?

- ***Four Distinct Seating Configurations***

The studies resulted in the characterization of the most common seating positions as "the corner position" (with two participants seated diagonally at a table end, to maximize cooperation, eye contact and friendliness), the "cooperative position" (with the two participants sitting on the same side of the table, to maximize the sense of a joint goal), the "competitive/defensive position" (with the key participants seated directly across from each other at a table, with a table representing a psychological barrier between them) and the "independent position" (which you might use at a library where you're forced to sit near others but wish to minimize contact. This has you sitting several chairs down, and across the table from, the other person).

- *The Corner Position is Ideal*

Choose the corner position for examining deponents whenever possible. This encourages a sense of cooperation with witnesses even if they are true adversaries. It also sharply minimizes the physical and psychological barriers between you and deponents.

The court reporter might give you a look, but there is nothing that requires reporters to take an end-table seat. Reporters need line-of-sight; that is available from any chair in the room. The corner position makes the most sense anyway because it speeds document reviews in the deposition. It also places you no closer to the witness than the opposing lawyer, who will also be seated in the corner position relative to the witness, but on the other side of the table from you (appropriately, in the "competitive/defensive" position).

- *Corner Seating in Other Settings*

I evaluated examination techniques in other quasi-coercive environments, including law enforcement interrogations, in writing this book. Among them were books on the Reid Technique, a widely-used police interrogation method.

Take a moment and search online for videos of actual interviews conducted in these and other high-stakes settings. You will find corner-position seating used in almost all of them. It's an effective and proven component of the interview/examination process.

You will also find the tone used by law enforcement interrogators to be quite a bit more respectful than that used by many lawyers in depositions, but that's a topic for another day.

- ***Uncomfortable? Practice at Work***

Try this with a coworker. Instead of sitting behind your desk, or at a conference table directly across from someone, walk around the desk and sit in a chair next to your colleague – the "cooperative position."

In another meeting, sit diagonally in the "corner position." Feel the difference? It's amazing. You'll both likely sense a degree of discomfort you didn't feel before. This is because your seating indeed implicates long-recognized psychological principles about your roles relative to each other. It's still the two of you, still just sitting in chairs. But the psychological dynamic is very different.

I remember once going to a deposition where the tables were configured in a large circle, as if the room had been used for training and the moderator stood in the middle of the row. (Psychologist Sommer would call this the "King Arthur" configuration. This classic, roundtable configuration, according to psychological principles, places everyone on equal footing because there is no "head" to the table.)

Anyway, the opposing party had me on one side of the large circle and the witness across the room from me. We were about 35 feet apart. It was simply too far. I politely got up and moved inside the circle to the same table as the witness - now about two feet away – and we began the deposition. The King Arthur configuration is not suitable for depositions.

Seating matters. It has a subtle but significant impact. There are favorable configurations, neutral configurations, and unfavorable configurations. Know which is which. Choose the one that best suits your needs. This is another essential element in the process of managing every component of the deposition process. Everything counts. Everything contributes to success or failure. Nothing is too small or too unimportant to warrant your attention.

§9.04 Discuss the Oath with the Witness

Discuss the oath briefly with witnesses at the outset of your depositions. At least one recent study revealed stark differences in the honesty of study participants when they were reminded about principles of honesty and morals before undertaking the tasks in the study. The role of the oath is rarely discussed with deponents, but you should do so.

The study I found involved a group of five hundred participants. They were divided into two groups. During the preliminary instructions, one group was asked to recall the

Ten Commandments, and the other to recall ten books they had read in high school.

They then began answering a series of math problems. The testing was designed so participants believed the exam proctors could not tell if they had cheated.

There was widespread but moderate cheating in the group asked to recall any ten books from high school. But in the group asked to recall the Ten Commandments, there was no observable cheating whatsoever. This experiment was run again, this time using not the Ten Commandments but their schools' honor codes instead.

The result was the same.

It was then run a third time, this time on a group of self-declared atheists who were asked to swear on a Bible. Once more it led to the same cheat-free results.

The bottom line? People were more truthful when reminded of the importance of being truthful.

- ***How to Present the Oath***

Your preliminary dialogue could go something like this: "Do you understand, Mrs. Jones, that you have been placed under oath?" Many witnesses will respond that it's because it's important to be honest. Reply that honesty is always important, of course, but because our judicial system depends heavily on absolute honesty - and that the system will break down if witnesses shade or distort the truth - witnesses are reminded of this obligation.

End by saying it is similar to the honor code from high school or college. That is enough.

You should not have this discussion in a loud or overbearing tone. A matter-of-fact tone is appropriate. And you should entirely skip discussions of perjury. There is no evidence a heavy hand is necessary to accomplish this objective. But discussing oaths and truthfulness will make a difference, and there is research to prove it.

- ***Why This Conversation Comes First***

The study I referenced showed, from a different experiment, that it is essential for discussions of oaths and honesty to take place before the witness begins testifying.

In that integrity experiment, the study's authors had participants complete insurance forms certifying how many miles a year they drive. This information is used to calculate insurance premiums. The sole variable in this test was the placement on the form of the certification of truthfulness.

One group was given forms with the certification at the top. It required them to sign and certify that the information was truthful before they added their information. The second group was given the same form with the certification at the bottom. That group completed the entire form and then certified its accuracy.

The group that filled out the form before certifying its accuracy was far less truthful about their annual mileage than those who promised to be honest before completing it.

The study concluded that moral reminders and honor

pledges, like the oath administered to witnesses in depositions, has a measurable impact on truthfulness if they're given before a person begins providing information.

- ***But the Oath Doesn't Affect Everyone***

The study's authors observed that these reminders are unlikely to deter committed liars. They do positively affect most people, who are generally honest but who will who fudge around the edges. So discussions of oaths, honor codes and morality will deter minor or modest acts of dishonesty, and that is sufficient justification to give those reminders.

The majority of your deponents are people who are honest and moral. Even so, they may feel pressure in the moment to overstate, understate, concoct or forget. It is precisely these witnesses - the "fudgers" - that benefit from your preliminary discussion. Think of this discussion as the equivalent of baseball's brushback pitch, a throw purposely meant to come very close to batters without hitting them, as a message to play straight.

Reporters administer the oath, but they often rush through it and so the moment loses its significance. Don't assume that will suffice. Keep your discussion of the oath brief and respectful, but have it.

One last point. What if the witness refuses to be sworn in? This situation arose in *Watkins v. Matarazzo*, 2015 WL 13745762 (S.D.N.Y. Sep. 22, 2015), an excellent decision that also cites similar cases. There the *pro se* plaintiff bizarrely refused to be sworn in unless the examining lawyer was also sworn.

The court held that "in a case where a deponent physically appears at a deposition but refuses to be sworn and testify, then the proper procedure is first to obtain an order from the court, as authorized by Rule 37 (a), directing him to be sworn and testify." The same rule applies to party deponents. Evans v. Griffin, __ F.3d __, 2019 WL 3720917 *2 (7th Cir. Aug. 7, 2019).

The testimony you obtain may be of little value if it is unsworn, so while it may delay progress and cost you additional time and expense, it is essential that you seek a court order directing the witness to swear or affirm to tell the truth. Subsequent failure by the witness to do so will expose him or her to sanctions by the court.

§9.05 Let Other Lawyers Take Depositions First

I know it is heresy among some, but let me say it: Consider letting the opposing lawyer depose witnesses first. Listening to the examination of deponents by an opposing lawyer will educate you on facts, strengths, and weaknesses about which you were previously unaware. The result? Your own examinations will be more thorough and effective.

Many trial lawyers believe it is critical to go first - to depose witnesses before the opposing side does. The thinking is that lawyers who go first might have a better chance of getting witnesses to give testimony favorably to them. In fact, the order in which lawyers conduct depositions doesn't often affects the testimony.

- ***You'll Learn their Battle Plans***

Allowing opposing lawyers to go first will sharpen your understanding of the case, and sharpen your own examination of those and other witnesses. Why? Because lawyers' questions necessarily reveal their thinking, their evidence, and their theories. They also reveal what they do not know.

Viewed another way, lawyer examinations are unavoidable disclosures of nearly everything the lawyers know and have gathered: facts, documents, protected work-product information and even matters likely within the realm of attorney-client privilege. It is impossible to frame questions to avoid leakage. Some questions reveal more than others, but the game plan becomes clear.

Caveat: I am neither a particular fan of military history or of sports, but sometimes analogies help because litigation involves principles of conflict just as much as those other endeavors. But in the same way the battle plan of an army becomes evident once the conflict starts, so does the litigation plan of your adversaries. Lawyers *cannot* conceal the contours and content of their plan once they begin deposing witnesses.

- ***The Valuable Insights You'll Glean***

An opponent's questions will tell me the central theme of their case, the facts and evidence they think are important and unimportant, the witnesses they've have interviewed, and the documents they have. In fact, an opponent's examination provides me so many insights that I often draft supplemental interrogatories or requests for production right in the midst of depositions, as the opposing lawyer's examination proceeds.

That can be an ideal time to draft follow-up discovery. Your requests will be more precise because they'll be based on information revealed directly by the opponent. If you have a portable printer in your briefcase – do you? I hope so - you can print them on the spot and hand them to the opposing lawyer when the deposition is done. I type discovery requests into a shell document on my laptop and then print them on breaks.[1]

In order to take more effective depositions, let the opposing lawyer go first. Their questions will be an intelligence bonanza.

§9.06 Use Spreadsheets for Methodical Notes

Consider setting up a spreadsheet or simple chart to collect key facts while questioning witnesses. This is a more effective way to collect some kinds of information than jotting notes on your pad or in a Word file.

Deposition testimony usually evolves in an unorganized way. Topics are covered in unpredictable ways and sometimes out of sequence, unintentionally or by design. The order of your notes will mirror the order in which testimony is given. Deposition transcripts are the same. They capture the testimony in whatever order it comes out.

We all reorganize the data after the transcript is received

and in preparation for motions or trial, but there are ways to do it while the deposition is still in progress. Better organization on the fly will sharpen your examination as it proceeds with the witness. It will also improve your examination of witnesses that follow.

An Excel spreadsheet is an excellent tool for systematically capturing information during your examination. Consider pre-configuring an Excel spreadsheet or a self-created chart before your depositions begin. Give thought to the information you will be uniformly gathering from each witness in developing your spreadsheet or chart.

You may want to capture the names of all known witnesses to specific events. Or, each witness' answers about their roles in a disputed transaction, and the names of other witnesses they spoke to.

As you work through the day's depositions, the data systematically captured this way becomes tremendously useful for each subsequent deposition. This contrasts with notetaking the traditional way, on a legal pad or in a Word document, which is simply to write down information in whatever order the witness testified to it. The shortcoming of that method is evident from the nonstop flipping of pages on the legal pad (or the scrolling up and down in the word-processing document) you see lawyers doing as they try to find specific information.

There are computer programs or applications that do the same thing. I am a strong advocate for the use of technology in every phase of litigation. But some programs require you to capture more detail than is possible while questioning a witness. This is why, for this purpose, I recommend a spreadsheet or chart. It allows you to gather information more effectively than the traditional way, but it is not so complicated that you get bogged down moving from field to field in one of the more complex case management programs. This approach is a balance between too much and not enough.

In every case I give thought to the critical information I will gather during depositions, and ask: What information or data will I be collecting from the deponents – names, dates, roles, sources of documentation – that are capable of being quickly captured in a simple chart or spreadsheet? If you routinely bring a paralegal or assistant to depositions, ask them to complete the charts as you proceed.

§9.07 Memorialize Inappropriate Nonverbal Conduct

Memorialize improper nonverbal conduct in the room by noting it on the record the moment it happens. This serves two purposes. First, it creates a written record of the conduct. Second it serves as a warning to the offender. That is often enough to stop it. I document anything I see or hear that the transcript will not reflect and that would not be tolerated by a judge if it occurred in a courtroom.

The deposition room is your operating theater. Distractions affect the development and collection of evidence. Common improper behaviors include eye gestures, words spoken under a person's breath (so-called "stage whispers"), grunts or huffing, head-shaking to signal agreement or disagreement, table-tapping, and note-taking that is unduly disruptive *e.g.*, the taking and passing of notes in an overly-conspicuous way or in a way that is intended to cue the deponent.

- *Witnesses Looking for Guidance*

It could also be something the deponent is doing, such as constantly looking at their lawyer before answering a question. I say nothing if deponents occasionally glance at their counsel. That is normal. But if they are looking, hoping, inviting some kind of input, i speak up. “Mr. Hannah, I see you’re looking at your counsel. Do you understand they cannot help you answer the question?”

Expect that the witness will deny doing so and that many lawyers will likewise deny the witness did so. No matter. Point made, and record made. I will repeat my comment if it occurs again. It generally doesn’t, but you’ve got to speak up and address it or you’re going to quickly find the witness regularly looking around for subtle help.

- *Who’s On First, Second, and Third*

I will also note the location of people in the room if it is contributing to or facilitating disruptions.

On occasion I see opposing lawyers pull their chairs tightly against the deponent’s chair, so close that the lawyer is physically touching the witness. A judge would not allow that in a courtroom, so I note it for the record during the deposition.

On occasion I also see attendees, just observers, rolling their eyes at the testimony. It is sometimes enough to cause witnesses to look over. So I make a note of that as well.

This is a particular problem if the deposition is being videotaped. A jury watching the video might wonder why the deponent keeps looking oddly off camera. If I speak up, the explanation is obvious (and the conduct stops). If I don't speak up, the witness just looks odd. Even I may otherwise eventually forget what was happening, and then wonder myself why the witness was repeatedly looking away.

Whatever it is, if you feel it is important, comment about it while on the record. It does not matter if the person or opposing lawyer denies it. You should assume they will. Most judges will assume your observations are accurate.

My rule is, if the conduct is affecting the deponent, me, others in the room, or the general environment, I speak up in a firm but professional tone, e.g., "I want to note for the record that Mr. Jones is seated so close to the witness that they're touching, " or to the witness, "Ms. Williams, would you tell us why you're looking at the agency's lawyer before you answer each question?" or, "Mr. Ford, what is the note on your lawyer's pad that he just pointed to and that you read? What does it say?"

Never let nonverbal behavior go undocumented. If you do, you are unlikely to get relief later. Judges will want to know why, if the conduct was so odious that it now requires judicial attention, you made no mention of it during the deposition.

§9.08 In Phone Depositions, Memorialize the Room

When conducting telephone depositions, begin your examination by asking about, and documenting for the record, the details of the deposition environment. This includes the address and office location, the specifics of the room environment, and the people, devices, and documents present.

Superior deposition management requires you to be aware of everything that affects the deposition process. That's true whether you're in person or on the phone.

I recall sometimes being surprised, when I first began practicing, about the room environment when I conducted phone depositions. Sometimes I learned, too late, that witnesses were testifying from documents I did not know they had. Sometimes I learned there were more people in the room than I ever imagined; I discovered that only after I got the transcript and saw the reporter's notations of those present.

How did I miss that? I missed it because I didn't ask. Worse, I didn't even think to ask. Rule 30(b)(5)(A)(v) requires reporters to identify those present, but I can't remember any reporter ever doing that. So now I treat it as my job.

- ***Things to Ask on the Record***

Here are the questions I now routinely ask:

1. What is the full address of the place where you are right now? (Are they where I think they are?)

2. Have you ever been there before? (Prior deposition experience?)
3. What kind of room are you in? Office? Conference room? Restaurant? What's the suite number? And the name of the business? (Assume nothing.)
4. How many doors are there in and out of the room? Are they open or closed? (This tells me whether others might be listening.)
5. Did you come with anyone today? (May provide all kinds of clues.)
6. Is there anyone sitting just outside the room that you know?
7. How many people are in the room with you now? (Tells me about unannounced observers.)
8. Tell me their names and who you believe they are. (Provides insights into the deponent's contact with the persons.)
9. What is the shape of the table you are seated at? How many chairs are there on your side of the table? How many at each end? How many on the other side? How many of the chairs in your side have people sitting in them? How many chairs at each end of the table have people in them? What about the chairs on the other side of the table? (Gives me a sense for how people are situated, who will be staring at who, the relationship between those present, and possible witness intimidation.) I will usually map out the table shape on my pad, marking each chair location

and the name of everyone in them. It is useful to visualize the seating and location of all present.

10. Is there anyone listening in on any kind of electronic device belonging to anyone in the room, as far as you know, other than the phone I am speaking on right now? (Self-explanatory.)
11. Have you discussed with anyone the sending or receipt of messages of any kind during your testimony? (Smartphones, laptops, tablets, Bluetooth earpieces)
12. What electronic or battery-powered devices did you bring into the room with you?
13. Tell me what is on the table, and who it is in front of. (Anything that may be used to guide the witness?)
14. Did you bring anything with you today? (Files, notes, pictures, memos, reports – anything?).
15. Will you tell me if you believe someone is trying to communicate with you while I masking you questions?

Even if you are videotaping the deposition, or watching a live stream, you will not have a complete understanding of the environment unless you ask. The cameras will not catch everything. In fact, the use of video might give you false confidence that you are fully aware of the things that will affect the deposition.

Even if a reporter were to note the identity of everyone in the room, they will not note their seating location, or even whether they are engaging in misconduct. As part of my preliminary instructions, I emphasize for telephone depositions that the witness may not receive verbal or nonverbal assistance of any kind from anyone else in the room. I ask the witness if they understand that, and I also ask the witness to tell me if they observe anyone attempting to communicate with them or otherwise affect the testimony.

I fully understand that not every witness will alert me even if they have agreed to do so. But, as with the discussion about oaths, a clear agreement by the witness to report misconduct will dampen efforts by others to do so.

§9.09 Protect Clients from Exhaustion

Be proactive to ensure your clients are free of circumstances that affect their testimony. Prolonged examinations under oath are nearly as exhausting as physical activity of the same duration. Many deponents are thoroughly exhausted by midafternoon.

One reason is that many deponents do not sleep well the night before. Another is that many skip breakfast and lunch because of anxiety. So as the day drags on, your clients may begin to suffer from fatigue-induced symptoms: grogginess, an inability to concentrate or focus, confusion and temper flare-ups. They may also have children or family waiting at home, further distracting them.

Be prepared to halt the deposition once your client is no longer able to focus. Some jurisdictions do not impose time limits on depositions, unlike the federal courts. That there is no time limit does not mean you should allow clients to testify past the point of exhaustion. And beware clients who "just want to get it over with." Testimony from a mentally-drained clients can prove disastrous. Answers at 9:30 PM count just as much as answers given at 9:30 AM.

The same holds true even if your clients become exhausted by mid-afternoon. Never permit them to continue once you decide they are no longer capable of focusing and paying attention.

Most opposing lawyers will agree to resume the deposition on another date. If an opposing lawyer objects, you may contact the court if a judge is still available. If not, then outline your reasons for halting the deposition on the record, and make clear your willingness to stipulate to continuation of the deposition.

§9.10 Use Your Smartphone Proactively

Use your smartphone's tremendous evidence-gathering capabilities to capture all the evidence that presents itself on deposition day. I am not referring to testimony. I am referring to evidence *outside* the deposition room, as I outlined previously in my discussion about having total awareness of the deposition environment, inside and out.

Your smartphone or tablet is a powerful collection of evidence-gathering tools:

- A high-quality still-photo camera
- A high-quality video camera

- A high-quality audio recorder
- A high-quality transcription device
- A stop-watch or timer
- A calculator
- A calendar that can retrieve every day and date in the last century
- Mapping software showing every street in the U.S., from above or at street-level
- A live-video chat device (e.g., Skype or Zoom)
- A video and audio playback device

These tools have many uses on deposition day. You should consciously look for opportunities to use them. None of the following examples refer to events inside the deposition room.

Some sample still-photo opportunities:

- To take photos of vehicles in the parking lot that might bear on an issue.
- To take photos of the vehicles in which witnesses arrived.
- To take photos of arriving witnesses, for identification purposes, among other things. Be sure witnesses have no expectation of privacy at the time and be doubly sure you are not doing anything that might intimidate the witness in any way.

Some sample video opportunities:

- For the same purposes as the still-photo opportunities, as above
- To take an on-the-spot witness statement

Some audio-recorder opportunities:

- To capture on-the-spot witness statements

Some live-video conference capabilities:

- To show off-site clients specific vehicles or other observable evidence
- To allow your client to speak with others, or to allow a witness to speak directly with your client

Smartphones and tablets are powerful evidence collection tools. Have them ready. Use them.

§9.11 (Mostly) Ignore Evidentiary Objections

Don't get bogged down in objections from opposing lawyers, or in the technical minutiae of the evidence code. For the most part I ignore both when examining witnesses.

First, many objections have no basis and are made specifically to disrupt you, the witness, or the flow of the testimony.

Second, and related to the first point, many litigators don't actually know when a legitimate objection should be made, so they make a slew of them just in case.

If you take a peek at the case history of your opposing counsels on PACER.gov, you will see just how little trial experience they have, if any. Often they have none, or at least no first-chair trial experience. It sometimes seems there is an inverse relationship between the frequency with which lawyers object and the extent of their trial experience. Third, and related to the first two points, most testimony gathered during depositions will be admissible even over objection.

So focus on your goals. Ignore everything else. Objections rob you of interaction with deponents.

Further, I also recommend you *generally* disregard the rules of evidence. Despite all our best efforts, most testimony is admissible. The rules of evidence are informed by common sense, to ensure juries hear the evidence that matters. If you have a critical set of questions that absolutely must be admissible, you should, of course, take pains to ensure that.

Otherwise, focus on the *conversation* with your deponent and tune out the procedural and technical noise.

During my examinations, I may use slang, colloquialisms and analogies. Lawyers that have book experience, but have never seen the inside of a courtroom, may object. Fair enough. Have at it. It does not change my style, and it has never prevented my examinations from being read to a jury when I am impeaching a witness on the stand.

Nor will it prevent yours. You need not use legal phraseology, or the King's English, in order for your questions and the deponent's answers to be admissible. Often the most effective examinations are those conducted in ordinary conversation and that your jury can easily relate to.

This is true even if you think the opposing lawyer's objections have a good-faith basis. Tune them out. Of course, if the frequency, tone or content of the objections become disruptive, you will need to address it.

Otherwise, you should view opposing lawyers as observers, like anyone else in the room. Do not give their presence weight. In a courtroom, the lawyer would not be permitted to make comments or speaking objections during testimony.

Use the same rule of thumb in depositions. You will lose control over the environment if you treat the opposition as a legitimate voice to be heard during testimony. The witness will sense that as well. Stay focused on your examination.

§9.12 Bring Observers Who Make a Difference

Consider whether you should bring someone with you who can add value with their observations. Deponents provide a flood of verbal and nonverbal information. You may not be able to absorb it all.

Contrary to widespread belief, the rule of sequestration does not apply to depositions. A party must seek agreement or court relief in advance to exclude someone. Some lawyers think they can simply "invoke the rule" and command observers to leave. That is incorrect. As I noted above, the 1993 Comments to Rule 30(c) specifically say requests from lawyers that people leave the room carry no weight. Check your state rules and governing case authorities, but states following the federal rules reach the same result.

People to consider bringing include staff familiar with the case, staff who are unfamiliar with the case (if you're more interested in possible juror reactions), an expert you retain, or a psychologist or psychiatrist, if it is important to know more about the motives and truthfulness of the witness. Insights from these people will be useful in shaping your theory and themes.

There are almost always empty chairs in the deposition room. Use them. Give your observers laptops, iPads, old-school notepads – whatever works. Open Facebook Messenger or a similar program and allow your guests to send you comments as the testimony develops. Instant feedback is invaluable.

If for whatever reason others cannot attend in person, consider a video feed or even a simple speakerphone to stream the testimony back to the office. I have found staff to be excellent mock jurors and good sounding boards in general. In my view, it isn't necessary to pay a professional jury consultant in most case. Juries aren't professional jurors. Your *ad hoc* jury pool might be more representative than professional mock jurors.

§9.13 Consider Deposing Your Own Client

Consider deposing your own client, if you have the opportunity. I have done this on some occasions when opposing counsels dragged their feet in deposing a client.

Is this acceptable? Does it strike you as inappropriate?

In at least one reporter decision, a defendant complained that a plaintiff's "self-deposition" was improper, rare and done only in exceptional circumstances. *Leamon v. KBR, Inc., et. al.*, 2011 WL 13340583, at *1 (S.D. Tex. Nov. 1, 2011).

- ***The Rules Allow It***

But the rules contain no such limitations. Rule 30 (oral depositions) and Rule 31 (depositions on written questions) both expressly allow a party to depose any party, while Rule 33 (relating to interrogatories) only allows them to be served on other parties. *Compare* Rule 30 ("A party may, by oral questions, depose any person, including a party...") and Rule 31 ("A party may, by written questions, depose any person, including a party...") *with* Rule 33 ("Unless otherwise stipulated or ordered by the court, a party may serve on *any other party...*") (emphasis added).

Thus while you cannot serve interrogatories on yourself, you can depose yourself. The clear import of the wording has not gone unnoticed. *Smith v. Morrison-Knudsen Co.*, 22 F.R.D. 108, 113 (S.D.N.Y. 1958) (court rejected as meritless defendant's argument that deposition rules mean a party can only be deposed by an *adverse* party).

- ***There are Several Benefits***

One benefit is that your client's testimony will develop as you choose. Another benefit is that this forces your adversary to essentially conduct a cross-examination in deposition, and deprives them of the convenience of working from a self-serving, highly selective script. If you set the deposition and conduct the direct examination, the opposing lawyer will have no reason to go through hours of preliminary, background questions. This will force them to conduct whatever they can muster in the form of an actual cross-examination on the fly.

This strategy consistently sets off fireworks, and that reaction is a good indication of the technique's power to alter the outcome. If smart people go bonkers at your legitimate strategies, pay attention. You are doing something right.

I began occasionally deposing my own clients after I noticed, while preparing some for depositions, that most were quite comfortable with the examination process. I grilled them using the same examination style and substance as an opposing lawyer, and they did well. I thought about the fact that at trial, I am of course the first person to question my client, and then asked: Why shouldn't I depose my own client? Why am I waiting for them to be ambushed by the opposing lawyer?

The first time I tried this, the opposing lawyer thought I was kidding. I had asked the lawyer many times to set my client for deposition so that we could get rolling. I prefer to have my client deposed first so that I can educate myself using the opposing lawyer's examination. Despite multiple requests, the lawyer did nothing. So I issued a notice setting my client for deposition.

On the day of the deposition, the opposing lawyer

showed up and spoke as if she was about to start the examination. I politely interrupted and reminded her it was my deposition. The lawyer responded by saying she thought my notice was a gentle nudge to her that I wanted her to get the case moving.

In other words, she did not think I was seriously deposing my own client. After taking some unnecessary verbal jabs by the lawyer, I spent the next four hours conducting a full-blown examination. The end result was an excellent deposition transcript, and the case settled swiftly afterward. My examination disrupted both the opposing lawyer's frame of mind and planned examination. It also laid out my client's case and allowed the opposing lawyer to more fully outline the case for their client.

The transcript was no longer a one-sided affair. It was the complete trial testimony of the key witness, in the order it will unfold at trial.

The most common justification lawyers give for avoiding examination of their clients in deposition is that they need to minimize their client's exposure to cross-examination before trial. Now, if your client is a weak witness, limiting his or her exposure to examination is wise. And if your client's story has a fatal defect, you might also pass on this technique.

You might also consider settling.

Otherwise, it is something to consider. Remember most cases never go to trial. Holding back means the adversary never hears your client's story first-hand. And if the story is solid, you'll make better progress getting to resolution if your client's story is out there.

There is no magic to this. Prepare your client for the examination as you would for trial. Use the documents you would use in your trial examination. Cover both liability and damages issues.

Another benefit is that you will become better at conducting direct examinations of your clients at trial, since you will be doing it more often. Depositions sharpen our cross-examination skills, but they do little to improve our direct examination work.

Examining your own witnesses requires skill, too. But few litigators regularly conduct full-blown direct examinations of their own witnesses. This reminds me of boxers who can throw good punches with their left or right hand, but not both. Great boxers can knock you out with both. They have *range*.

This technique, apart from its deposition benefits, will develop your range, and make you a better courtroom boxer. It is not suitable in all cases, but it is in many.

§9.14 Use the Internet to Sharpen Your Examination

I often use the Internet to improve my examination during depositions. I can quickly verify facts discussed by the witness, clarify points for my own benefit, and develop additional lines of questions mid-deposition.

Many lawyers bring laptops or tablets but use them chiefly for note-taking – an expensive substitute for a yellow pad. A traditional legal pad is actually a better choice if you can get by with jotting down the occasional point. The court reporter is creating a vastly superior version of your notes anyway, and extensive note-taking is an impediment to quality examinations.

The real value of access to a computer during your examination is the Internet connection. You have at your fingertips the most incredible databases, processing power, and speed in history. Take a laptop or tablet to your depositions, but don't use it to take notes (unless perhaps you are defending, not taking). The reporter will take all the notes you need, and will do a far better job. Use it to sharpen your examination.

Some examples:

- Run searches of your deponents' names. Look for resumes, LinkedIn and Facebook profiles, personal websites, blogs, Twitter posts, photos, and videos.
- Search for images if the witness is talking about a place or thing. It may help you better understand the witness' testimony. In one of my cases the deponent, a road maintenance worker, said he drove a "John Deere tractor with an Alamo boom mower." I did not understand the combination but needed to know before I went further. I asked him to explain it, and his second response was, "It's like a bush hog." We laughed. That added nothing. I then ran a search for "John Deere tractor with an Alamo boom mower," though, and it brought up the exact configuration of machinery the witness mentioned. I turned my

laptop around, showed the witness the image to verify it, and called out the URL for the record, so everyone could find it. I also cut and pasted the link to the image in an email and immediately emailed it to the opposing lawyers. I have done the same thing many times when a tool, product or machine was at issue and I needed an image of the exact model and configuration.

- Use aerial images, like Google Earth or Google Maps, if your examination involves the layout of a building, an intersection, or the distance between two points.
- Look for relevant policies, procedures, and documents posted online by the opposing party or witness. In one case, the deponent was describing a piece of commercial equipment in a way that was hard to follow. Worse, the lawyer kept objecting that the design was confidential. I ran a Google search, found a detailed drawing of the exact equipment on the company's own website as part of a sales presentation, and then began a much more effective examination with the actual image.

Be sure when agreeing to a deposition location that you will have an Internet connection. If that isn't an option, bring a Wi-Fi hotspot as a backup. Also, it's useful to be familiar with multiple search engines and the best way to search each. There are differences in the databases of Google, Yahoo and Bing, for example. Third, use a metasearch engine, which runs simultaneous searches in multiple search websites at the same time.

Some other tips:

- Once you've located useful images online during your deposition, consider printing them on the spot. I always have a portable color printer with me for this reason. The moment I find a relevant image, I print it and hand copies to the opposing counsel and witness. That way, I can instantly create, mark and distribute valuable exhibits I did not have when I arrived. In some depositions I found photos of machinery online that were exact duplicates of machinery at issue in my case. By spinning my laptop around and showing the deponent the image, I was able to get the witness to agree (under oath) that the image was the same as the machinery at issue. I right clicked, printed the image, and passed out copies to the other lawyers in the deposition. Had I not done this, I would have needed consent or a court order allowing me to travel to the defendant's location, requiring the defendant to produce one of the machines, and then photograph it. I did the same thing in seconds because I had an Internet connection and a color printer.
- Whether you print the image or not, download it and attach it to an email to your opposing

counsel. This ensures they have the exact image you printed. You can also copy and paste – into the same email – the link to the page where you found the image.

§9.15 No Confidential Talks in the Deposition Room

You should never discuss privileged or confidential matters in the deposition room. Even if the reporter is not typing, their back-up digital recorders may continue to run. Some reporters are afraid of forgetting to turn the recorder back on when testimony resumes, so they just leave it running. Even inexpensive recorders have large capacities. I found one online for the price of lunch that can store 1,073 hours of audio - about six and a half weeks of nonstop recording. Even if you see a reporter reaching to turn the recorder off, there is no assurance the device has stopped. They might have pushed the wrong button.

Even if it has stopped, there may be another recorder built into the reporter's stenographic machine that continues to run. It is also possible someone else in the room has a recording device in operation. Smartphones, tablets, even digital pens can all easily capture conversations from across the room in high quality.

Sometimes, too, there are representatives of one party or another listening by speakerphone. I have seen lawyers forget about the adversary's representative on the phone and engage in very sensitive conversations.

So, the best rule is an absolute one: *No conversations in the deposition room.*

To illustrate just what might happen otherwise, consider the situation in July 2018 in *Wellin, etc. v. Farace, etc.,* 2018 WL 724056 (D. S.C. Dec. 5, 2018), Case No. 2:16-CV-00414. There, a lawyer in the New York office of a top-flight global law firm was in her conference room - with her expert witness - listening by phone to a deposition of the opposing expert.

Multiple other lawyers were listening in from remote sites. The pending lawsuit, unfortunately, was a malpractice claim against her firm. During a break in the phone deposition, the lawyer opted to disconnect from the call to prepare her own expert. But she pressed the wrong key on the high-tech phone and the call was not disconnected. She merely muted *incoming* sounds, and thus could not tell that her phone line remained open. Everyone else could still hear her. Both the plaintiff and her counsel stayed on the line and listened to the prep session.

Predictably, the plaintiff's counsel, in later deposing her expert, spent time grilling the expert about the deposition prep session. That led to a motion for a protective order, a motion to disqualify the plaintiff's law firm, and in December 2018, a court ruling addressing the mess caused a the simple mistake in failing to disconnect the call. The court eventually ruled that the disclosure was accidental and that no privileges were waived. But so what? You can't unring a bell. Valuable confidences were lost and cannot be regained.

The lesson: Disaster can follow if you do not actively

consider the security of the environment in which you hold confidential conversations.

Even your own office can be problematic, as that case shows. Check every device in the room before you begin prepping your deponents. Check desktop phones to make sure they're not connected. Insist that those present remove all devices from their jackets, pockets, purses, and briefcases, place them on the table, and confirm they're inactive. Turn them off if needed. Or leave them in another room.

When having confidential conversations, you must ensure the room is safe. Grievous consequences follow otherwise.

§9.16 Location, Shmocation

Don't waste time fighting over deposition locations. There are exceptions to this, but they are few. All things considered, the location where the deposition takes place has very impact on the testimony.

I realize some lawyers disagree with this view. You will have opponents who will do anything to ensure depositions take place in their office or, at least, not in yours, and not even in a neutral location. The most common reasoning given for fighting over location is that they don't want to be "in the enemy's camp."

For me the opposite is true. I thoroughly enjoy going to an opposing lawyer's office. I learn a lot about opposing lawyers, their staff and their firms by being in their offices. If the defendant owes me documents, I can ask them to walk down the hall and get them. It eliminates the excuse that the things I need are "back at the office." So being in their offices is another valuable intelligence tool and excuse-eliminator.

Rather than battle over the location, consider the benefits of taking the fight right into the opposing lawyer's home base.

When do I haggle about location? I might if:

- The location will cause my client anguish, such as where my client was injured at or near the location, or where there will be people who caused emotional distress.
- The environment is not suitable for taking testimony. It may be too small, too loud, or too full of distractions, or perhaps there is a dynamic that might intimidate witnesses.
- The location has no phone, Internet access or available signals.
- The deponent is dangerous or violent, and the location offers no protection.

A good deposition requires both the examining lawyer and the witness to focus. If in my judgment the location and room will allow that, I don't care where it is. You shouldn't, either.

§9.17 Have a Deposition Misconduct Kit Handy

Keep an expandable folder in your car with published decisions on common types of deposition misconduct. This will allow you to swiftly retrieve it if a problem develops and cite the cases to a disruptive opposing lawyer. You can then ask the lawyer on the record to justify his or her conduct in light of the authorities declaring the conduct improper. You can also provide a copy of the case to the lawyer and attach it as an exhibit if needed.

- ***The Basics***

My basic kit contains about ten subfolders, each touching on a specific type of deposition misconduct. The tabs are labeled. For example, some deal with improper objections, such as "I Don't Understand Your Question," "If You Know," "Lengthy Objections," "Speaking Objections," and so on.

I label them with the actual offending conduct because it allows me to quickly sort through them. If one of those behaviors surfaces, I can ask the lawyer to stop it and cite to a case on point if needed.

And if that doesn't work, I will have the case authorities at my fingertips in calling the court. Even if you don't wind up calling a judge mid-deposition, the transcript will document your efforts to solve the problems with actual case authority. It will also document the opposing lawyer's continued obstruction. Your on-the-record conferral will help you if you must later file the transcript.

You should also know that some courts have held that, where there is a rule requiring you to confer with opposing counsel before filing motions to compel, you can satisfy that requirement by conferring at the deposition itself. You do not have to wait until you get back to the office. So having a deposition toolkit satisfies that obligation fully. Even better, the entire discussion will be on the record.

Having cases ready is far more effective than attempting to debate the propriety of a particular objection or behavior, which usually goes something like this:

You: You can't do that.

Opposing lawyer: Yes I can.

You: No you can't.

Opposing lawyer: Yes I can.

You: No you can't.

This is the short version. This usually continues *ad nauseum*, until both lawyers are worn out. In fact, many of the opinions on deposition disputes quote the entire colloquy, going on for pages and pages, perhaps to show their brethren in the profession what childish bickering looks like.

These stalemates can be avoided with a folder of decisions on the most common types of problems. Deposition misconduct typically falls into about one of five categories. There are only so many ways a lawyer can disrupt your examination, and there are cases on all of them.

I recommend you assemble your own kit and include reported court decisions, local rules and the rules of ethics governing your state bar.

Many state and federal courts have one or more rules

governing lawyer conduct and proceedings, including depositions, so you should check for that in your jurisdiction. There are also aspirational guidelines, such as the American College of Trial Lawyers' *Code of Pretrial and Trial Conduct.*

- ***Sample Cases on Misconduct***

I have collected a few sample cases and authorities below. They are representative of the cases you can find, and should give you a jumpstart in looking for appropriate headnotes and citations:

Frivolous objections, telling the witness to only answer questions you understand, and general coaching: *Ofoedu v. St. Francis Hospital*, 234 F.R.D. 26 (D.C. Conn. 2006)

Interrupting without objections, speaking objections, cautioning witnesses not to answer when not representing the witness, suggesting answers through the objections, and exchanging whispers: *Phinney v. PaulShock*, 181 FRD 185 (DC New Hampshire 1998)

Collection of citations to improper deposition conduct: *Federal Practice and Procedure, Chapter 6, Depositions and Discovery, Wright and Miller, 8A Fed. Prac. & Proc. Civ. 2d §2113*

Speaking objections, conversation, and argument: *Damaj v. Farmers Insurance Company, Inc.*, 164 FRD 559 (D.C. Oklahoma 1995)

Lawyer saying, "If you know," or "If you remember": *City of New York vs. Coastal Oil New York Inc.* 2000 WL 97247 (S.D.N.Y. 2000)

Lawyers who repeatedly call for breaks to huddle with the witness: http://apps.americanbar.org/litigation/committees/pretrial/email/spring2012/spring2012-0612-discoverability-deposition-breaks.html; and http://scholarship.law.campbell.edu/cgi/viewcontent.cgi?article=1021&context=fac_sw.

Interrupting witnesses' answers by telling the witness they already answered a question, then objecting when the lawyer asks the witness to finish the answer: *Soken v. Fieldcrest Cmty. Unit Sch. Dist. No. 8,* 2014 U.S. Dist. LEXIS 6109, 32, 2014 WL 201534 (C.D. Ill. Jan. 16, 2014)

Coaching by writing witnesses notes during testimony: Ryan v. Astra Tech, Inc., 2014 U.S. App. LEXIS 21628, 2 (1st Cir. Mass. Nov. 14, 2014); and *Tucker v. Pacific Bell Mobile Services,* 186 Cal. App. 4th 1548, 1562, 115 Cal. Rptr. 3d 9, 19, 2010 Cal. App. LEXIS 1255, 21 (Cal. App. 1st Dist. 2010)

American College of Trial Lawyers, Code of Pretrial and Trial Conduct, often cited by federal judges as outlining the models of attorney behavior: http://www.vawd.uscourts.gov/media/3143/pretrial_and_trial_conduct.pdf

§9.18 Take EUOs Whenever Possible

I touched on this topic earlier, where I outlined the different choices for taking sworn testimony from witnesses. That section covered EUOs in some detail.

I mention them again here to stress their value in gathering evidence outside the presence of opposing lawyers. This has two beneficial effects on your deposition strategy.

First, you may decide formal depositions of those witnesses are not necessary. Second, this process will sharpen your examinations of these witnesses if you (or the opposing lawyer) proceed with a formal deposition.

- *Identifying EUO-Viable Witnesses*

As I briefly explained elsewhere, I use the following approach.

First, I determine which witnesses I can contact directly, without needing to clear it with opposing lawyers. That may require you to research the law in your jurisdiction. This is not complicated, but getting it wrong could result in your disqualification as counsel. In other words, if you contact and take a statement from someone that you are not ethically permitted to contact, the result could be a motion seeking your disqualification as counsel, and an order granting the motion. In some jurisdictions, currently-employed managers and senior policymakers are generally off-limits to *ex parte* contact, but lower-level employees are fine to interview. And in many jurisdictions, former employees are fair game regardless of prior rank.

- *Explaining the EUO to Witnesses*

I tell witnesses that an EUO is entirely voluntary. I say they did not have to come, can get up and walk out right that moment, and can refuse to answer any questions they choose without any consequence whatsoever.

I explain that the EUO is not a court proceeding. I thus ask them to confirm that they have not been subpoenaed, that coming was voluntary, and that staying and answering questions is also entirely voluntary.

Finally, I ask again if they understand this is a voluntary statement and not a deposition. Once they agree, I start the examination as I would a deposition. It may be short or it may run for several hours. I may or may not use documents. Either way, I treat it like a regular deposition once we are underway, except for the differences I have explained here. I do not engage in informal chats or discuss off-topic subjects. I want to preserve the right to disclose the transcript if it benefits me, so I do not want to turn it into a chatty social hour. It remains a relatively formal examination.

- ***Explaining EUOs to the Reporter***

I also remind the court reporter that an EUO is not a deposition. This means the cover page must simply say that it is an examination under oath, list the date and time, and the witness' name. There must be no case style on the first page because it is not a proceeding, technically speaking, within the case.

I also remind the reporter that none of the standard deposition-style language should be included in any portion of the transcript. Sometimes reporters use generic pages inside the front cover that say the proceeding was a deposition pursuant to the rules of court. Well, an EUO is not a deposition, and it was not conducted pursuant to any rule of anything. It is simply an interview under oath. I may use it in the case, and I may not. This is a critical distinction. The ultimate transcript must have no reference to the pending case or to rules of court or procedure. I don't want anything associated with the EUOs to have the accouterments of an actual deposition.

I also remind the reporter that the EUO is work product. It must not be produced to anyone without my permission. That is another reason why I do not want any reference to the case in the transcript.

I may not even tell the court reporter which case it pertains to. Why? Because months from now, it is possible an opposing lawyer will call and order transcripts relating to the case. I do not want a clerk in the court reporter's office to run a word search for the case name and accidentally produce my transcript. If there is no link to a case, the court reporter cannot make that error.

- ***EUOs Enjoy Work-Product Protections***

The majority of my practice is in federal court, and I have taken the position these statements do not need to be produced unless and until I choose to do so. I disclose the existence of EUOs on my Rule 26 disclosures, but I do not say from which witnesses.

You must determine for yourself the level of disclosure required in your jurisdiction.

No judge has ordered me to release EUOs, but they do want some disclosure of their existence and the approximate date they were taken. The rationale expressed by one judge is that revealing the month or year establishes that the statements were taken after the commencement of litigation and enjoy *prima facie* work product privilege.

Check out the following orders and cases for guidance on taking and disclosing EUOs. *See* Order on Defendant's Motion to Strike, ECF Doc. 41, *Heffernan v. North Florida Workforce Development Board*, Case No.: 4:14-cv-85-MW/CAS (N.D. Fla. Dec. 16, 2014) and *Bagwell v. Peachtree Doors and Windows, Inc.*, Case No. 2:08-CV-00191-RWS-SSC [Doc. 222].

§9.19 Don't Be Shy About Calling the Judge

Never hesitate to call judges or magistrates and ask for help if the deposition is out of control. They can be the most powerful tool you have. You will only have to do this once with a lawyer before they stop the offending conduct. Otherwise, you may never gain control in depositions if obstructive lawyers sense you are afraid to call the court.

The deposition is our operating room. It must be a sterile environment, free of bacteria, figuratively speaking. It is the only setting in most lawsuits where testimony will be heard. Fewer than five percent of all lawsuits wind up in a courtroom. Your case, like most, will be won or lost in discovery. You cannot afford to let opposing lawyers hijack your depositions, or get the proceedings so off course that they destroy your efforts.

But because judges do not like to get involved in lawyer

bickering, you must be sure the issue is serious and warrants the call.

Here's how.

First, do your best to work it out with the opposing lawyer. Second, make sure you have stayed on the record so the transcript fully captures the problems and efforts to solve them. Third, take time after stopping the deposition, before calling the judge, to make sure you can quickly quote specific passages in the testimony for the judge. This third point will require you to work with the reporter during the break to find offending objections or comments.

Remember the judge has no idea what happened. He or she is coming in cold, and might be distracted if you called in the midst of a trial. So it is your job to provide the court with the ammunition to rule in your favor. It is not sufficient to paraphrase what happened.

If you know before depositions start that problems are likely, call the reporter's office in advance. Ask the reporter what to say on the record, when a problem surfaces in the deposition, that will allow the reporter to mark specific spots in the testimony you'll refer to during the phone hearing.

I also recommend calling the judge's office before a potentially troublesome deposition and asking if the judge will be available that morning or day. Knowing the judge is available could get you the confidence to resolve it on your own.

Don't be shy. Obstructive lawyers bank on the hesitation of ethical lawyers to involve judges. Even if the judge doesn't ultimately side with you, the fact you called in the first place will send a message that will benefit you in the future.

One last thought. While I encourage involving the court if you decide it is justified, don't get baited into doing so. Sometimes harassing lawyers will taunt you into calling the judge. They might appreciate that the situation has not reached the point where you will succeed. Use your own judgment. Don't hesitate to call, but make the decision based on your own conclusions, and not because an obstructive lawyer is shouting "Go ahead! Call the judge! Call right now!"

§9.20 Play the Phone Game When Using Exhibits

When your deponents refer to exhibits, they'll often say something like the following:

> I dropped off supplies here, over there, and then right there. I never even stopped at these two. As for the map, our building is this one. Michelle's office is here, Ashley here, and mine, there. This is where I left the excess inventory.

Was that answer important to your case? I hope not. Your judge will have no idea what the witness is talking about. Nor will the jury.

Witnesses naturally do not appreciate how their testimony will appear in the transcript, or how it will be used later. They're trying to be helpful. But if your witnesses speak in this manner when referring to exhibits, you'll have problems later in relying on these kinds of answers.

You've got to make sure the witnesses refer to physical exhibits in a way that makes sense to someone who can't see what the witness is doing. That "someone" is the judge, the jury and everyone else who will be reading the transcript.

My technique is to tell deponents I'm going to be showing them documents and asking them to find and refer to specific paragraphs or places on them. I then discuss the transcript and that readers obviously will not know what I'm referring to if I just point to the document and say, "Right there."

Witnesses get that.

Then I tell them to imagine I'm in another location on the phone, with the same maps and documents, and to think about how they'll describe the same points to me over the phone. I then ask them to refer to all exhibits by their number first, to documents by their page, paragraph number and section, and to maps or photographs by marking specific references points on them or by describing specific points with great specificity. Examples:

On Exhibit 71, I signed on the line on page 22, and those are my initials in the lower left corner on each page.

> Yes, Exhibit 229 is a map of our complex. When I get to work, I clock in here, which I'm marking as "1" for my first stop. I go to the long building in the very center next, and I'm putting a "2" on the roof of that building because that's my second stop. Michelle Hines' office is here, and I'm

putting an MH to mark that, and Ashley Morgan's office is here, so I'll put an AM right where her office is.

Better? Yes. Now, everyone knows which exhibit to look at for this piece of the deponent's testimony. And everyone knows exactly where the offices of key managers are because he specifically labeled them.

This is such an easy problem to overlook, but it's a fatal one if the answers matter. Asking witnesses to imagine being on the phone for exhibit-based testimony solves the problem. I use this because everyone at some point has had to describe something over the phone and they can easily make the mental adjustments needed.

§9.21 Never Take A Non-Answer for An Answer

You must insist on direct answers to your questions. You will lose control of the deposition, possibly all your depositions, if you do not. Lawyers who sense that you will let witnesses evade your queries may share that observation with future witnesses. They may also share it with other lawyers in their firm or field.

You can insist on direct answers without being unpleasant. Some witnesses do not give direct answers because they're not used to listening or speaking with precision. The typical social conversation has no consequence beyond the end of the conversation itself. It is imprecise by nature.

Giving quality testimony, on the other hand, is high art. The required degree of precision is one hundred percent. To someone who's never engaged in anything but casual conversation, the rigors of testimonial exactitude can be a shock. Even mild efforts to get witnesses to answer questions directly can seem like harassment.

So give the witness the benefit of the doubt, at least initially. Start with a respectful repetition of the original question, and explain why you're repeating the question. Here's an example where the witness does not answer the question at all:

> Q:Did you talk to your neighbor about what you saw?
>
> A:Let me put it this way.....I hate my neighbor.
>
> Q: I understand, and thank you. Let me ask it this way. Sometimes even people who aren't friends wind up talking about an incident like this. So, even if you're not friends, I want to know, did the two of you ever talk about what you saw?

By explaining how there could be a way for them to talk even if they have no regular interaction, you can soften the blow of your pursuit for a responsive answer.

Here's an example where the witness doesn't answer the question but perhaps *seems* to, because he says that discussing the termination is something he is required to do. But the question asked if he *did* discuss it, not whether he *might have*, and not whether the rules require it:

> Q:Did you discuss your decision to fire her with your boss?
>
> A:Well, our process requires us to talk to our own

supervisors before we prepare a recommendation for termination. So I'm pretty sure we would have done that.

Q: I appreciate your explanation of the process. I know in some situations that, even though an employer has a specific procedure, it isn't followed. Sometimes written procedures are never followed. Now that I know the *procedure*, my question is this: are you telling me that you did, in fact, discuss your decision to fire her with your boss *here?*

This witness might well believe he squarely answered your question. On the other hand, he may know he did not, and he may be playing games with you to avoid saying he violated policy by failing to run the firing by his supervisor.

There's no reliable way to tell if you have never met this witness before.

But motive doesn't matter. You must secure direct, complete responses. You forfeit the value of the deposition if you allow witnesses to get away with loose responses, regardless of motive. It's fine to initially operate on the assumption the witness is answering in good-faith, but it is not okay to overlook it. Get direct answers to your direct questions.

If this is a common problem in your depositions, consider explaining the need for precision in your preliminary instructions to witnesses at the start of the deposition. Give an example of a non-responsive answer and explain why it doesn't respond to the question. You can use an example like those above - that telling you what was likely done, what should have been done, isn't telling you what was done in this situation.

You might need to make this point more than once - that unless you say otherwise, *you will not be asking the witness at any time to tell you what could have happened. You will only be asking the witness to tell you what he or she knows to be true.*

Providing witnesses examples of non-responsive answers can minimizes problems once the deposition is under way. It also helps clarify whether continued non-responsiveness is inadvertent or intentional.

§9.22 Use Witness-Centric Hypotheticals

Use hypothetical examples involving the witness' own interests for better answers in depositions.

Psychologists say this tactic implicates a cognitive bias called the "framing effect." Put simply, decades of research shows people draw different conclusions from the same information depending on how you present it. If you ask an opposing witness to help you understand something, the witness' tendency will be to avoid doing so to the maximum extent possible. You're the enemy.

But if you reframe it as a hypothetical in which the witness' boss wants to know the same thing, you're much more likely to get a helpful answer.

Here's an example. I ask witnesses to imagine they're out of the office on a month-long vacation. The phone rings. I continue with something like this:

> It's the CEO of your company. She has a board meeting later today, and she needs your urgent help. She needs to know [how many accidents company drivers had in 2019] [how many hospitals bought your company's coding audit software last year]. The CEO asks you, 'Where can I find the answer? Do we have documents? A database? I need it right now!" Where will you tell her to look? Which file cabinet, which shared drive, or which person should they talk to? If you couldn't answer the question, who would you tell them to speak with instead?"

You can tell from this hypothetical that witnesses are not likely to respond flippantly, such as "I'd tell the CEO to go jump in a lake because I'm on vacation!" That might get them fired. After all, it is their sworn testimony that they would blow off their own chief executive. So even though I am the adversary, my frame of the inquiry incentivizes the witness to provide the information i need.

In effect, you are rewiring the witnesses' perception from seeing a useful answer as harmful (by helping me) to seeing it as beneficial (by helping the CEO).

So when you need a witness' help in tracking down information, frame your questions so the witness has a motive to be helpful.[2]

§9.23 Pursue Selective Memory Failures

Pin down witnesses who make tactical use of memory failures, such as those who repeatedly claim, "I don't remember" or "I can't recall at this time." You must foreclose any possibility the witness can later claim recovered memories. The goal is to create a record that will lead jurors to see subsequent recollection (or the prior amnesia) for what it is: a sham.

- ***Genuine Memory Failure is Usually Obvious***

The genuineness of memory failure is usually apparent. Factors to consider include the passage of time, the importance of the event to the witness, and, as it relates to your case, the likelihood that testimony on a topic will cause problems for the witness. If your instincts tell you that memory failure is legitimate, there is very little you can do absent a way to refresh their memory.

If the memory failure is suspicious, you should politely but firmly press the witness for as many specific details about the event, and surrounding events, as possible. This should be done in a series of questions, beginning with events during the days, weeks or months leading up to the core event in question. The goal is to either help the witness recall memories - allowing for specific testimony - or to show a jury that the person's testimony is not reliable because at least some of those events would not have been forgotten.

For example, suppose you are in an employment discrimination case and are deposing the hiring official. You want to know what the hiring official took into account, how many times she interviewed your client, and what factors she considered in making the decision.

She might say she is involved in many hiring decisions and doesn't remember this one. That should trigger a series of questions about the number of hiring decisions she was involved in that year, or the year before, and the year after; whether she is even sure she was involved in this hiring process and, if so, how she remembers it if she remembers nothing else?

Further, ask what documents likely exist that might shed light on her role. (emails, memos, forms, background checks, applications from others) and so on.

This same framework can be applied to any substantive area of law.

- ***Break Details Down Even Further***

You can take each of these questions and break them down even further. If our hypothetical hiring official continues to claim memory failure beyond the bare fact of involvement, you can show her the resumes of the winning candidate and of your client, and walk through both to ask what qualifications would stand out for the position in question. It is unlikely that the desired credentials will have changed over a year or two. If the hiring official declines, by saying that her reasoning might be different now, ask why.

This can be a slow, painful process but commit to it. Use external parameters, such as the position description, the timeframe over which the hiring process took place, and the role of others, to box the witness in.

- ***The Goal: Create a Complete Memory Map***

The goal is to develop a complete, detailed record of everything the witness can and cannot recall.

The mistake here that many litigators make is moving too quickly onto other topics when witnesses claim memory failure. If you have good cause to believe witnesses are feigning amnesia about a significant event, you cannot abandon your inquiry after a simple "I don't recall."

Instead, create a record of all the facts the witness remembers, and all the facts the witness claims to forget, about both an event and the period generally just before and just after the event. That could be the hours before and after, the days, or the weeks, depending on the event. This fuller portrait of before-during-after will either paint a clear picture of the falsity of the memory failure, or make plain that it is legitimate . The key here is pinning the witness down on all relevant events before, during and after the single event about which the witness claims memory problems.

I mention this because I see transcripts from lawyers who abandoned a line of inquiry the moment the witness said they did not remember an event. Often, memory failures are engineered, to avoid giving you the information you need. Absent a brain injury or other diagnosed cognitive impairment, few people suffer amnesia about nontrivial events in the last three to five years. When I hear witnesses say "That was a year ago! I don't remember that," I immediately suspect coaching. It has a very practiced ring to it, more so if multiple witnesses use the same phraseology.

There are formal tests for testing memory malingering - the TOMM and ASTM among them - but you cannot administer them. So your best bet is to conduct an examination that shows the witnesses' claimed amnesia is at odds with the jurors' probably experience.

- *Objections to Malingering Inquiries*

As you press your inquiry about the witnesses' memory - testing them about events around the time of the forgotten fact - you may hear objections that you are harassing the witness. The louder the objections, the more likely you have a witness who was coached to forget a key fact, but not coached to deal with your test of its authenticity.

Such objections are of no moment to me. I respectfully explain that it was the witness, not me, who made amnesia a good-faith issue for examination. I am obligated to be thorough; when a witness offers memory loss as an explanation, I must explore it. It is a fair inquiry, and one you skip at your peril.

It is also fair to ask whether the witness has been diagnosed with a brain injury, with amnesia, or with a cognitive impairment associated with amnesia. (Amnesia isn't a sarcastic term. That is the accepted label for memory loss.) It is also fair to ask if the witnesses generally have trouble remembering events X years past. The answer is always no.

In the *Bigham* case, cited in the next paragraph, one of

the reasons the court rejected the claim of memory loss was the absence of any medical records and diagnosis to support it.

Courts have held that even absent a refreshed memory, a witness should not be allowed to testify later about specific matters where the witness claimed memory failure repeatedly in deposition. Later testimony, whether based on documents or not, is treated as a sham.

- ***Examples of "Shamnesia" Cases***

One of the most well-known examples involves famous military test pilot Chuck Yeager. He claimed memory failure 185 times during his deposition, and then later signed an affidavit later addressing the same topics in great detail. Yeager claimed he'd looked at documents he wasn't shown in his deposition. The court didn't buy it. *Yeager v. Bowlin*, 683 F.3d 1076, 1078 (9th Cir. 2012). *See also Chase v. Ivan Dietrich & Norco Corp.*, No. 3:14-CV-581-HTW-LRA, 2017 WL 4400018, at *1 (S.D. Miss. Sept. 30, 2017), *dismissed sub nom. Chase v. Dietrich*, No. 17-60709, 2018 WL 1935930 (5th Cir. Mar. 6, 2018) (lawsuit dismissed with prejudice as sanction for false deposition testimony, where explanation of "memory loss" appeared to be a sham); *United States v. Bigham*, 812 F.2d 943, 947 (5th Cir. 1987) ("Despite his ability to remember in detail some of the events of the night the inmates were beaten, Byrd claimed no memory of other details. The district court reasonably could have concluded that this selective memory loss was more convenient than actual. Similarly, the fact that Byrd's grand jury testimony and his trial testimony were separated by only seven months, while the underlying event occurred several years earlier, casts doubt on Byrd's claimed loss of memory. As Professor Wigmore observed, "the unwilling witness often takes refuge in a failure to remember." *3A J. Wigmore, Evidence* § 1043, at 1061 (Chadbourn rev.ed. 1970)").

As an aside, some courts have held that where a corporate representative in a Rule 30(b)(6) deposition claims not to remember why the company did or did not do something, the company will be prohibited from presenting testimony on that point at trial. In other words, a memory failure from the corporate representative is a memory failure for the company as a whole.

§9.24 Explore the Selectively Perfect Memory

You must be as aggressive in pursuing witnesses with selectively perfect recall as you are witnesses with selective memory failure.

These witnesses claim a perfect recollection of specific events that just happen to be very damaging to your client. They can't recall anything else, but they do remember the fact in question. These are difficult to attack because they sometimes appear to have no motive to testify falsely. Even so, your instincts tell you the witness is a plant or someone driven by a misguided duty of loyalty to wreak havoc.

Such testimony may begin like this: "I don't really know why it stands out in my mind, but I definitely do remember sitting there and hearing Dan say he was going to take our customer lists. I was shocked. I don't remember anything else, but I sure do remember that. In fact, I'll never forget it."

This can destroy your case. So how to confront these folks? In effect, testimonial hitmen?

As with witnesses who suffer event-specific amnesia witnesses with event-specific total recall must be confronted, not head-on but from the side. You won't get them to admit their dishonesty. Instead, you must develop enough detail to cast so much doubt on the truthfulness of the before-and-after testimony that it casts doubt on testimony about the event itself.

Again, pin the witness down on as many details about the conversation, the day, and the week as you can. Some examples: "Tell me what the last remark you or he made just before this comment was made? What was the comment immediately after? How long did this entire conversation last? Tell me everything else that was said during the conversation, from start to finish. What were you doing just before this conversation, and just after, as well? Who was the first person you spoke to after my client left? What time of day? Did you email anyone?"

A prepared witness might have answers to some questions. They won't have answers to all. The better your ability to show memory failure concerning everything but the comment in question, the better your ability to show the key facts are concocted. This kind of examination takes time and is exhausting, but it must be done. This will be the only opportunity you have before trial to lock that witness in and to prevent further "recollection."

Authentic memory is usually complete. Spot memory failure is unusual. More common is complete memory failure after a specific event (anterograde amnesia) or complete memory failure before an event (retrograde amnesia).

§9.25 Your Appearance Affects the Testimony

Your appearance matters. It can materially affect your interaction with witnesses and the quality and quantity of testimony you get.

You and I judge people everywhere we go based on their appearance. Those judgments affect how we interact with them. If their presence makes us uncomfortable, we react negatively. If their presence says we share common interests, we react positively. Such judgments govern our interaction with deponents as well. Some lawyers give limited thought to their own appearance, though, on deposition day because they don't see their apparel as a factor.

But if we assess and interact with others based on their presence, why can't we see that others assess us the same way? Our deponents are judging us from the moment we meet. Their assessments inform both what they say and how they say it.

I recommend apparel that sends a message of "professional but slightly understated" as the norm, with non-flashy apparel and accessories. An examining attorney, male or female, should consider a jacket. Jackets convey authority. My research into apparel worn by investigators and interrogators in other professions suggests that jackets are an important element of the examiner's appearance. It doesn't have to be a power suit; I don't recommend one that says "hedge fund tycoon."

But jackets send a message of authority in our culture and that is a positive dynamic for you in depositions. The first impression deponents draw is based on what they see. They do not have time to get to know you, so their assessments are instant and superficial.

On the other hand, it is important not to overdo it. Most deponents appear in their work clothing or uniforms, or in apparel that reflects their lifestyle and financial status. This is why I recommend a middle-of-the-road, professional appearance that sends no particular message except that you are an authority figure. Deponents of limited means will resent you if they see a $5,000 watch and high-end designer accessories. The same is true if your clothing is loud, garish or conveys an obvious social or status message. The witness won't relate to you. The disconnect will affect the testimony.

This applies at both ends of the spectrum. Witnesses of limited means react one way and witnesses of great wealth another. The point is that the quality of testimony you obtain depends on your ability to relate to, and be trusted by, your deponents.

§9.26 Create Powerful Exhibits for Depositions

Use existing documents and data to create your own exhibits for use in depositions. Use the same approach as you would at trial - if data can be summarized in a chart, spreadsheet or infographic, do it and use it in examining deponents. Useful demonstrative exhibits or summaries include timelines, collections of email excerpts, or charts showing comparative data. Witnesses often testify about facts as they perceive them, right or wrong. The use of demonstrative exhibits in deposition can change and correct misperceptions, and have a powerful impact on the strength of your case while still in the discovery phase.

Lawyers often wait until discovery closes, and trial approaches, to begin synthesizing data. Synthesis, as I use it here, means stripping away extraneous data and organizing the remainder into a cohesive, powerful presentation.

This synthesis ordinarily begins at the summary judgment stage and is fully complete by the start of trial. While discovery is still under way, however, lawyers simply use documents as they were produced. It is possible to score points this way, but it is less effective than synthesizing the evidence and using it in depositions as you would at trial. Witnesses who came prepared to quibble about the contents of a single document, or the timing of events, are unprepared for a powerful graphic or spreadsheet containing undeniable proof of your contentions.

- ***Start Your Synthesis Early***

Don't wait until trial to organize the evidence. Strike your most powerful blows in depositions. Demonstrative deposition exhibits can entirely alter what witnesses admit or deny.

Virtually no one does this, which is why it can be a case-altering strategy. Few lawyers defending your depositions have prepared their witnesses to deal with strong compilations and summaries.

Your compilation might be a timeline of events, footnoted to document the referenced emails. It could be a chart listing emails by witnesses that all discuss a single topic, with their date and a blurb showing what each person said about a specific topic, with footnotes tied to deposition or document pages.

Time depending, you could attach supporting documents to your summaries with tabs for easy verification. Hostile witness will find it unavoidable to admit the obvious. Ambivalent witnesses – those who weren't sure about events - will move solidly in your favor. Witnesses fearful of running afoul of their bosses will feel more comfortable giving supportive testimony because you've given them a basis to stand their ground.

- ***Consider Low-Case Freelancers to Help***

I use sites like upwork.com to find graphic designers and animators. They can prepare graphics from your raw data at very low cost. Sites like this allow you to post projects for bidding by freelancers all over the world.

I used them recently to create an infographic similar to a wheel, illustrating that a senior corporate manager – the center of the wheel - was behind all major events. I also hired an animation expert to create a short video clip to show collaboration between two employees in making false complaints against a third employee. The two testified they had not collaborate to craft their complaints, even though their forms mirrored each other. The animation expert I hired, for less than a hundred dollars, created a short video clip slowly superimposing one form over the other, showing that not only did the two employees use the same form and language but that handwriting on both forms was identical. In other words, one of the two wrote both of them.

Synthesizing raw information also often leads to revelations. How many times have you had a genius moment in the days before trial because seemingly unrelated events were now clearly related? These moments come because of your synthesis. You'll have the same moments much earlier in a case if you organize and compile the evidence before depositions.

I suspect some lawyers are afraid to use compilations or synthesized material out of a fear that the compilations or testimony might not be admissible. They use the individual documents alone, without demonstrating the broader picture the documents paint. But if your compilations or summaries are accurate, they will be admissible. The rules of evidence specifically allow compilations and summaries. They make life easier for everyone, including the judge. Objections during deposition are often unfounded.[3]

§9.27 Maintain a Neutral Affect

It is essential *in general* that you minimize observable clues to your thoughts and emotions while examining witnesses.

Hostile witnesses look for signs their conduct is getting under your skin. Other witnesses, perhaps trying to avoid getting drawn into the conflict, will scrutinize your reactions to see if their answers seem controversial or surprising. Their testimony may change based on your reaction. As you know, witnesses are often determined to tilt in favor of one party or another. They will use your reactions if possible to help them calibrate their responses.

If you are a parent, you can relate to this feedback loop. When children fall on the sidewalk, the first thing they do is look at their parents' reaction, intuitively using Mom and Dad's reaction as a gauge for what their own reaction should be. If Mom reacts in shock, the child feeds off that and starts crying. ("Mom's upset! I must be hurt!") On the other hand, if Mom laughs, and urges the child to stand up, the child laughs. ("Mom's laughing! This must be fun!")

We all learn at an early age to judge our circumstances in part by the reactions of others. That holds true with deponents.

It pays to maintain a neutral affect throughout your examination, even when angry, shocked, surprised or thrilled. It is not difficult to develop this skill, but it takes practice. Witnesses unable to discern your emotion will focus on answering questions because you've given them nothing to latch onto. A good poker face is a valuable skill for litigators.

This will benefit you in other ways. First, you will avoid unnecessary arguments with opposing lawyers. Second, even opposing lawyers will glean nothing from your reactions. Experienced lawyers, like witnesses, use your demeanor as a gauge. Noncommittal outward appearances deprive opposing lawyers of valuable feedback, too.

There are of course occasions where displays of emotion will help. My point is that a neutral or noncommittal demeanor should be the norm and will suit you well under most circumstances.

§9.28 Never Go Off the Record for Discussions

You should never agree to go off the record - meaning, to instruct the court reporter to stop typing while you discuss a matter with the opposing lawyer - for anything of consequence that relates to a deposition in progress.

If the discussion has any significance, stay on the record. This includes conversations about permissible or impermissible lines of inquiry objections or waivers of objections, time remaining in the deposition, the production of documents or other discovery, or anything else that could be important. The absence of a record is a serious problem. You have court reporters sitting right there. Use them. Memorialize the agreement.

This is especially true if the opposing lawyer is known to be obstructive or if the topic is controversial. Never agree to off-the-record conversations simply to get along. Nor should you worry that you're sending a message that you don't trust the other lawyers. Your relationship is not trust-based. Litigation is an adversarial process. It is the opposite of trust-based. Everyone understands that. If a lawyer tries to goad you into making it personal - "What? You don't trust me?" - the best response is simply, "We're staying on the record."

Have all significant conversations about the deposition or case related matters on the record.

§9.29 Scale Your Examination to the Witness

How long should your depositions last?

The depth and duration of your depositions should roughly match the relative importance of the witness, if you're looking for a gauge to decide how long your depositions should run.

The deposition of a witness whose testimony centers on a single minor fact might not last ten minutes. You can establish their identity and get right to the point. It may be unnecessary to even go through the preliminary instructions. You should not be concerned that it will appear you wasted the witness' time. Judges will applaud you for having the common sense to scale your depositions up or down according to the roles and relevance of the witnesses.

Some lawyers prolong examinations of even nominal witnesses. This wastes time and money and accomplishes nothing. I have had judges compliment me for taking fifteen or twenty depositions in a single day. After listening to the opposing lawyer argue that I could not possibly conduct effective examinations this way – during a hearing on the lawyers' motion for a protective order, to stop me from setting so many in one day - the Harvard-educated chief judge responded, "Why not?"

The dialogue reflected the judge's belief that most depositions take far too long, much as many trial examinations stretch to the breaking point. The judge's comments reinforced the notion that what matters is the evidence obtained, not how long it took to get it.

Resist the temptation to show your client how detailed you can be in every deposition. Once you achieve your objectives, bring the deposition to a close.

§9.30 Summarize and Cap Witness Testimony

Be sure to properly wrap up key lines of inquiry with each deponent. This will minimize the risk that witnesses will surprise you at trial with new recollections.

Here is a sample examination involving comments made by your client:

> You: Did you ever hear my client directly say anything you felt was discriminatory?
>
> Deponent: Yes.
>
> You: Tell me any single comment you claim to have heard.
>
> Deponent: Okay. I remember in our sales meeting he said......

You: [After the witness explains that comment in detail]: Thank you. Have you now told me every comment you heard my client say that you believe was discriminatory?

Deponent: No.

You: Tell me the next/another comment you claim to have heard.

Deponent: Okay. I remember we were at lunch at Sam's Diner, and when everyone sat down he said....

You: [after the witness explains that comment in detail]. Thank you. Have you now told me every comment you heard my client say that you believe was discriminatory?

Repeat this summarization question after each recollection by the witness. Once witnesses say they have now told you every comment they heard, you can safely move to the next topic.

Sometimes witness try to leave the door open with a comment like, "Well, I've told you everything I can remember at this time. There might be more that I am forgetting."I

This isn't a claim of memory failure. It's a *potential* claim of memory failure. If this happens, you must summarize and cap that as well. Here's one way to deal with that:

You: [After the witness offers last recollected event.] Thank you. Have you now told me every comment you heard my client say that you believe was discriminatory?

Deponent: I've told you everything I remember right now. There might be more I've forgotten. I'm just not sure.

You: Thank you for the clarification. Tell me why you cannot say right now with certainty that there is nothing more.

Deponent: I'm just not sure. I don't want to say that's it and then realize I left something out.

You: I don't want you to do that either. So I have some additional questions for you.

Deponent: Okay.

You: First, as you sit here now, there are in fact no other comments of any kind you can tell me about that you consider discriminatory, correct?

Deponent: Correct.

You: You came to the deposition today having given thought to the events involving my client and you've told us about three comments you say you do remember, correct?

Deponent: Correct.

You: Did you document any alleged comment by my client in an email, a memo, a document or in any other written or electronic form of any kind?

Deponent: I might have. I'm not sure.

You: As you sit here now, there are in fact no documents you can recall in which you memorialized any discriminatory comment by my client, correct?

Deponent: Not right now. I'm just saying there might be.

You: I understand. Tell me each and every email address you have used in the last three years.

Deponent: Why do you need those?

You: I need them to serve subpoenas on the email services. You have testified there could very well be emails you have about alleged discriminatory comments by my client. In order to be thorough, I must now serve subpoenas on your email providers to make sure we have everything you say exists or could exist. Please provide me each full email address you have used in the last three years.

This line of examination can continue substantially longer as you expand into every conceivable source of information the witness may rely on. You can ask for each and every document, email, person, account - whatever it is. This need not take long. Most such witnesses will quickly run through the people and places where more information could reside, and usually confirm that more information is unlikely. Indeed, witnesses will swiftly close these doors themselves when they realize you have the power to dig deep (and are about to do so through the use of subpoenas.)

Do the same thing for memos and documents. If the witness has left doors open to the possibility there are unproduced memos or documents, ask for the location of every computer the witness has used in the last three years. Explain that, as with emails, you will now serve subpoenas to obtain mirror copies of their hard drives for an analyst to inspect. Explain that this will allow your expert to search for documents the witness testified “might” be there.

Alternatively, you can ask your deponent to identify each and every file or location in their office where memos or documents are currently being stored in my contain documentation about this matter.

Make no mistake about it. A witness who leaves doors open to brand-new testimony is a trial risk. You must bolt these doors shut before ending the deposition. The good news is that doing it while the deposition is still in progress - when witnesses can be made aware that leaving doors open comes at a heavy cost - may motivate them to admit there are no emails or documents on the topic.

9.31 Don't Hold Back Bombshells

If you have evidence of great value, use it in your depositions. This is where it will have its greatest impact, because most cases never make it to trial.

This is a fundamental rule in my practice and one that underscores the purpose of this book. Whether in mediation or in a less formal setting, negotiations are driven by what happens in depositions, not what will happen at trial. Your efforts and resources should be poured into winning at deposition.

Many lawyers withhold their best evidence for as long as the rules permit. They do so for many reasons. But because of disclosure requirements, true bombshell surprises at trial are rare. And if you've improperly withheld or delayed disclosure of critical evidence, you could face potential sanctions, including the exclusion of your evidence entirely.

Use your best evidence during depositions.

§9.32 "The Usual Stipulations?" Huh?

In some depositions, the court reporter or opposing lawyer may ask you almost in passing to confirm that "the usual stipulations" will apply.

Huh?

The Most Common Meaning of "Usual Stips?"

Typically, this refers to objections, specifically that you will only object to the form of the question while the deposition is in progress; all other objections are preserved for trial. Absent such a stipulation, objections to questions that could have been corrected at the time of the deposition are waived and cannot be made later. *See* Rule 32(d)(3). This principle equally applies to objectionable answers by witnesses. [4]

One notion of such a stipulation, I suppose, is that such an arrangement allows the deposition to proceed without a barrage of objections. *E.g., Otis v. DeMarasse,* 2019 WL 1778955, Case No. 16-C-285 (E. D. Wis. Apr. 23, 2019) (declining sanctions against lawyer, based on frequent, disruptive deposition objections, because objections were in good faith).

But there is no way to know what an opposing lawyer means by "the usual stipulations" unless you ask. One court pointed to the cryptic "Usual Stips?", and the equally-unhelpful response, "Yes" as unclear but for the fact that in a prior deposition the same lawyers had made reference to the "[standard] objections" included "[o]bjections to the form, all others preserved." *Beard v. Kenan Transport*, 2005 WL 8154710, Case No. 1:04-CV-2299-BBM (N.D. Ga. Nov. 23, 2005).

Always Require Explicit Clarification

You should never agree to such a generic declaration without articulating its meaning on the record in the deposition where the "usual stip" applies. Confirm each and every stipulation explicitly. If you are in a jurisdiction where there are common stipulations, the court might hold you to them, even if you did not understand what the term meant. I can appreciate that you might feel some pressure to agree, perhaps to appear sophisticated and experience. But it could cause you problems if the opposing lawyer later argues that the stipulation meant something very different and that you forfeited objections as a result.

I have taken more than 20,000 depositions, and I never presume that I know what opposing lawyers mean by "the usual stipulations." I always ask.

Can "The Usual Stips" Hurt You? You Bet.

If you are conducting the examination of witnesses, permitting the defending lawyers to hold their substantive objections for trial can backfire on you.

Why? Suppose at the time of trial the deponents are

"unavailable" as defined by the rules. That means you need to read the transcript to the jury, in lieu of the deponents' live appearances. Because you agreed to let the defense hold their substantive objections, they're going to make them now. And you can't fix the problems through better questions because your witness isn't there. Your transcript is frozen in time. You're stuck. Your questions and the critical answers to them are inadmissible.

Some lawyers have been known to craft their trial strategy around this tactic. They'll hire an expert in another jurisdiction, knowing full well that the expert will meet the test of unavailability at trial and that you're going to have to read the transcript to the jury. Then they'll suggest "the usual stipulations" at the expert's deposition, to hold back their killer objections until you're in the courtroom.

Who do "the usual stipulations" benefit? Lawyers defending depositions. With the agreement, they need only make their form objections. The objections most likely to be fatal to you - like witness competency - will sit in silence until trial.

By the way, "form" objections, typically, are leading, lack of foundation, assuming facts not in evidence, mischaracterization, vague or misleading questions, no personal knowledge, speculative, asked and answered, argumentative and compound. *Otis v. DeMarasse,* 2019 WL 1778955 *5, Case No. 16-C-285 (E. D. Wis. Apr. 23, 2019) (listing sample form objections).

§9.33 Insist Documents Be Marked as Exhibits

When I first began practicing, I encountered a few opposing lawyers who would pull documents out of a folder, quickly show it to the witness without marking it and, after asking several questions, grab the document and put it back in their in their folder. The result was that we had testimony about a document, but not the document itself.

Never let this happen. The proper way to protect the witness, and your record, is to require the examining lawyer to mark each document as an exhibit before showing it to the witness. This eliminates doubt about what the witness was shown.

Once a lawyer returns a document to his or her folder, you will never again be able to determine whether the document the witness testified about is the same one that the lawyer later uses.

§9.34 Address Deponent Misconduct

What if the person creating havoc is the witness? What if witnesses become obstructive, angry or threatening, or refuses to answer questions or review documents?

Generally speaking, there are two options. One is to remain calm, and to stress the importance of cooperating, as well as the reasons you need their testimony. Talking through concerns with obstructive witnesses often results in cooperation, and that's the fastest path to getting what you need. And, frankly, if you can get witnesses to cooperate on essential points, you may overlook their failure to cooperate on marginal issues.

If the witness utterly refuses to cooperate, I will thank them for their time and explain the steps the law requires me to take, including filing papers asking the judge to issue an order compelling their cooperation (and, possibly, awarding costs against them). I explain this in the most respectful way possible, to avoid further angering them. Sometimes it solves the problem and the witness becomes cooperative. Sometimes not. But it is better to have that discussion, and to have it on the record, so the court can see you did your best to avoid motion practice.

You gain little ground by returning fire against an uncooperative witness. Most of the time, you lose ground.

If the witness is threatening, however, and you deem the threat genuine, you should end the deposition after an appropriate, limited discussion on the record to confirm it. Then seek court relief. There are no circumstances where you should press on with a witness who poses an immediate, legitimate physical threat to you or anyone else in the room.

§9.35 Remove Unnecessary Deponents From Your Notice as Soon as Feasible

Some jurisdictions allow adversaries to seek fees and costs if you serve a deposition notice with multiple witnesses and then drop some from your lineup at the last minute. The principle behind this is that parties should be compensated if you unnecessarily forced their counsel to expend time and resources preparing for depositions that will not take place. This also serves to curb constant lineup changes and substitutions as a tactic to grind adversaries down.

There are of course legitimate situations where you must change your lineup. When this becomes apparent, swiftly amend your notice, and alert opposing lawyers so they can stop all preparations relating to the dropped witnesses. This will minimize the risk of a motion seeking fees against your client.

And if a motion is filed, it will minimize the amount that may be fairly claimed or awarded. See F*lores v. Entergy Nuclear Operations, Inc.*, 2018 WL 2452769 (S.D.N.Y. 2018) (judge distinguished between time spent "preparing" for deposition and expenses "caused" by late-noticed cancellation; sanctions awarded for just 30% of time defense counsel spent preparing, after opposing lawyer sent text at 7:32 AM advising that plaintiff would not appear later that morning).

§9.36 Strategic Deposition Cancellations

In some instances, lawyers will, as a tactic, drop witnesses from a deposition lineup at the last minute, but not because of legitimate problems. Rather, they do this as a *strategy,* to leave you without testimony from key witnesses before discovery closes.

It's important to consider this possibility and to take steps to protect against it.

Suppose the discovery deadline is close. Your adversary has noticed key witnesses for deposition, and they're witnesses you need, too. So you're pleased the opponent set them. The night before the deposition, however, you receive an amended notice dropping several major witnesses on the list. Or maybe they canceled the entire day. Now what?

Now you might be out of luck, unless you cross-noticed those witnesses and subpoenaed them to appear.

That is how to protect against scheduling shenanigans involving eleventh-hour discovery depositions. A cross-notice is nothing more than a deposition notice you serve after the witnesses have been noticed by another party. In effect, you are independently scheduling the same witnesses at the same time.

When cross-noticing key depositions, you should also subpoena each witness that you must depose. By serving a cross-notice, literally titled Cross-Notice of Depositions, and by subpoenaing the witnesses, you have independently obligated each of those witnesses to appear, even if your adversary opts to cancel their plan to depose them.

This is the way to guard against tactics designed to leave you short of the discovery you need.

Keep in mind that by cross-noticing the depositions, each may count toward your limit if you are in a jurisdiction that sets a ceiling on the number of depositions you can take.

§9.37 Be Wary of Making Judicial Admissions

Are you making "judicial admissions" in depositions without realizing it?

I'd put this on my Top 10 list of deposition mistakes litigators make, because I suspect few lawyers consciously appreciate how their offhand comments may bind and sink their clients.

A judicial admission is generally regarded as a clear and unequivocal statement of concrete fact that removes a fact or issue from contention. Judicial admissions, while perceived as something done in pleadings, can occur in any stage of litigation, including in paper discovery, in depositions and in open court. They can be purposeful or inadvertent. In other words, you need not declare in a formal or grand way that your client is or is not making or conceding a point. Something offhand and loose is enough, if a court finds you clearly caused a fact, issue or claim to be withdrawn from the case.

Examples?

A lawyer representing a woman in a sexual harassment case under the Jones Act (because she worked on a gambling ship) interrupted deposition questioning about the woman's physical condition by saying, "[We're] not making any kind of physical injury claims here...." Based on the comment, the opposing lawyer asked no further questions on that topic.

That seemed reasonable enough. Many sexual harassment claims arise from the infliction of emotional distress alone. But in Jones Act cases, a sexual harassment claim only arises if the harassment amounts to physical battery. While plaintiff's counsel was likely thinking of general Title VII principles of sexual harassment, which do not require physical contact, his deposition statement was deemed a judicial admission that erased a mandatory element of the claim. The result was the entry of summary judgment and affirmance by the Fifth Circuit. (*Martinez v. Bally's Louisiana, Inc.*, 244 F. 3d 474 (5th Cir. 2001).

Yikes.

In one of my cases, an opposing lawyer volunteered during my client's deposition the following: "I think it's true, we can agree that you reported a workplace injury as having occurred on July 2nd, and we can agree that you were terminated on July 8th, six days later." Up to that point, the defendant itself had taken the position in workers' compensation proceedings that my client never reported her injury. This judicial admission dramatically strengthened our retaliation claim.

Things to watch out for in depositions that might amount to a judicial admission, for you or against you:

- If you represent the plaintiff, beware of informal questions posed to you mid-deposition about whether your client is claiming some specific nuanced angle ("Christine, you're just claiming basic disability discrimination, right, and not a failure to accommodate?"), or whether you are seeking specific types of relief ("You're not seeking reinstatement, right?"). This kind of friendly colloquy between lawyers is common in depositions. But you can lock yourself out of the house this way.
- If you represent a defendant, be careful about offhand questions about defenses you are asserting (e.g., after-acquired evidence, mitigation,

unclean hands), or about facts you might be contesting.

- Comments to the deponents by the examining lawyer that appear to remove a fact from dispute, such as "Ms. Jones, no one from my client is going to claim you were a poor performer. That had nothing to do with your layoff," or "Ma'am, my client agrees that the loss of your job/spouse/child caused you tremendous hardship and emotional grief." Statements of sympathy on the record like this are understandable, but they can be sufficiently specific and factual enough to constitute a judicial admission.

Courts have said judicial admissions can be formal or informal, intentional or inadvertent, as long as they are ((1) clear, (2) unequivocal, (3) statements of fact which have the effect of removing an issue or fact from the case. What you say as counsel in a deposition matters - and binds your client. FRE 801(d)(2) says statements made by a party in their individual "or representative capacity" are not hearsay. So your statements may be deemed an admission of your client.

If you think this is an arcane or rarely-used principle, let me assure you it is not. It is used frequently and successfully by savvy litigators to narrow the issues and scope of the lawsuit. And for the unwary, it is a malpractice trap. Teach your litigators about judicial admissions, and be sure they're looking for opportunities in comments made by opposing counsels in depositions.

An excellent overview of judicial admissions can be found in a Pepperdine Law Review article titled *Your Honor, What I Meant to State was....": A Comparative Analysis of the Judicial and Evidentiary Admissions Doctrines as Applied to Counsel Statements in Pleadings, Open Court, and Memoranda of Law,* Vol. 22, Issue 3 (1995)

§9.38 Telling Deponents About Other Testimony

There is generally no prohibition against telling a deponent what other witnesses said in their depositions.

Ax expressly provided in Rule 30(c), the rule of sequestration does not apply to depositions, absent agreement or a prior court order. So not only are other people permitted to attend depositions, you may also tell a deponent during a deposition in progress what other witnesses said in their depositions.

The best way to do this is to provide your deponent a copy of the actual deposition excerpts. You can trying verbally summarizing the testimony, but you are likely to get objections if your summary is off even by a word.

You should mark the deposition excerpt as an exhibit. You may get objections from a less experienced opposing lawyer, even suggestions that what you are doing is completely improper, but they are wrong. Deposition exhibits need not be admissible in court.

§9.39 Cross Far Beyond the Scope of Direct

A common question is whether your opponents, in a deposition you noticed and which they did not cross-notice, can ask questions far beyond the scope of your direct examination. The key is "far." Courts allow some latitude in the extent to which adversaries can exceed the contours of your examination. So the question here is, how extreme can a follow-up examination get?

- ***The Basic Rules on Follow-up Cross***

We start with Rule 30(c)(1), which says "The examination and cross-examination of a deponent proceed as they would at trial under the Federal Rules of Evidence, except Rules 103 and 615." (Rule 103 pertains to court rulings on evidence; 615 is the sequestration rule.) We go next to Rule 611(b), generally applicable to the presentation of evidence at trial, which tells us, "Cross-examination should not go beyond the subject matter of the direct examination and matters affecting the witness's credibility."

So, does this mean deposition examinations are strictly limited to direct, cross and redirect, as is common at trial in many jurisdictions? And that, similarly, cross-examinations in depositions are limited to the scope of the direct?

Generally, no. The approach in depositions is much more fluid, chiefly because the goal is to allow reasonable efforts at discovery to proceed without the exceedingly rigid boundaries of a trial examination.

- ***Be Practical, and Pragmatic***

Rather than think of the answer in terms of bright lines, think of it in terms of what makes sense. What's practical? What a judge would expect? Would a judge prefer lawyers cooperate and show flexibility, so witnesses need not be brought back multiple times? Or run each other into a ditch the moment a question goes outside the lanes painted by the examining lawyer?

In *Smith v. Logansport Comm. Sch. Corp.*, 139 F.R.D. 637 (N.D. Ind. 1991), the judge rejected the notion that there is a definitive, universally-applicable limit to the manner and mode of deposition examinations, and indeed sanctioned the plaintiffs' lawyer for stopping depositions on that assumption. The judge instead urged lawyers to use common sense, saying:

> Although Rule 30(c) states that the "[e]xamination and cross-examination of witnesses may proceed as permitted at the trial under the Federal Rules of Evidence," this provision, when considered in light of the Rules of Evidence, has no practical effect upon the scope of cross-examination during a deposition, see 4A J. Moore, J. Lucas, *Moore's Federal Practice* ¶ 30.58 (2nd Ed.1991), and "the examiner may ask about anything relevant to the subject matter of the action, regardless of whether it was raised on direct examination. 8 C, Wright & A. Miller, Federal Practice and Procedure 2113, at 420; Spray

Products, Inc. v. Strouse, Inc., 31 F.R.D. 211, 212 (E.D. Pa. 1962).

Next, the judge pointed out that while FRE 611(a) addresses the mode of examination at trial, it mostly leaves the order of examination to the discretion of the trial judge. In other words, FRE 611(a) expressly gives the judge control "over the mode and order of examining witnesses..." to "(1) make those procedures effective for determining the truth; (2) avoid wasting time; and (3) protect witnesses from harassment or undue embarrassment."

Also check out *Spray Products, Inc. v. Strouse*, 31 F.R.D. 211 (E.D. Pa. 1962), which quotes a salient passage from Moore's Federal Practice:

> Moreover, if the party taking the deposition examines the deponent only as to one issue in the case, it would seem that another party may examine the deponent on any other issues by direct examination without the necessity of serving a prior notice of the taking of deposition.

- ***Some Rules of Thumb***

So how to figure out when the adversary's examination is too much - that it's time to cry foul? Here are some rules of thumb, but always be sure to check specific case authority and rules governing your jurisdiction, too:

- If you're going to stop a deposition in progress,

you'll likely need to meet the standard set forth in Rule 30(d)(3)(A), showing that the deposition is being conducted "... in bad faith or in a manner that unreasonably annoys, embarrasses, or oppresses the deponent or party." The correct procedure is to announce the suspension of the deposition and then to immediately file your motion for a protective order. This rule only applies "during" the deposition. If you wait until the deposition ends to seek relief, you've lost your leverage under this subsection. And if you stop the deposition but don't actually seek a protective order swiftly, you're subject to sanctions. You can't just talk the talk. Once you stop it, you've got to walk the walk. And before you walk, pause. Can you persuade the judge that the extended cross is being conducted in bad faith or in a manner that unreasonably annoys, embarrasses, or oppresses the deponent or party?

- If, *before* depositions begin, you think an adversary might conduct an excessive or improper cross, Rule 26(c) provides you a basis to seek a protective order issued in advance ("The court may, for good cause, issue an order to protect a party or person from annoyance, embarrassment, oppression, or undue burden or expense. . .").

These are not easy standards to meet. Things the judge may ponder:

- How long was your examination? Are you complaining about an opponent's one-hour cross-examination after you deposed the witness for six hours?
- Was your examination broad and wide-ranging in scope, such that cross-examination might reasonably be just as broad, even if not a perfect match?
- Does it make sense, for judicial efficiency, to just let the adversary explore the topics, so a second noticed deposition isn't needed? If the adversary could notice the witness and bring everyone back anyway, what was your point in stopping it? Which approach wastes more time and causes more inconvenience?
- Is the witness a crucial figure in the case, or a minor figure?
- Is there a possibility the witness is going to be unavailable for a second deposition? Did the witness travel from a distant location? Would the witness have trouble, for health or other reasons, coming back for a second deposition, if you halt the extended cross? In other words, did you create more problems than you solved?
- Is the opponent using the same documents you used? Or are they working from a stack of hundreds of new documents, clearly exceeding any reasonable notion of a legitimate cross?
- Is the extended cross-examination

inconveniencing other witnesses waiting for their deposition? Did everyone agree to a dozen minor witnesses in a single day, setting them back-to-back every fifteen to twenty minutes, and now lawyers are conducting three-hour crosses of each witness?

- Were there discussions between you and the opposing lawyers about the schedule, and about the likelihood of extended cross-examination? Did the opposing lawyer object to your lockstep scheduling of multiple witnesses? Or did the lawyer say nothing, implicitly approving the tight schedule as a viable one?
- Is there plenty of time available to allow extended cross? For example, if you have just one witness, and your examination runs from 9:00 AM to 10:00 AM, is the balance of the day open, such that a cross of the witness that lasts twice as long is easily doable?
- Did you have an understanding with the opposing lawyer that depositions would end by a specific time because you had other commitments?

I rarely stop depositions because of extended crosses. It's will have to be something extreme. The standard for stopping a deposition is high, and the last thing judges want are discovery and scheduling squabbles. Further, good cross-examinations reveal things I don't know and, occasionally, opposing lawyers wind up developing some great testimony for me. It also benefits me if I don't have to come back for a second deposition of the same witness, newly noticed by the opponent.

It's all a balance.

Now, if you think your opposing numbers might take unbridled advantage of follow-up examination, consider building in some protection. For example, set the deposition on a day when you have other events scheduled two hours later; be sure to let the other lawyers know about it. Or set it a few hours before your client's medical appointment, or before your clients have to pick up their children from school. An early-morning deposition with nothing but open calendars the rest of the day might invite prolonged cross.

Better to plan ahead like this than to find yourself bogged down in the deposition equivalent of the Tour de France.

§9.40 Making Unsworn Documents Sworn

If you have an unsworn document authored by the deponent, and want to convert it to a sworn document, just show it to the deponent and ask the deponent to verify that the information in it is true and based on the deponent's own personal knowledge.

It could be an email, a written statement, or even an EUO you previously took. But this is an easy way to convert a work-product statement that was not taken pursuant to the rules into deposition testimony.

In your deposition, show the witness the prior statement, email or document. Ask the deponent to review it, and allow the witness ample time to do so. If necessary, ask the reporter to note the time the examination pauses, and to note the time the questions resume. This way, the transcript shows how long the witness had to review the document.

Next ask the witness if the document is a true copy of their prior writing. Then ask (to avoid hearsay problems) if the statements therein are based on his or her own personal knowledge. There should be no hearsay problem if witnesses admit on the stand that they made the statement and that it was true. They therefore adopt the statement and eliminate a hearsay problem. It is now their present testimony.

Even if hearsay, it can still come in to rebut an express or implied charge of fabrication, or an accusation that the witnesses are testifying from a recent motive to fabricate. *Botey v. Green et al*, 2018 WL 5985694 (M.D. Penn. Nov. 14, 2018).

As to EUOs you previously took, this also allows your adversary an opportunity to cross-examine the deponent about the statement.

§9.41 Jury Instructions as a Deposition Tool

Most jurisdictions have standard jury instructions. The instructions cover not only the substantive elements of claims and defenses but many other critical matters, including damages, motive, intent, knowledge, and the mitigation of damages. The instructions tell juries how to figure things out, and they do so in a clear, user-friend way. They are a very useful tool in constructing your deposition theme and questions.

I don't rely on pattern instructions exclusively, obviously, but they help ensure your examinations are oriented to the claims or defenses you must prove.

§9.42 Phrase Questions to Match Trial Themes

World-classes examiners don't just develop facts in depositions. They lay the linguistic foundation for trial openings, examinations, and closings.

They do this before depositions begin by imagining the adjectives and phrases that will make for great courtroom theatre. Deponents don't think ahead to trial, and they're far more likely to agree with your planted adjectives and phrases in relatively relaxed deposition settings than they are if they hear them for the first time in a courtroom before a jury. So don't miss this golden opportunity.

In an upcoming trial, I needed to convince the jury that senior officials from the opposing party saw obvious, dangerous warning signs of a problem and ignored them. In depositions, I asked witnesses in a low-key manner if they were a little alarmed by a series of events. It seemed a reasonable enough question. All said yes.

And that was how I began assembling testimony to match my trial theme of alarm, alarm bells, and warning signs. At trial, the testimony came together nicely because all the witnesses had used the verbiage I choose very early on.

If you know your general trial theme when you begin

taking depositions, you can use consistent concepts, words, and synonyms, so the testimony as a whole will perfectly mesh with your arguments to the jury. If the deponents agreed to words matching your theme, your closing will seem tailored to the testimony, rather than the other way around. It is very effective.

§9.43 Physical Demonstrations by Deponents

Can you ask your deponent to physically demonstrate something of relevance? Yes, in most cases.

But there isn't a lot of law on the topic, and the cases go both ways. It may depend on your facts and your judge. The better view is that demonstrations are as permissible in depositions as they are in trial.

So why not try? There are lots of things witnesses can demonstrate during a deposition that will be helpful to your evaluation of the case. Demonstrations can help you (a) understand the facts better, (b) conduct more precise and effective deposition examinations, (c) help your experts, (d) educate the judge rule on key points and (e) argue to the jury. They can also help the parties evaluate settlement.

Demonstrations can include police tactics during an arrest, how an accident occurred, physical behaviors in a sexual harassment case, or how an employee should have performed a task or used a computer program to enter data.

Most every lawsuit involves something that can be demonstrated. You might be losing valuable opportunities to persuade the jury if all you have is an explanation, and nothing to visually persuade the jury about a particular event or claim.

More generally, whether the deposition re-enactment is itself admissible evidence at trial in court is an aside. I learn a great deal from watching demonstrations by key witnesses. It also sharpens my examinations in depositions and trials ,and if the demonstration proves admissible, or if I can then safely have the witness do the same re-enactment in front of the jury, all the better.

Some authorities to get you started, in no particular order:

- Opponents of deposition demonstrations sometimes cite *Hall v. Clifton Precision*, 150 F.R.D. 525, 528 (E.D. Pa. 1993) (saying generically that a deposition "is meant to be a question-and-answer conversation between the deposing lawyer and the witness.") On the other hand, Rule 30(c)(1) says "The examination and cross-examination of a deponent proceed as they would at trial under the Federal Rules of Evidence...." If a demonstration is allowed at trial, it should be allowed in deposition.
- See how pro-and-con arguments were presented by litigants in the case *Crossroads Systems (Texas), Inc. v. Dot Hill Corporation*, Case No. 1:03-CV-00754-SS (W.D. Texas) in CM/ECF documents 197 (motion to compel demonstration by deponent), 204 (response in opposition to

demonstration) and 208 (reply in support of demonstration).

- Limited videotaped deposition re-enactment **allowed** in *Carson v. Burlington Northern, Inc.*, 52 F.R.D. 492 (D. Nebraska 1971).
- Videotaped deposition re-enactment **allowed** in Roberts v. *Homelite Division of Textron, Inc.*, 109 F.R.D. 664 (N.D. Indiana 1986).
- Videotaped deposition re-enactment **allowed** in *Emerson Electric Co. v. Superior Court*, 16 Cal 4th 1101 (S. Ct. Calif. 1997) (threatening deponent with sanctions if he refused to cooperate in re-enactment; further holding that since demonstrations at trial are allowed, they are certainly allowed in depositions).
- Some useful discussion in *Getting a Witness to "Walk the Line": Accident Demonstrations at Videotaped Depositions*, 30 Am.J.Trial Advoc. 487 (2007) by Robert A. Sachs, available on Westlaw.
- More in *Underused Defense Tool: Videotaping Accident Demonstrations at Discovery Depositions*, 50 No. 12 DRI For Def. 18, by Robert Sachs (2008), available on Westlaw.

§9.44 Explore Witness Tampering

We think of "witness tampering" as threats or actual violence.

Often, though, the intimidation or tampering is more

subtle. It can occur in many forms. Sometimes it's positive – a sudden promotion or pay raise for a key witness whose deposition is a few days away. Sometimes it's negative - suggestions the witness might not get a promotion or raise, again just a few days away from testimony. In one federal trial, a witness I was cross-examining volunteered that she had been promoted by telephone on her way to the courthouse.

Sometimes the tampering isn't something the witness even appreciates, such as when an opposing lawyer fills the witness with wildly false information. It's important to explore this with key witnesses to ensure you get the most out of your depositions.

For an example of an actual civil lawsuit filed against three individual lawyers and their law firms for alleged witness tampering, and the lawyers' conduct that triggered it, see *Chance v. Cook*, et al., Case 4:19-cv-00335-MW-CAS (N. D. Fla. filed July 22, 2019).

- ***Sources of Authority on Tampering***

Both state and federal laws forbid any effort to adversely influence witness testimony. Here's the language of a typical statute, to give you a sense for the vast scope of conduct that can constitute tampering. I've **bold-faced** key elements:

> A person who **knowingly** uses **intimidation** or **physical force**, or **threatens** another person, or attempts to do so, or **engages in misleading conduct** toward another

> person, or **offers pecuniary benefit or gain** to another person, **with intent to cause or induce any person to:** a) **Withhold testimony, or withhold a record, document, or other object**, from an official investigation or official proceeding; (b) **Alter, destroy, mutilate, or conceal an object with intent to impair the integrity or availability of the object** for use in an official investigation or official proceeding; (c) **Evade legal process summoning that person to appear as a witness, or to produce a record, document, or other object**, in an official investigation or an official proceeding; (d) **Be absent from an official proceeding** to which such person has been summoned by legal process; (e) **Hinder, delay, or prevent the communication to a law enforcement officer or judge of information** relating to the commission or possible commission of an offense or a violation of a condition of probation, parole, or release pending a judicial proceeding; or (f) **Testify untruthfully** in an official investigation or an official proceeding, **commits the crime of tampering with a witness, victim, or informant.**

Under this particular law, the "official proceeding" need not be pending or about to be instituted at the time of the offense, and the testimony or the record, document, or other object need not be admissible in evidence or free of a claim of privilege.

All fifty states have anti-tampering laws. There are federal statutes on point as well. E.g., *42 U.S.C. 1985(2)*

(Obstructing justice; intimidating party, witness, or juror); 18 U.S.C. 1512(b)(1) (Tampering with a witness, victim, or an informant).

- ***Suggested Inquiries on Tampering***

I recommend inquiry about potential tampering for any deponent you suspect might have been a target. In my experience, conduct that meets at least the technical definition of witness tampering is more common than anyone imagines.

Sample topics and questions include the following:

- Actual or promised pay raises, bonuses, promotions or other favorable job-related treatment, *e.g.*, "When was the last time you received a raise? Has anyone at your employer discussed raises with you since then?"
- Actual or promised demotions, pay cuts, write-ups or other adverse action. Witnesses who believe their jobs are in jeopardy will not be as forthcoming. Look for anything resembling a warning to the witness, *e.g.*, "Have you ever been disciplined, suspended or experienced a pay cut? Have you been told in the last several months that something like that might be in the works for you?"
- Actual or perceived physical threats to the witness or someone close to the witness
- Actual or perceived offers of compensation. This

could include something as simple as a free lunch when the witness met with the opposing lawyer or party to discuss the case

- Suggestions that the witness avoid a subpoena or summons to appear for a deposition
- Suggestions to the witness that there was a technical flaw in the subpoena or summons that might have allowed them to avoid coming
- Group meetings involving the witness and others associated with the case where it appears there was a collective effort to shape upcoming testimony
- Documents provided to the witness to shape or influence perceptions
- Documents not provided to the witness
- Misleading information provided to witnesses to shape their perceptions. What does the witness think the case is about? (*E.g.*, "If I told you this was a case about a car accident, would you know if that is true or not true? If you believe it is not true, what would you tell me you think the case concerns?")
- It isn't unusual for deponents to be given information even in the hour or so before their depositions, sometimes by other witnesses who are leaving the deposition locations. Ask if they've heard anything more about the case from witnesses whose depositions just ended.
- Suggestions to the witness by anyone that they

should avoid a topic, destroy documents, avoid looking for documents, or pretend not to know the relevant information

- Suggestions of retaliation for harmful testimony. In one recent case, a witness sat silent for a full thirty seconds when I asked him if he feared retaliation for what he had just said. His boss sat at the end of the table. The intimidation could not have been clearer. By the way, this illustrates why audiotaping depositions is useful. Absent audio, that long silence would have vanished into the ether. With audio, the pauses tell the judge and jury a great deal about the truthfulness of the witness' eventual response, "No." Lengthy pauses and silence by a witness in response to specific questions matter. *See In re Asbestos Litig. Carter Trial Grp.,* No. CIV. A. 91C-07-61, 1992 WL 390617, at *3 (Del. Super. Ct. Oct. 26, 1992) (noting importance of intangible elements of a witness' testimony when evaluating truthfulness and credibility, including "...demeanor, attitude, body language, inflections, cadence, and all of the other myriad of intangible characteristics of the witness which allow jurors to make decisions about both the truthfulness and the depth of knowledge of that particular witness; excluding use of witness' stumbling deposition transcript at trial because "...the jury will not be able to judge the demeanor of this witness, the difficulty or lack of difficulty

> he had in answering the questions, the pauses or lack of pauses in his answers, the tone of his voice, etc.")

I have had considerable success in getting deponents to open up about intimidation efforts. An empathetic tone and demeanor works wonders. Often deponents will reveal such efforts either in their answers or by their body language, which can provide further guidance to you in examining the witness. Witnesses under attack need to know they have an ally.

§9.45 Never Use False Facts with Deponents

Can you falsely state or imply facts to a deponent - such as "There are tapes of that conversation, just so you know" - as a tactic to encourage witnesses to testify truthfully?

The short answer is no. Making false representations of material fact to a deponent might trigger serious disciplinary charges against you.

In *Cincinnati Bar Assn. v. Statzer*, 800 N.E. 2d 1117 (Oh. Sup. Ct. 2003), a lawyer allegedly placed a bogus, and bogusly-labeled, stack of cassette tapes on the table in front of the deponent. The purpose was to suggest the witness shouldn't lie because there were actual recordings of conversations to prove otherwise.

But there weren't.

Disciplinary proceedings followed. Ultimately, the Ohio Supreme Court saw it as an integrity-of-proceedings issue.

The lawyer argued there was a legitimate basis for the bluff. Here's a blurb and the court's response:

> "Here the Respondent, however, urges us to distinguish trial conduct from "discovery depositions," arguing that the latter require greater freedom of inquiry into matters that may be relevant but inadmissible.....She argues that wide latitude was imperative.....to draw honest testimony from a theretofore untrustworthy witness and that use of the audio cassette tapes was merely a tactic intended to achieve this legitimate end. We recognize that the discovery process, particularly the pursuit of information through deposition, cannot be overly restricted if it is to remain effective. We must draw the line, however, when an attorney engages in subterfuge that intimidates a witness. While respondent's primary purpose [was] to elicit the truth, her tactic also tricked the legal assistant into thinking that the revelation of embarrassing confidences was at stake. [The] the success of her tactic is not at issue....while such deception may induce truthful testimony, it is just as likely to elicit lies if a witness believes that lies will offer security from the false threat. Respondent's deceitful tactic intimidated her witness by creating the false impression that respondent possessed compromising personal information that she could offer as evidence. For these reasons, we agree that respondent violated DR 1–102(A)(4) and 7–106(C)(1)."

The lesson to be learned is that bald-faced lies on a material point should be avoided. It might be kosher in a law enforcement interrogation, where bluffing is high art, but not in court proceedings. There are lots of ways to enhance truthful deposition testimony, but making your own false statements isn't one of them.

§9.46 Documents Deponents Used to Prepare

Many witnesses review documents to get ready for their deposition. Sometimes opposing lawyers provide documents, by email or in hard-copy folders or binders. Sometimes the witnesses independently go back and look at documents.

Either way, you're entitled to know what they are and to obtain them. Federal and state courts are clear. Information provided to a witness specifically to prepare them for deposition testimony is subject to disclosure. This is an elemental impeachment issue.

I previously wrote about this topic, specifically the extent to which lawyers can verbally inquire about a deponent's preparation efforts, including the duration of and attendance at preparation sessions, and whether specific techniques like a mock deposition examination were used to get the witness ready.

You should consider subpoenaing the documents deponents used to get ready. You may need to see everything the witness used or was given. Often the opposing lawyer supplied the documents and might have forwarded a package that is highly-selective or misleading. There are occasions, too, where witnesses saw documents you've never seen.

Further, some witnesses claim to forget what they've reviewed. I had one witness tell me she reviewed counsel-supplied documents earlier that morning but could not remember what they were. I immediately served a subpoena for everything she was provided.

I recommend a laid-back, calm approach when questioning witnesses about preparation efforts, lest they get wise to your intentions. You should do this early in the deposition before things become contentious. I've discovered some real gems this way.

Few litigators serve subpoenas for materials deponents reviewed in preparation. There's a perception that we can't deeply probe about a witness' deposition preparations. As a result, we miss blockbuster opportunities to see documents that neither the witness nor their counsel expected would be produced. There is real potential impeachment value in them, beginning with the significance of the specific documents chosen, the implications of documents not sent to the witness (which might change the witness' view) and the impact of any markings on the documents for emphasis.

Juries are fascinated by behind-the-scenes documents an adversary feeds witnesses to shape their thinking, especially if the documents were very misleading.

§9.47 Preparing Unrepresented Witnesses

How far can you go in preparing witnesses for a deposition when you don't represent them?

Pretty far, it appears, according to a federal judge in her January 20, 2017 Memorandum and Order. In *United States v. Malik*, 2017 U.S. Dist. LEXIS 8439, Case No. 15-CV-9092-CM-TJJ (D. Kan. Jan. 20, 2017), Judge Teresa J. James ruled there was nothing improper with an Assistant U.S. Attorney's actions in preparing an unrepresented witness for her deposition. The witness was a former immigration officer, and her testimony was key to an ongoing naturalization-revocation proceeding. Lawyers for the defendant, Ahmed Malik, complained that the Justice Department's lawyer went too far in meeting with the witness, discussing the case, and suggesting that the defendant had engaged in fraud.

The judge disagreed. In her Order, she relied on section 116 of the *Restatement (Third) of the Law Governing Lawyers* (2000). I'd not heard of this treatise, so I ran a quick LEXIS search to see how often it is cited. That search retrieved more than 1,000 state and federal cases citing it.

Judge James quotes from the treatise to illustrate just how far you can go in preparing - *influencing, shaping* - a third-party, unrepresented witness. Keep that in mind the next time you're meeting with a witness you don't represent. It's no time to be shy:

> [A] lawyer may invite the witness to provide truthful testimony favorable to the lawyer's client. Preparation

> consistent with the rule of this Section may include the following: discussing the role of the witness and effective courtroom demeanor; discussing the witness's recollection and probable testimony; revealing to the witness other testimony or evidence that will be presented and asking the witness to reconsider the witness's recollection or recounting of events in that light; discussing the applicability of law to the events in issue; reviewing the factual context into which the witness's observations or opinions will fit; reviewing documents or other physical evidence that may be introduced; and discussing probable lines of hostile cross-examination that the witness should be prepared to meet. Witness preparation may include rehearsal of testimony. A lawyer may suggest choice of words that might be employed to make the witness's meaning clear. However, a lawyer may not assist the witness to testify falsely as to a material fact.

But exercise caution when prepping non-client witnesses for deposition, as your conversations probably do not qualify for a privilege to shield them. One federal court observed pertinent to former employees that disclosures of facts "... developed during the litigation, such as testimony of other witnesses, may not be privileged, particularly given their potential to influence a witness to conform or adjust her testimony, consciously or unconsciously."

One decision widely cited on this point is *Peralta v. Cendant Corp.*, 190 F.R.D. 38 (D. Conn. 1999). Also check out an excellent free article on prepping former employees, by googling "*Attorney-Client Privilege and Deposition Preparation of Former Employees,*" by Baker & McKenzie LLP lawyer Meloney Cargil Perry. It was published in 2007 but is still of value in assessing this issue.

§9.48 Last-Minute Document Dumps

There will be times when your adversary drops an unexpected load of documents on you the day or evening before your depositions. There is clearly no time for you to properly prepare. What's the right thing to do under the circumstances?

One seemingly-exasperated federal judge would tell you, *do something.* Postpone the depositions if appropriate, or proceed and ask to retake the depositions if you later determine after review that the documents would have informed your examination.

This situation arose in a 2016 case. Lawyers for approximately thirty disabled plaintiffs filed a motion for sanctions alleging a wide range of litigation-related misconduct by defense lawyers, including the release of 10,000 pages of documents just days before plaintiffs' counsel was to begin depositions. The sanctions motion described the situation thusly:

> Approximately one week before the scheduled depositions of Defendant's witnesses, Defendant dumped 10,000 pages of documents onto Plaintiffs. Having already scheduled flights and accommodations, as well as the

> depositions themselves, Plaintiffs proceeded with the scheduled depositions while simultaneously attempting to digest approximately 10,000 pages of document production.

The plaintiffs subsequently asked the federal district court judge to sanction the defendant for "defense counsel's bad faith conduct." But until the plaintiffs sought sanctions, they had done nothing relating to the last-minute flood of documents. The district judge refused to impose sanctions:

> Plaintiffs object to Defendant's production of 10,000 documents on the eve of depositions. Notably, plaintiffs never objected to the timing of the filing of the documents, never requested to reschedule the depositions, and never sought to re-take any of the depositions based on documents contained in that production. Plaintiffs never filed any motions objecting to the document production or its timing. Under these circumstances, no sanctions are warranted.

At first blush, the plaintiffs' lawyers' decision to proceed with depositions seems reasonable. Most judges will urge lawyers to proceed under these circumstances. One reason is that the lawyers may discover that the document dump did not affect the testimony. Another is that, if the late production does impact the examinations, the examining lawyers can seek sanctions more precisely tailored to the harm caused. And, here, the fact that the plaintiffs' counsel had incurred substantial expense for travel and lodging seems to support their decision. On the other hand, the judge does imply that the plaintiffs' counsel could have, following depositions, asked to retake them.

What's the lesson here?

First, if the last-minute production of documents is likely to affect your examination, act swiftly to postpone the depositions either by agreement with the adversary or with the help of the court.

Second, if you opt to proceed with the depositions, move quickly to seek court relief - either to allow the re-deposition of those witnesses or to exclude the documents – if your depositions show that the last-minute document dump hurt your examinations. The decisive factor for the judge was the lack of swift action by the plaintiffs' counsel, either before the depositions or after.

The case is *Schwarz, et al. v. Vills. Charter Sch.*, No. 5:12-CV-00177, 2017 U.S. Dist. LEXIS 3449. (M.D. Fla. filed 2012). The motion for sanctions, filed in December 2016, is Document 282 in the case docket on PACER. The defendants' response, filed January 3, 2017, is Document 287. The order denying the motion, filed January 10, 2017, is Document 292.

§9.49 Make Digital Evidence A Deposition Priority

Consider including the location, storage and retrieval of digital evidence a topic in your Rule 30(b)(6) deposition, in order to understand the universe of potential evidence the adversary has.

Much discoverable evidence is now digital. This includes emails, texts, database records, digitally-created images, metadata, and office-suite files (e.g., Word, Excel, Access, Outlook) that tell the real story about what happened.

- ***Obstacles, and Getting Around Them***

There are difficulties in conducting digital discovery. One is the widespread tactic by adversaries of converting electronic evidence from its original, "native" form into some other form. In the process, they strip valuable information from the files and impede the ability of electronic evidence to reveal the truth. I know few lawyers who routinely set depositions of corporate representatives to learn how the adversary creates, stores and retrieves electronic records. We need to know that - what programs are used, what devices are used and how information from them can be found.

Litigators must be fluent in digital evidence in three ways:

- *First*, lawyers must be intimately familiar with the major file formats used in business and consumer applications and devices.
- *Second*, they must know what information each format stores and how it can be searched.
- *Third,* they must know when to demand the information in native format - meaning the original file format used to create and store the information - and when some other format is okay.

There are lots of free resources online for lawyers to learn about these areas. It isn't necessary to hire a digital-evidence expert in most situations. It is only necessary to read enough about digital file formats, storage, and retrieval to be reasonably fluent in the jargon.

This proficiency will allow you to properly query an adversary's 30(b)(6) witness, and then to frame discovery requests accordingly. Some motion practice may be needed if an adversary refuses to produce files in the format requested.

Further, judges need to know why you need evidence in native formats, such as the fact that files in native format are often field-searchable. This means you can keyword-search millions of files quickly because you can limit your search to relevant fields, as opposed to the entirety of the production. Native files also typically contain all original metadata - the how, where, when and why of file creation and modification.

I recommend a few steps to get started:

- Become well-versed in the ten or so major file formats used by businesses and consumers. There are a huge number of formats in use, but the actual number you'll need to understand is less than a dozen. Understand what each format stores, and how it can be retrieved. Consider making a chart of this information for easy reference.
- Draft your document production requests according to the file format you need for each type of document. As I've said, it isn't always

necessary to have productions in native format; sometimes this can lead to productions in proprietary formats that will require you to invest in software or expert fees to read.

- Develop a good working 30(b)(6) statement of the topics you'll want the opponent's IT witness to discuss. This should be attached as an exhibit to your deposition notice. You can build on it as you learn more about the subject. Here's a sample I've used to get you started. Don't assume this will work for you in all cases. But here it is: "Topic: Digital Storage, Retrieval and Destruction: A person who is knowledgeable and can to answer specific questions about how [Adversary] stores, maintains, retrieves and destroys information on mail systems, archives, local drives, shared networks, portable devices, removable media, and databases. Many devices require different search terms because they store and retrieve information differently and often use or require different search term characteristics (e.g., Boolean constructs, proximity searches, "stemming," and fielded searches, to name a few that come to mind. Each device and system may require different approaches to ensure all data is retrieved properly. This examination will last approximately three hours and will inquire into [Adversary's] network infrastructure, meaning the hardware and software resources of [Adversary's] systems that enable network connectivity, communication, operations and management of an enterprise network. Plaintiff seeks to determine how information generated at the store were plaintiff worked is stored, both locally and on the corporate network; how the information is archived; and how it is retrieved, including the software used to search for and retrieve emails, memoranda, career-preference documents, personnel documents such as evaluations; and how it is deleted, altered or destroyed.")

- Be ready to seek help from the judge if opponents refuse to produce documents in the desired format. Don't assume your judge understands any aspect of digital file format creation, storage, and search-retrieval. Assume the judge knows nothing, or even has a mistaken belief, and start from there.

§9.50 Asking Questions From Interrogatories

Can you ask opposing party witnesses the same questions you asked in your interrogatories?

Sure. There is nothing to stop you from questioning a live witness in a deposition setting just because the topics are the same or similar to those contained in documents already provided or interrogatory questions answered. *Bernardi Ortiz v. Cybex Int'l, Inc.*, No. CV 15-2989 (PAD), 2018 WL 2448130, at *9 (D.P.R. May 30, 2018)

§9.51 Catch-All Concluding Questions

In some situations, a witness may be less than candid because of the specific wording you use. Sometimes your phraseology isn't spot on - as the deponent sees it, anyway - to trigger the response the witness knows you are looking for. Clever or reluctant witnesses may provide an answer that is technically correct but that is untrue given the spirit of your question. Now what?

This is definitely frustrating. I cover this in my common wrap-up questions at the end of each deposition:

- Did you ask for clarification each time I asked you a question that was in any way unclear?
- When you answered questions, did you understand the question you were being asked?
- Were your answers all based on your own personal knowledge?
- I realized that some time has passed since these events took place. Sometimes when we discuss older events, we start to remember details that we had forgotten. So here's my question: Is there anything that you've recalled during this deposition that you would like to now add to your answers, or that you would like to offer in order to change an answer that you have given me today to make it more accurate?
- Finally, were there any questions I asked you today that you would have answered differently,

> or in response to which you would have provided more information, if I had asked it a slightly different way?

While there is no way to prevent a deponent from answering more fully at trial in response to an opponent's "perfectly-worded" question, this last question will help you impeach the witness. You can on cross remind the witness of the question your opponent asked and the answer given, and then read your question and the witness' answer from deposition.

10

CREATING INVINCIBLE DEPONENTS - PART 1

EXPLAINING THE DEPOSITION PROCESS

Covered in This Chapter:

- ***§10.01 Preliminary Overview***
- ***§10.02 Poor Preparation Destroys Cases***
- ***§10.03 Bullet-Proofing Your Witness***
- ***§10.04 The Training Must Mirror the Battle***
- ***§10.05 Your Witness Must Be Stronger than Needed***
- ***§10.06 A Sample Client Prep Session***
- ***§10.07 "Good morning. Thanks for coming in."***
- ***§10.08 "You must answer every question."***
- ***§10.09 "Depositions on TV are not realistic."***
- ***§10.10 "The opposing lawyer is not your friend, and is not neutral.***
- ***§10.11 "The lawyer will try to put words in your mouth."***
- ***§10.12 "Your deposition is not a practice run."***

- *§10.13 "The judge will read every word you word."*
- *§10.14 "Here's how deposition transcripts are used."*
- *§10.15 "Let's talk about how to answer questions."*
- *§10.16 "A deposition is not a social conversation."*
- *§10.17 "Listen to the preliminary instructions."*
- *§10.18 "Answer questions fully and completely."*
- *§10.19 "If you don't know the answer, say so."*
- *§10.20 "If you don't remember something, say so."*
- *§10.21 "But don't use 'I don't recall' as a crutch."*
- *§10.22 "Never change answers under pressure."*
- *§10.23 "If you don't understand a question, say so. Say nothing else."*
- *§10.24 "If the lawyer interrupts you, keep talking."*
- *§10.25 "Do not answer until you hear the entire question."*
- *§10.26 "Read all documents with great caution."*
- *§10.27 "People do alter documents and it may not be obvious."*
- *§10.28 "If you're unsure about a document's authenticity, do not take a stance on it."*
- *§10.29 "Opponents might have altered your documents."*
- *§10.30 "Some questions may be very personal."*
- *§10.31 "You'll be asked about prior cases."*
- *§10.32 "They'll ask about your criminal history."*
- *§10.33 "They'll ask about acts of dishonesty."*
- *§10.34 "You'll be asked who's helping you."*
- *§10.35 "They'll ask if you've removed data."*
- *§10.36 "They'll ask if you've recorded calls."*

- *§10.37 "They'll ask about texts, emails and social media."*
- *§10.38 "They'll ask about your medical history."*
- *§10.39 "They may ask about substance abuse."*
- *§10.40 "Some anxiety is a good sign."*
- *§10.41 "Take hourly breaks to clear your head."*
- *§10.42 "Never reveal our communications."*
- *§10.43 "Be truthful about everything."*

In this section I focus chiefly on preparing your own clients and witnesses to have their deposition taken.

§10.01 Preliminary Overview

Because most cases never make it to trial, I urge lawyers to invest *heavily* in preparing clients and witnesses for deposition testimony. It is their performance in that arena that will power your case into the Winner's Circle.

Your opponents will use depositions not only to make judgments about the merits, but also as a gauge of the overall calibre of your clients. Are they confident? Is their testimony unequivocal? Are they easily angered? Do they exaggerate? Do they pay attention?

The presumption, sometimes correct, is that a witness' deposition performance will mirror their performance before a jury. In other words, all you see is all there is. So the value of cases tend to rise or fall in the aftermath. Thus the time you invest rendering your witnesses invincible will return dividends in multiples.

§10.02 Poor Preparation Destroys Cases

A surprising number of lawyers arrive at their offices on the day of depositions, or at the reporter's office, without having spent one moment getting their client ready. They offer the thinnest of guidance: "Tell the truth." "Pay attention." "Watch out for trick questions." "Just answer yes or no." "Don't expand on your answer."

These trite, threadbare platitudes offer clients no lifeline. *Of course* your client should pay attention. *Of course* your client should watch out for trick questions, whatever those are. *Of course* your client should tell the truth. So far, lawyers using this approach have said nothing of value. As for lawyers who tell clients not to expand on their answers, or to "just answer yes or no," it's hard to tell who has been to fewer depositions, the client or the lawyer.

Your clients will sit for hours on end; answer many different types of questions; review and testify about documents; defend and explain their answers; and fend off aggressive declarative statements, not to mention a barrage of taunts, innuendo, and hints if not accusations of misconduct or incompetence.

A deposition is a complex and lengthy intellectual sword fight. If your client's blade has not been sharpened, the ensuing contest of wills may well be disastrous.

§10.03 Bullet-Proofing Your Witness

There are three elements to best-in-class deposition preparation. You must:

Explain the process, start to finish. Explain what a deposition is, how it is used (case evaluation, summary judgment, impeachment), who reads it, who will be present and their roles, and where everyone sits. Stress that the opposing lawyer is the opposing team's coach.

Offer numerous examples of tricks and traps. Offer numerous examples of tricks and traps, with anecdotes from actual depositions. This includes tricks to lower their guard, misstatements about the case and the many forms of misleading questions.

Conduct at least two thorough, aggressive mock cross-examinations. Stay in character as the opposing lawyer, and insist your client do likewise, as the deponent. Use multiple tricks and traps. I aim for a total of five hours of mock examination, including background questions and breaks. Make your mock examination identical to the actual experience. Finally, and once you understand the ten to twenty case-critical questions that could make or break the case, ask them over and again through the deposition, slightly varying the way you ask the questions each time. Get your client used to recognizing those questions no matter how they're worded. Your opposing number will ask them many times and in many different ways.

I generally break the preparation sessions into two days, and I do a final, highly-condensed one the morning of.

The goal is to expose clients to the approach they will face in the actual deposition. This includes introductory instructions, background questions, and documents. In general, it is not difficult to figure out most or all the questions likely to be asked, and to pose them to clients in the mock deposition session.

§10.04 The Training Must Mirror the Battle

In preparation sessions I use the style of the opposing lawyer.

If the lawyer's style is aggressive, I am aggressive.

If the lawyer is given to putting words in witness' mouth, I rely heavily on leading questions and unfavorable declarative statements.

If the opposing lawyer tends to smirk, interrupt, feign shock or disbelief during depositions, I do that as well.

Clients do best when exposed to the exact experience they will face. And I will reword questions to see if the client has absorbed the concepts, or gets confused if I ask the same thing a different way. It is great if they answer a softball question in a solid way; not so much if I rephrase the exact same question and the clients have no idea what to say.

I will also rush the clients, interrupt them, push documents in front of them or pull them back quickly, suggest that the client's testimony has been dishonest, and suggest that the client's claims or defenses are a sham.

I may use documents that have nothing to do with the case, to see if the client is even paying attention.

I want to develop the clients' range, so they can easily adapt to anything thrown at them. I also want to see if I can get the clients to admit they are speculating (especially when they are not), and agree they have no idea whatsoever whether their views have any basis in fact whatsoever (when they clearly do).

I may ask clients if they are willing to change their minds based on what other witnesses are going to say, and I then make up "mystery meat" testimony to see if the client bites or knows how to respond to supposed testimony no one has given or ever will give.

§10.05 Your Witness Must be Stronger Than Needed

When depositions of my clients start, they are ready to fight. There will be nothing asked that they cannot answer. Lawyers who interrupt my clients will find my clients talking over them until my clients have finished their answers. Lawyers who are disrespectful will hear aggressive objections from the clients. Lawyers who attempt to rush my clients through documents will be shut down.

This is how to prepare your clients. This is how you win cases through your depositions.

§10.06 A Sample Client Prep Session

Let's work through a sample deposition preparation session for the typical client. Your client may be more or less sophisticated than this sample fits, so adapt accordingly. The approach here presumes a civil case, a client who is fairly sophisticated and understands the basic concepts, but who has never been a witness before and is generally unfamiliar with court proceedings, depositions or trials.

This is a summary. It does not include all the things I cover every time. But if you use this as a starting guide, and then develop your own preparation session from there, you will be in great shape.

§10.07 "Good morning. Thanks for coming in."

What we're going to do today is get you ready to be the best possible witness you can be. Since you've never had your deposition taken before let me give you an outline or framework of the process. It's important to understand what a deposition is, and how it will be used.

Your deposition will be a question and answer session about all of the relevant claims and defenses in the case. It will be in a conference room just like this one. At one end of the table will be the court reporter, who is going to take down every word you say. The record created will be preserved for all of time.

Across from you will be the lawyer for the opposing side. He or she will be asking you questions. There may or may not be a representative of the company there, but don't worry. The representative cannot say anything, and cannot engage in behavior of any kind that will distract you. If they do, I will put a stop to that immediately.

he lawyer will ask you a series of questions, typically

beginning with background questions about you, your education, work history, and family life. The lawyer will then turn to the facts relevant to your claims or defenses. The first segment on background issues may take an hour or two. The balance of the deposition will be about the case.

§10.08 "You must answer every question."

There are some exceptions to this, but the lawyer on the other side is solid and is not the type of lawyer who will ask wildly inappropriate questions. So whether you think the questions are relevant or not, you must answer them unless I tell you otherwise. And it is highly unlikely I will instruct you not to answer a question, so you should not look at me every time you're asked a question to see if I want you to answer it. If I do not, I will let you know.

Focus on the question and on giving your best and most accurate answer. You may have heard some people say the best way to respond to questions is with a simple yes or no, and nothing else. That is not how depositions work. Most of the questions will require you to give explanations. There will be some questions that call for a simple yes or no answer, but most will require detail.

§10.09 "Depositions on TV are not realistic."

A real-life deposition is very different. You should not look at me for signals on how to answer anything. No blinks, no winks, no hand gestures, no nothing. The purpose of our conversation right now is to get you ready. Once the deposition begins, the answers must come from you. A court would likely fine both of us, or worse, if we engaged in that kind of conduct. TV lawyers might do that, but real lawyers who want to remain lawyers do not.

§10.10 "The opposing lawyer is not your friend, and is not neutral."

Lawyers sometimes start depositions in a very friendly way, with something like "I'm just here to find out what happened."

Know this: That is not true. The only neutral participants in a lawsuit are the judge and jury. Lawyers are advocates for their client. Think of the opposing lawyer as the coach for the opposing team. I am the coach of your team. Never confuse the role of the lawyers. We are not neutral. We are there to win. The opposing lawyers were hired to hurt your case, and they need your help. They need you to assume they're neutral, maybe even your friend. They need you to relax your guard, and to pay very little attention to what they're asking. The minute you lower your guard is the minute you start getting hurt. The opposing lawyers are there to do you damage. They have no other purpose.

§10.11 "The lawyer will try to put words in your mouth."

There are two ways that lawyers can ask questions. Let me explain both.

One style of questioning is what I call the "pull" method. This is where the lawyer frames questions to *pull* information from you. These are questions like the following: "So what did you do next? What did he say? Tell me what happened?"

The other type of examination involves what I call "push" questions.

This is a more aggressive, antagonistic form of questioning that requires you to be stay sharp and be very firm. Example: "You never made a complaint to human resources, *did you?*" "You looked away before the light turned, *didn't you?* " "You knew the content was a trade secret, *didn't you?*"

This form of question does not ask what you know. *It tells you what you supposedly know to be true and demands you agree.* You must listen with great caution to this form of examination. You must speak up if any piece of the question is inaccurate. You must never agree to an aggressive statement that is simply *close* to what you would say.

If it is not 100% correct, if it is only 99%, you must speak up and explain why it is wrong and why you do not agree.

§10.12 "Your deposition is not a practice run."

Everything you say counts. It is critical that you understand that most cases never go to trial. Most are settled, or thrown out, based on what the parties and witnesses say in depositions.

So this is not a situation where you work out the kinks in your deposition, get a feel for what's important, and then do your thing at trial. If your deposition testimony is not solid, you will never have another chance to tell your story. There will be no trial. So this is it.

§10.13 "The judge will read every word you say."

The judge will eventually get a copy of the transcript of your deposition and review every word you said. That's who matters most.

It is useful to imagine the judge is listening in on the phone as you testify. He or she won't be of course, but it's useful to think of it that way, because in a very real way, that is who you are talking to during your deposition.

If the judge reviews your transcript and thinks your testimony is weak, untruthful, unfounded or speculative, your case is over. You will never see the inside of a courtroom. This is why the opposing lawyers will be doing everything they can to confuse you, to trip you up, to get you to lower your guard, and to force admissions out of you that may not even be correct. Those lawyers know how your transcript will be used, and they will do everything they can to make sure that it is useful to them and harmful to you.

§10.14 "Here's how deposition transcripts are used."

First, this isn't a criminal case, but I'm sure you've heard the expression,"Everything you say can and will be used against you in a court of law." The same is true here. Once the deposition is over, everyone will get a transcript, a word for word account, of what you said today. And here's how they're used.

First, the opposing lawyer will try to have your case thrown out at some point down the road. In doing so, the lawyer will rely heavily on your deposition testimony - *your own words.* That's one reason why it's important to pay attention. Lawyers may even use small snippets of your testimony, present them to the judge, and use them as a basis for the court to throw your claims or defenses out. For opposing lawyers, that is a key function of your deposition - as a tool against you. Because you are a party in the lawsuit, your words matter more than most. If you offer damaging testimony, it is far more likely to hurt the case at its core than testimony offered by others that have an obvious bias against you.

Second, your deposition testimony can be read out loud to the jury at trial to make you look dishonest or incompetent. This is because opposing lawyers are allowed to tell the jury what you said in deposition if you are asked the same question at trial and give a different answer.

So if you give a different answer in court, the lawyer will hand you a copy of your deposition while you are on the stand, ask you to turn to the page that has the same question, read the question out loud, and then demand that you read your prior, *different* answer to the jury.

At that point, the jury may think you can't keep your story straight. This will cause the jury to lose faith in your truthfulness. If it happens enough - if there are multiple occasions where your answers at trial differ from what you said in deposition - the jury is likely to reject what you say and rule against you. The transcript, in other words, will be used to embarrass you, and to paint you as dishonest, if you're not careful and consistent.

In virtually all trials, juries hear two very different versions of events. They have no way to know who is right and who is wrong except by deciding who is believable and who is not. That is where deposition testimony comes in. The party that has more inconsistencies in what their witnesses say is the one that usually loses.

§10.15 "Let's talk about how to answer questions."

The basic rule of thumb is this.

Listen to the question.

Answer the question fully and completely.

Then stop.

A question that calls for a yes or no response is fully answered by a yes or no. A question that asks you to recount a conversation is fully answered when you have recounted the conversation. Once you have done that, stop. If the lawyer is pushing facts on you and asking you to agree, you must listen carefully and agree only if the assumptions in the question are 100% accurate. If they are not, you must say so.

§10.16 "A deposition is not a social conversation."

A chatty approach to answering deposition questions will get you into trouble. It is unlikely you will fully appreciate how certain questions are intended to trigger harmful answers.

For example, some questions might be tied to legal standards about which you know nothing. If you're not careful, you might give an exceedingly clever answer that literally sinks your own ship.

You must answer all questions truthfully, fully and completely, but once you have given a complete answer, stop talking. In a social conversation, if I ask whether you have children, you might answer not only by telling me yes, but also by telling me their names, how old they are, and what they are doing in life right now. In a deposition, if I ask you whether you have children, the full, complete and correct answer is "yes" or "no."

That's the approach to take. Your deposition is not the time to show how everyone smart you are, or to show how much you know. It is to answer questions put to you and, when the questions are done, to leave the room.

§10.17 "Listen to the preliminary instructions."

The lawyer questioning you will generally ask you if you are suffering from medical conditions, or taking any medications, that will affect your ability to tell the truth. The lawyer will tell you to speak up if you don't understand a question and that, unless you do, the lawyer will assume you understood it. This goes back to what I said before: if you are not sure what a question means, ask the lawyer to rephrase it.

If you answer a question without asking for clarification, the lawyer, judge and jury will assume you understood the question and you will be stuck with your answer.

§10.18 "Answer questions fully and completely."

You should not play word games or hold back information responsive to the questions. "Yes" or "No" is not a complete answer if the question calls for you to elaborate. If you fail to elaborate and provide all information called for by the question, you may not be able to use the additional information later. And if you are allowed to expand your answer in trial, the opposing parties will paint you as dishonest for not answering completely in your deposition. Juries do not like dishonest or game-playing witnesses.

§10.19 "If you don't know the answer, say so."

Do not guess. Guesses count as real answers even if they are wrong, even if you say you're guessing. And if they are wrong, they will be used against you at trial.

Here are some telltale phrases that you're derailing your case:

- *You start your answer with, "Well, I don't really know, but I'd say...."*
- *Or, "Not sure. Maybe a hundred."*

- *Or, you give a full answer, and then say, "But don't hold me to that."*
- *Or, "I can't swear to it, but...."*

I should never hear you say any of those things in your deposition. If I do, it means you are answering questions with guesses, not facts. This is how cases are lost. You are not required to guess.

Sometimes opposing lawyers will invite you to guess. For example, after you say you do not know something, the lawyer may respond immediately with "What's your best guess?" The only answer you should give after that is, "I just told you that I do not know."

§10.20 "If you don't remember something, say so."

If you knew the answer at one point but do not remember at the moment you are asked the question, you can simply say "Sitting here right now, I don't remember." The opposing lawyers might get frustrated, and might even think you are pretending not to remember. Of course, you should not pretend to suffer memory failure in response to any question.

But if you do not remember at the moment you are asked the question, that is a legitimate answer. I do not care whether the opposing lawyer thinks you remember the answer or not. I only care that you answer fully and correctly about those things you remember and that you refrain from answering when you do not remember.

§10.21 "But don't use 'I don't recall' as a crutch."

Remember this. You cannot use "I don't remember" as a crutch to avoid a question when you actually do recall the answer. Once you say "I don't remember" or "I don't know," you may be stuck with those answers for the rest of the case, including at trial.

These answers leave a hole in your case. That hole will be filled, in most circumstances, by an opposing witness who will clearly recall the answer, especially if the opponent knows you can't offer a different version of events. And their recollection will not be beneficial to you.

When a jury has to decide which version of an event to believe, and it must choose between (a) an opposing witness who gave a clear, specific answer, and (b) you, who said "I don't remember," who do you think gets the jury's vote?

Right. Our opponent.

Holes in our case created by lots of "I don't know's" and "I don't remember's" do tremendous damage. You are stuck with those answers. And it can get worse if, at trial, you suddenly have all the information that you claimed you didn't have in your deposition.

§10.22 "Never change answers under pressure."

Lawyers are generally only allowed to ask you a question once. Do not change your answer just because the lawyer repeats the question.

Court rules generally forbid lawyers from repeatedly

asking the exact same question. Doing so is almost always an effort by the lawyer to get you to change your answers. Sometimes, I see witnesses getting nervous when a lawyer repeats a question, and they actually change their answer. Such witnesses find themselves in deep trouble because they've now given two different answers to the same question (and both can be read to the jury to imply confusion or dishonesty).

You should never change your answers unless you made a legitimate mistake, which is unlikely. If I catch the lawyer repeating the same question over and over, I will speak up, and I will take steps to prevent you from being subjected to the same question again.

Indeed, some lawyers will openly press you to change answers. For example, if you say you do not remember something, the lawyer might retort, "Well, this is my only opportunity to question you before trial, so I need an answer. If you need to take a break, that's fine, but I need you to answer the question." But if you do not remember, "I don't remember" is a complete answer, and you have satisfied your obligation.

Never concoct an answer under pressure from a lawyer. Sometimes situations like this are caused by the failure of the opposing lawyers themselves. They could have easily anticipated that you might not remember an event or document from several years ago and could have provided you documents to refresh your memory, for example. Now in deposition, and having failed to construct an examination with documents to refresh your memory, the lawyer either goes away empty-handed on key questions or decides that pressuring you is a good alternative.

I cannot say it enough. Your obligation is to answer questions fully and completely at the moment you are asked them. You are not required to have a perfect memory. No one has one.

§10.23 "If you don't understand a question, say so. Say nothing else."

You should never answer a question when you are unsure what is being asked. You should only say you do not understand the question. Then stop talking and wait for a rephrased inquiry.

You may not know *why* a lawyer is asking a question, but you are entitled to understand what a specific question seeks. If you do not understand the question, say so. Then ask the lawyer to repeat it or reword it.

Never reword the question yourself, such as "Well, are you asking me [A] or are you asking me [B]?" If you reword the question, the lawyer will likely insist that you answer both the question you came up with and the lawyer's original question. That means you just turned one question into two - congratulations! - and your rephrasing might do you more harm than what the lawyer asked.

§10.24 "If the lawyer interrupts you, keep talking."

Lawyers may interrupt you if you begin offering an answer that is particularly damaging to their client. Why? A half answer counts as nothing to a judge and jury.

If you allow interruptions, the transcript will look something like this:

> Q: Did he tell you the company had approved your removal of the documents?
>
> A: He said, well, you can take the strategy papers and customer lists if you - -
>
> Q: That's not what I asked you. I asked if he told you the company had approved your removal of the documents?

The reporter will note that you were interrupted with two dashes. But that's it. The rest of your answer is nowhere to be found.

Lawyers who use interruption as a tactic won't admit their motives. They may actually blame you, saying you weren't answering the question asked. And after cutting off your response, the lawyer may swiftly jump to another topic as a distraction, hoping you never finish your answer.

Whether your answer fairly responded to the question isn't for the lawyer to decide. You are entitled to complete your response. If the lawyer thinks your answer doesn't meet the question, he or she can try it a different way. But interruption is not proper.

Sometimes interruptions are unintentional. Often, they are not. There is no easy way to tell. So here's the rule: Never allow an opposing lawyer to interrupt you and cut off your response. Once you begin a response, finish it.

§10.25 "Do not answer until you hear the entire question."

You must let the lawyer finish his or her question before you start to answer. Just as the lawyer must allow you to finish your answers, you must allow lawyers to finish their questions. The transcript will become a mess if each of you interrupts the other.

But just as an incomplete answer is harmful to you, responding to an incomplete question can also do you harm.

Why?

Because you're likely to wrong about what was about to be asked. Sometimes answers blurted out in haste are actually worse than what the lawyer was about to ask. You must wait to hear the entire question, reflect, and then give your best and most powerful answers.

This isn't the lightning round in a game show. In this setting, speed kills.

§10.26 "Read all documents with great caution."

As I said before, all your answers count. This includes answers about documents.

All things considered, depositions proceed at a fairly

swift pace. Years of events may be covered in the span of a few hours. Likewise with documents. You may be shown thousands of pages of documents in the course of a single day of testimony. Handbooks, manuals, contracts, long email chains - you name it.

And because your deposition is limited to one day of seven hours, the lawyer is likely to pass documents across the table to you without any intention whatsoever of letting you properly review them. They just want a yes or no as to its authenticity before they take it back.

You can't buy into that. If you are asked to review a document and agree to its authenticity - meaning it is a complete, unaltered version - you must go through it with great caution. Once you answer yes or no, you are bound by the answer. There's no "Well, I didn't read it" later.

In fact, the transcript will not show how long you took to review the document before you said it was a true copy. A judge and jury will assume you took all the time you needed, unless you said otherwise.

If I were shown a lengthy handbook or manual and asked to quickly agree it is authentic, I'm certain I would look at the lawyer, incredulously, and say that I must review every page before I can say so - and maybe not even then.

How can I verify a document's authenticity without time to reflect? Without comparing it to the copy I have? Without looking at every page? Without conferring with others, if need be? And if the document contains signatures, check-boxes, or handwritten notes or narratives, then quickly attesting to its authenticity *under oath* is simply impossible.

Should I just trust that the documents haven't been tinkered with? No. Nor should you. If you cannot properly review them and then give an accurate answer, you cannot attest toothier authenticity.

By the way, there is another, more appropriate way for lawyers to show you lengthy documents and ask for your agreement that they're genuine. The lawyer could send you copies and allow you thirty days to review them before you give a thumbs up or thumbs down on authenticity.)

You do not have to admit a document is authentic just because it is put in front of you. If you cannot say so, you must not say so.

§10.27 "People do alter documents, and it may not be obvious."

It is not unheard of for parties to alter documents. Be suspicious. *So you cannot assume anything.*

Parties sometimes do alter documents. It could be anyone from an entry-level employee to the CEO. Lawsuits are contentious; parties may see the act of fraudulently altering documents as an act of true justice, or even vengeance. Someone might also alter a document to protect themselves.

And changes can be subtle. Some examples:

- A handbook may be a newer version with an older cover slapped on it, suggesting it was in effect during the relevant period
- A guide may have individual pages substituted, so

while the overall guide is correct, key pages are the wrong ones

- Some signatures may have been added; others might have been removed
- Boxes that were checked may now be blotted out
- Boxes that were blank may now be checked
- Email chains may be missing key responses and replies
- Documents may have been created on dates other than those shown
- Digital files may have been modified

When the stakes are high, some people will do whatever it takes to win. This is why you must be absolutely certain the document is what it claims to be before you say so. "It looks right," or "It's probably right" are not acceptable answers.

§10.28 "If you're unsure about a document's authenticity, do not take a stance on it."

If you refuse to say a document is authentic, the lawyer may try the next best thing, which is to say,"Well, do you have any basis to believe the document is *not* authentic?" This is the same question, coming in the back door.

In fact, if you were not given the time and opportunity to carefully assess a document, you have no basis even to say "Nothing stands out," because that implies some level of complete, appropriate review took place. And if you do buy into that, your answer will be portrayed like the following in court papers as if you'd said the document was genuine:

> *Even Mr. Hernandez admitted in his deposition that "Nothing stands out" to suggest the contract was altered in any way whatsoever.*

So refrain from informal assessments of documents shown to you in deposition, just as you must refrain from informal guesses in questions generally.

§10.29 "Opponents might have altered your documents."

Once we turn copies of our documents over to our opponents, there is a risk that someone has altered them. Thus even if you are handed copies of your own documents in deposition, you must view them as skeptically as documents created by anyone else. They are no longer *your* documents; they are *copies* of your documents that have been in the possession of your adversary.

During most lawsuits, parties exchange documents. We produce our supporting documents to them; they produce theirs to us. But once our documents are in the hands of a foe, we cannot say without review that they remain unaltered. They may have been scanned in and altered in numerous ways.

So even if you are shown copies of your own documents, exercise the same caution as if they came from a hostile party

- because they just did. The lawyer may seem exasperated at your stance - "*These are your own documents*!" - but disregard the show.

All documents, once in the hands of an opponent, must be viewed with suspicion, regardless of their initial origin.

§10.30 "Some questions may be very personal."

You will be asked a series of background questions once the deposition begins. This is normal and you should answer them without flinching unless I specifically tell you not to.

Courts allow some degree of intrusion into the backgrounds of opposing parties. This ensures that, within reason, details that might shed light on the case come to light.

Initial questions may seek information about where you live, who you live with, the names of your children, how old they are, and the names of current or former spouses. I appreciate that these questions can seem like an invasion of privacy.

But here's one reason why lawyers ask about these things. They want to know if anyone related to you shows up on the jury pool or on a witness list. Even close family members may have different last names, and they want to make sure that your brother-in-law, for example, isn't chosen to sit on the jury without their knowledge.

Another reason lawyers ask about the people in your immediate family and social circles is to learn the identities of those you've probably talked to about your case. You should not be offended if you are asked for this information. You must generally provide it.

§10.31 "You'll be asked about prior cases."

The court files from other cases you've been involved in can provide a wealth of information to an adversary. (We make use of opponents' prior cases, too.)

This includes cases where you have sued others, where you have been sued, where you have filed for bankruptcy, or where you have filed for government benefits, such as unemployment compensation, Social Security Disability benefits, or workers' compensation benefits. All can provide relevant information. You should be prepared to reveal prior matters in which you were involved.

§10.32 "They'll ask about your criminal history."

Criminal histories can have some bearing on the issues in a case, depending. If you have ever been arrested, charged or convicted of a crime, tell me now. I'll decide if you should acknowledge the incidents or whether we should object.

And if you have successfully petitioned to have prior criminal histories expunged, let me know that, too.

If we decide you must answer questions about prior criminal charges, just answer the questions truthfully and completely. I will not let an opposing lawyer dig any deeper than the law allows (which generally stops at the nature of the charge and the outcome).

Sometimes lawyers ask questions like this simply to cause embarrassment. Once embarrassed, witnesses may become too distracted to perform well for the balance of the deposition.

It's just a tactic. I can assure you that everyone in the deposition room has dealt with people with every conceivable kind of criminal charge. No one cares.

Just answer the questions and move on.

§10.33 "They'll ask about acts of dishonesty."

You may be asked if anything on your resume or job application is inaccurate. Remember that *any* omissions, even of modest jobs, technically make them"inaccurate." So review your application or resume if a copy is provided you and note any omissions. If you are not provided a copy, insist on being provided a copy before you give a definitive answer.

You might also be asked whether you have engaged in any undiscovered misconduct pertinent to the case at hand. You might be asked about pending judgments or liens whether you've filed all your tax returns; whether you've accurately reported all your income; and whether ou owe child support or alimony.

Let's talk about these if you have concerns.

§10.34 "You'll be asked who's helping you."

Sometimes people employed by adversaries help my clients

confidentially. They provide insights, key information, and sometimes documents we didn't know about.

You will be asked about your contacts with current or former employees. If you have, the opposing lawyers may already know about them, and are simply testing your truthfulness.

Or they may have no idea and the question is a random question.

If you've had contact with people affiliated with our opponent, let me know. "Contact" includes emails, texts phone calls - anything of substance other than "Hi" in passing at the store. Your written communications might have to be produced.

And if anyone has provided you documents or sensitive internal information, we need to discuss it. In some cases the release of internal documents can lead to criminal charges, or lawsuits alleging the theft of trade secrets or company property. And it could certainly lead to the firing of the people who passed them to you.

§10.35 "They'll ask if you've removed data."

You will be asked if you took information from the opponent's computers. You will also be asked if you've logged on remotely since your authorization was terminated. Let me know if the answer is "yes" to either question.

In many situations, doing so may be illegal and could expose you to serious civil and criminal penalties. The list of acts constituting a computer crime has been vastly expanded in the last several years. It includes unauthorized access to a system; downloading or other copying of data; forwarding information stored on the system; and damage to the "integrity" of the system. The definitions of "loss" and "damage" are very broad.

If these are concerns for us, we'll need to talk about ways we can protect you. They may include asserting the Fifth Amendment or even abandoning our claims or defenses.

§10.36 "They'll ask if you've recorded calls."

You will be asked whether you surreptitiously recorded conversations, either on the phone or in person. If you did, let's talk about it. In some states, recording a conversation or call without the consent of all participants is a serious crime. In others, only one person to a conversation need consent. If you recorded conversations, let's pin down the details, including where you and each participant was physically located at the time of the recording. This could also require assessment of your potential civil and criminal liability.

§10.37 "They'll ask about texts, emails and social media."

You will be asked whether you have used text messages, emails or social media to discuss events relating to the case and, if so, with whom. Be prepared to produce them unless they're between you and me.

Further, you must not delete anything. You should know

that deleting posts or messages from your profiles generally does not eliminate them. Social media sites archive your profile data and usually have everything you ever posted, sent or received through your page. Deleting content does nothing more than show an effort by you to destroy evidence.

§10.38 "They'll ask about your medical history."

Depending on the claims and defenses, you might be asked questions about your medical condition, diagnoses, and the medications you take. That is something we should discuss in advance. In some cases, this kind of inquiry is appropriate. In others, it is not.

§10.39 "They may ask about substance abuse."

I'll provide you guidance about how to deal with this if it comes up and if your answer about prior illegal drug use will be "yes." I generally will not allow questions about drug or alcohol use or abuse, but again that is case dependent.

§10.40 "Some anxiety is a good sign."

Many clients arrive on the morning of the deposition experiencing great anxiety. Many do not sleep well the night before. Many do not eat lunch because their stomachs are in knots.

If you have some anxiety, that's a good sign, because it means you understand this is an important event. I would be more concerned if you came in this morning and told me "I've got this." *That* attitude is a sign that someone does not understand how important depositions are.

So a little nervousness and anxiety is a very good sign. We are off to a great start.

§10.41 "Take hourly breaks to clear your head."

I don't want you to get exhausted. Most deponents are slow to appreciate how exhausting prolonged examinations can be. Although it involves almost no physical activity, the stakes are high and extreme focus is required. You will get tired, whether you realize it or not.

Deponents who become exhausted do major damage to their case. Exhaustion in this setting will increase your susceptibility to influences by the examiner nd will impair your judgment and reasoning.

So you must ask for regular breaks. You need to get up, walk around, have snacks as needed and eat lunch when the time comes. Never skip breaks or meals while your deposition is in progress.

§10.42 "Never reveal our communications."

All our communications are protected by the attorney-client privilege. This means no one, including the opposing lawyer, is entitled to see our written communications or hear about our conversations.

Most lawyers will not ask questions that require you to

reveal our communications, but I mention this so you do not inadvertently include conversations with me in an answer.

If any answer you give begins with "Well, I told my lawyer..." or "Well, my lawyer said....", you are revealing confidential information. Now, you might be asked questions about when you first contacted me, and other similar questions, and those might not be protected by attorney-client privilege.

Even so, you must not respond until I have had time to object or call for a recess and discuss it with you. *Motorola Sols., Inc. v. Hytera Commc'ns Corp.*, No. 17 C 1973, 2019 WL 2774126, at *2 (N.D. Ill. July 2, 2019) (noting courts have consistently held that the facts surrounding attorney-client communications, including the fact that they occurred, their dates, topics and subject matter are discoverable and not privileged, and that privilege protects only the content of communications, not underlying facts). *See also, e.g., Westhemeco Ltd. v. New Hampshire Ins. Co.*, 82 F. R. D. 702, 707 (S. D. N. Y. 1979); *Upjohn Co. v. United States*, 449 U.S. 383, 395-96 (1981); *Motorola Solutions, Inc. v. Hytera Communications Corp.*, 367 F. Supp. 3d 813, 816 (N.D. Ill. 2019).

§10.43 "Be truthful about everything."

You must never say anything in your deposition that is untrue or misleading in any way. Even minor inaccuracies will be used to paint you as dishonest. And if it appears that you gave an answer you knew was untruthful, it could destroy your case and expose you to perjury charges.

The most important thing you can do is be honest.

You may see TV shows where lawyers encourage clients to omit facts or give false answers. That is never acceptable. And if I have ever said anything to you that you took to mean otherwise, let me assure you it is not.

In fact, I am obligated to withdraw from representation if you give false testimony. So please don't put us in that position. It is better to lose the case standing up that to win it on a bed of lies.

11

CREATING INVINCIBLE DEPONENTS - PART 2

PREPARING AGAINST TRAP QUESTIONS

Covered in This Chapter:

- *§11.01 Practicing for Unfair Tactics*
- *§11.02 "But you don't actually know that, do you?"*
- *§11.03 "So what facts do you claim to know?"*
- *§11.04 "Tell me every fact supporting your [claim] [defense]?"*
- *§11.05 "What if I told you Ms. Owens says she never told you that? Is she lying?"*
- *§11.06 [Impatiently] "What is your answer? It's a simple question."*
- *§11.07 "I don't care what you think. And I don't believe anything you're saying."*
- *§11.08 "I'm just here to find out what happened."*
- *§11.09 Questions Asserting Unprovable Facts*
- *§11.10 Influencing Testimony Through False Facts*

- *§11.11 "We've only got another hour or so. I'm about to wrap up."*
- *§11.12 "This is like a regular conversation."*
- *§11.13 "Remember, you're under oath."*
- *§11.14 "Okay. So what you're saying is...."*
- *§11.15 "I'm going to ask you again. Did you..."*
- *§11.16 "Have you ever used drugs or alcohol?"*
- *§11.17 "Did you record anything?"*
- *§11.18 "How much did your other cases settle for?"*
- *§11.19 "Have you ever filed for bankruptcy?"*
- *§11.20 "Have you ever sought Social Security benefits?"*
- *§11.21 "Did you take documents or material from the workplace?"*
- *§11.22 "Have you logged into computers or devices since your separation?"*
- *§11.23 "What did you tell your [lawyer] [accountant] [spouse] [doctor] [pastor]?"*
- *§11.24 "Do you have his number on your phone? Do you have those documents in your car?"*
- *§11.25 "Well, what would you have done if...?"*
- *§11.26 "You have other documents? Would you give them to your lawyer, so she can give them to me?"*
- *§11.27 "If you don't know, it's okay to say so."*
- *§11.28 "I'm going to stand beside you and go through these documents with you."*
- *§11.29 "Have you now told me everything that is important about your claims?"*

- ***§11.30 "Have you and your partner ever separated? Have you ever been unfaithful in the relationship?"***

At this point we've now covered some basics to help your client become a strong witness.

In this next segment of my deposition preparations, I work through common but unfair or harassing tactics lawyers use to undermine your clients' testimony and even their confidence.

§11.01 Practicing for Unfair Tactics

It is important your clients be able to spot questions and commentary intended to adversely affect their answers and performance. These include questions that rush or pressure deponents; that are premised on false or non-existent facts; that suggest the client's answers don't amount to anything; that exhaust the client; or that require the client to apply legal principles.

So let's walk through some of the most common tricks, and talk about how to combat them. In this section, each is presented in quotes and italicized to set the tactic up as a remark made to your client during the deposition.

§11.02 "But that's just your speculation or belief. You don't know that, do you?"

This is a common problem in all lawsuits. Lawyers seek to undermine testimony by demanding that deponents admit they don't "know" something to be true. Deponents can easily become confused about the meaning of "knowing" something, and may back away from even the most obvious facts they know to be true. And that's dangerous because a deponent who is no longer sure they "know" something may abandon many of their firmly-held beliefs.

I spend some time with clients to discuss this. By the time I am done, we have eliminated this as a problem.

Opposing lawyers key in on this issue by taking the position that knowledge gained from indirect or circumstantial evidence is a nullity – that it does not count and is not "knowledge" and "knowing." Lawyers who take this approach will attempt to force your clients to admit they do not "know," and cannot claim to know, certain facts unless (a) they personally heard it, (b) they personally witnessed it, (c) the opposing party has admitted it, or (d) it was captured on audio or video.

The lawyer will press your client to admit that their perspective is something well below knowing – that it is a mere suspicion, a belief, a feeling, a thought, a speculation. If your clients buy into that, the next stop is summary judgment.

The fact is that most of what we "know" and what we deem our "knowledge" is pieced together using information from a variety of sources. That is how life works.

Most of our knowledge does not come from a direct source, from an event we personally witnessed, from a confession. We operate almost entirely on knowledge we gain indirectly or circumstantially.

But some lawyers treat the deposition room as an alternate universe, where a person knows nothing that wasn't personally heard or observed. If your clients buy into this fallacy, you are in trouble, because from there it is a slippery slope to testimony from your clients that their views are pure speculation.

So you must prepare your clients to stand their ground, whether their knowledge and knowing come from circumstantial or direct evidence. In fact, this is how our judicial system works. Evidence can be direct or indirect.

Both count equally.

Federal pattern jury instructions inform jurors that as far as the law is concerned, it makes no difference whether evidence is direct or indirect. The jury can make its decision based on either. Put another way, jurors can and will "know" something to be true regardless of how the evidence was presented. And it will make a decisive finding – guilty or not, liable or not - based on that evidence.

This is so even though the jury has not personally witnessed or personally "known" anything. The very lawyers that tell your clients they do not "know" a particular fact to be true would probably say the same thing to a jury if they could. ("You don't know! You weren't there!") But they cannot, because that is not how the system works. And, to our point here, they cannot do that in a deposition because the same principles apply to evidence in a deposition as they do at trial.

So how best to prepare your clients against lawyers who assert that because your client's knowledge or position is based on indirect evidence, your client cannot testify that what they know is anything more than a wild guess?

I usually start by outlining this problem in broad terms for clients. I explain that the opposing lawyer is likely to challenge their knowledge about certain events if the knowledge comes circumstantially. But, I say, in court proceedings, as in real life, people legitimately "know" something even if the underlying basis for their knowledge is indirect or circumstantial. In other words, circumstance-derived knowledge counts the same as first-hand-derived knowledge: video proof, confessions, and direct observation.

I often quote the following passage to clients. It's drawn from the Eleventh Circuit Court of Appeals pattern instruction and perfectly illustrates the point:

> Some evidence may prove a fact indirectly. Let's say a witness saw wet grass outside and people walking into the courthouse carrying wet umbrellas. This may be indirect evidence that it rained, even though the witness didn't personally see it rain. Indirect evidence like this is also called "circumstantial evidence" – simply a chain of circumstances that likely proves a fact. As far as the law is concerned, it makes no difference whether evidence is direct or indirect. You may choose to believe or disbelieve either kind. Your job is to give each piece of evidence whatever weight you think it deserves.

So I help clients understand they can firmly testify they "know" something to be absolutely true by explaining the jury process and how juries also "know" facts with similar, absolute certainty. The umbrella example above is a good start.

I will sometimes also discuss the different burden-of-proof standards juries use.

The one all juries know is "beyond a reasonable doubt." I tell them to consider that the the 99%-certain standard.

I then talk about the "clear and convincing evidence" standard, which I loosely describe as the 66 2/3%-certain standard.

Finally, I describe the common civil standard of "preponderance" or "greater weight of the evidence," which I loosely describe as the 51%-certain standard.[1] I tell my clients that under this standard, a jury can doubt *almost half my evidence* – up to 49.999999% - and still reach a concrete, unqualified determination that they know which side is right.

I may also show them a sample verdict form to end all doubt in their ability to speak in absolutist terms about what they "know." Verdict forms are black and white; they contain no shades of gray. No jury checks a box that says "WE THE JURY *feel* the defendant is guilty." No juror has personal knowledge of anything they decided, I say, but they know who wins, who loses, who goes to prison and who goes home.

The point I impress upon clients is that the judicial system allows for doubt and uncertainty, allows for knowledge based on circumstance, and does not demand scientific proof or confessions of anything in order for judges and juries to know what is true and what isn't. Certainly, scientific proof is sometimes used, and is sometimes helpful. It is not required.

And clients should use the same approach.

Thus, I explain, the notion pushed by opposing lawyers that clients need some kind of scientific proof before they "know" something is misguided, and clients should reject it. They can say they know something to be true whether their knowledge is direct or indirect.

Taking this a step further, I talk to clients about what I call "wobble words." Wobble words convey a lack of confidence about what someone knows is true. Examples include *believe, think, suspect, feel,* and *speculate.* I explain that when judges are reviewing deposition testimony, they look for wobble words. Their presence tells the judge that the deponents weren't sure about their testimony.

I conclude by saying that if the client knows something to be true, based on direct or indirect evidence that likely proves the fact, it is perfectly acceptable to say they know that fact to be true, as in, "Yes, I *do* know that," or "That *is* what happened," or "They *did* discriminate," or "They *were* negligent," or "They *did* misappropriate our customer lists," rather than the wobble-word versions "I *think* that's what happened," "I *feel* like that's what happened," or "I *suspect* that's what happened."

Game, set, match for folks who answer that way.

Indeed, testimony infected by wobble words kinds accounts for the high summary judgment rate in civil cases. Many excellent cases are lost based on deposition examinations that were crafted to walk witnesses back from what they know. You and I have both seen dispositive motions that seize on this kind of testimony to argue that the party has no evidence whatsoever to support their position (*e.g.*, "Ms. Holloman admitted in her deposition that she does not know whether this is true or not. At best, she thinks/feel/speculates that it might be.")

So we work through that until clients are comfortable with the phraseology. But I caution them that even if they do not use wobble words, opposing lawyers may forcibly inject them into the examination:

- Q: I understand that's what you *feel,* but you don't have any *proof*, do you?
- Q: But that's your *speculation*, correct?
- Q: That's what you *believe*, but you don't *know* that to be true, do you?
- Q: Well, you just told me you didn't hear that first-hand, so you actually *don't know it to be true,* do you?

There are a dozen variations of this line of questioning. They're all premised on the hoax that indirect evidence is worthless - that only direct evidence counts.

I know of no field of law in our legal system that rejects indirect evidence as a basis for knowing something. In my judgment, this type of examination is gravely misleading because it implies, if not outright asserts, that only direct evidence can support knowledge and knowing.

Clients go into depositions fully aware that this line of

attack is intended to undermine and weaken their testimony. When lawyers inject wobble words into the dialogue, clients push back: "It's not what I *feel. That's what happened*," or, "It's not what I *think. That's why they did it*."

By the way, many courts have said that words like "proof" and "evidence" require legal analysis and are for judges and lawyers, not for witnesses. I object when a lawyer asks a client what "proof" or "evidence" the client has to support their claims or knowledge. (These are sometimes referred to as 'legal contentions.') Lay witnesses do not know what constitutes "proof" or "evidence." The better question is to ask a witness what *information* they have upon which they base their knowledge. Then the lawyers and judge can hash out whether the information is proof or evidence.

§11.03 "So what 'facts' do you claim to "know"?

Once the issue of "knowledge" is resolved, it helps to next teach clients how to explain the *basis* for their knowledge - the underlying facts that, when strung together like beads on a necklace, constitute their knowledge.

This is straightforward. The client should testify about what they saw, heard, and read, that led them to their knowledge and knowing.

I describe this as "eyes and ears evidence." That is circumstantial evidence: information seen and heard that tends to prove a fact. If I am upstairs at home, hear the cookie jar crash, and race downstairs to see my son standing in the middle of the broken ceramic pieces - with chocolate around his mouth and, further, knowing no one else is home - I "know" with absolute certainty he is guilty. I witnessed nothing. He confessed nothing. But I know it to be true.

Our hypothetical opposing lawyer would make the claim that while I *feel, believe, suspect* and *speculate* it was him, I don't actually *know* it. Maybe the jar was already on the edge of the counter and a pet or vibration of some kind caused it to slip off.

Right.

Yet this is precisely how some lawyers approach obvious truths. They seek to subvert your case by zeroing in on knowledge gained circumstantially, sometimes while offering up other explanations that sound plausible but have no basis.

I suggest to clients that they construct their "knowledge inventory" by writing down each and every fact - document, conversation, event, policy - that led them to absolute certainty.

For example, if a 65-year old female client in an employment discrimination case believes she was passed over for promotion because of age, she should build a list like the one below to prove she knows age was a determinative factor. I encourage clients to work hard to break their knowledge down to its smallest component parts, because obvious but ultra-basic elements - such as her own age - might be seen as understood and omitted from the list.

It might look like this:

1. Her own age - 65

2. The winning candidate's age – 31
3. The ages of the hiring panel – 22, 34 and 31
4. The ages of others who were granted interviews: 22, 24, 28, 31 and 33
5. Language in the job announcement: "Looking for fresh blood"
6. Stereotyping questions during the interview: "Are you sure you can use a computer?"
7. Stereotyping comments during the interview: "I see you've got typing experience, but our concern is that things have changed since you were in high school."
8. The ages of other employees already in the same position: 23, 24, 24, 26, 27 and 35.
9. Photos of promotional brochures about the unit, depicting nothing but very young people
10. The industry segment of the employer (e.g., clothing for millennials)
11. The complete lack of other employees in any position above the age of 40
12. Her credentials versus the winning candidate: 20 years' experience versus 2

This type of list could go on and on. But all of it is based on things she saw, read or heard. No one said, "We are going to hire someone young and we will not hire you because you are old." But she can say with absolute certainty, "I *know* I was passed over because of age discrimination," and that she *knows*, without doubt, her age was the decisive factor.

It is a useful technique where the knowledge is circumstantial to force your clients to make a physical list of the underlying facts supporting their "knowing." This exercise helps them become fluid in articulating the individual components of their case. It must be done before you conduct your first mock cross-examination so your client can practice verbalizing their facts.

The actual deposition should never be the first time your client verbally recites their listed items. It won't work. If they don't practice ahead of time, they will fail to detail even a fraction of the facts contributing to their knowledge.

You might have to help them do this. You should not spoon-feed them winning examples from other cases and urge your client to simply adopt them. Start with a conversation and illustrate how intuitive knowledge can be cataloged or broken down. Without your guidance, the client may not even appreciate the incredible number of facts they already know that support their claim.

So have them make a list. Try a few light, informal practice runs where you quiz them about the facts supporting their claims or defenses.

If they struggle to come up with more than a few, try my approach. I tell clients to imagine a necklace that has no beads on it. The bare strand represents their basic claim or defense, with no facts added. Each bead is one supporting fact. I tell them they must sell their necklace to a judge and jury, but that a necklace with just two or three beads is unsaleable - no judge or jury will buy it. They must fill the strand. A full necklace contains 25, 50, whatever number of beads - individual, concrete, logical, specific facts - and every empty spot makes the necklace less likely to sell.

Interestingly, the number of fact beads I say constitutes a full necklace will heavily influence the number they end up with. For reasons that are unclear to me, if you ask someone to come up with five reasons a customer should buy a product, they struggle to come up with two or three. If you ask the same person for fifteen reasons, they 'll now easily come up with ten, but struggle to think of five more. If you ask them for fifty reasons, they hit twenty-five quickly and then start struggling.

I don't know why this is. But I have seen it my entire life. So if you want your client to come up with as many facts as possible to offer in deposition, pick a number substantially higher than you need and tell your client to hit that target. Give them a few examples to get started, and then let them do their thing.

You should also explain the basic elements of the claim. I recommend reading the pertinent pattern jury instructions to your clients, so they hear exactly what the jury will be told. Some lawyers think of jury instructions as something for juries - correct - but they're also a phenomenal tool for clients. I begin talking about the core substantive instructions in my first meetings with clients.

Instructions are perfect because they're written for laypeople. A great deal of effort goes into making them both precise and very easy to understand. Once clients know what the jury is looking for, they can make sure they provide it.

§11.04 "Tell me every fact supporting your [claim] [defense]"

This kind of question – typically referred to a legal contention - is often asked in depositions, but improperly so. *Rifkind v. Superior Court*, 22 Cal. App. 4th 1255, 1259, 27 Cal. Rptr. 2d 822, 824 (1994) ("What authority there is almost uniformly condemns the practice"); *Charal Patterson v. Department of Corrections,* Order Denying Motion for Reconsideration, CM/ECF Doc. 111, Case No. 1:12-cv-00029-MW-GRJ (N.D. Fla. Apr. 1, 2014) ("Plaintiff is not bound by answers to legal contention questions put to her during her deposition. In the first place, it is unfair to ask such questions to a layperson"); *see also Bret Schyvincht v. Menard, Inc., d/b/a Menards,* No. 18-CV-50286, 2019 WL 3002961 (N.D. Ill. July 10, 2019) (same); *Miller v. Peter Thomas Roth LLC*, No. C 19-00698 WHA, 2019 WL 3817857, at *2 (N.D. Cal. Aug. 14, 2019) (Order noting that noted it is normally improper to ask for FRCP 30(b)(6) deponents to testify concerning the entire basis of a claim or defense).

Legal contention questions call on the deponent, almost always a lay witness, to figure out which facts go with which legal claim or defense. Courts have said that *contention interrogatories* are appropriate because lawyers help clients craft those answers. But *contention deposition questions* are inappropriate because the obligation to conduct the legal analysis falls solely on the lay deponent.

From the *Rifkind* case, above:

As one commentator put it, legal contention questions require the party interrogated to make a "law-to-fact application that is beyond the competence of most lay persons." (1 Hogan, Modern California Discovery (4th ed. 1988) § 5.9, p. 252.) Even if such questions may be characterized as not calling for a legal opinion (see *Singer v. Superior Court, supra,* 54 Cal. 2d at p. 326, 5 Cal. Rptr. 697, 353 P. 2d 305), or as presenting a mixed question of law and fact (see 4A Moore's Federal Practice (2d ed.) § 33.17[2], p. 33–85), their basic vice when used at a deposition is that they are unfair. They call upon the deponent to sort out the factual material in the case according to specific legal contentions, and to do this by memory and on the spot. There is no legitimate reason to put the deponent to that exercise. If the deposing party wants to know facts, it can ask for facts; if it wants to know what the adverse party is contending, or how it rationalizes the facts as supporting a contention, it may ask that question in an interrogatory. The party answering the interrogatory may then, with aid of counsel, apply the legal reasoning involved in marshaling the facts relied upon for each of its contentions.

That, we believe, is a principal basis of the Supreme Court's dicta in *Pember II,* and of the federal authorities. It is a major reason why, as Professor Hogan puts it, "[t]aking the oral deposition of the adverse party is neither a satisfactory nor a proper way to satisfy" the interrogating party's desire to learn which facts a party thinks support its specific contentions.

§11.05 "What if I told you Ms. Owens says she never told you that? Is she lying?"

I caution clients to watch out for questions that include commentary about what other witnesses have purportedly said.

It is not proper to ask deponents what they think about the testimony of other witnesses. *See Smith v. Crews*, No. 3:12CV326/LC/CJK, 2014 WL 1900695, at *14 (N.D. Fla. May 13, 2014), *aff'd sub nom. Smith v. Sec'y, Fla. Dep't of Corr.*, 626 F. App'x 246 (11th Cir. 2015).

In fact, this kind of testy exchange is so common in depositions that I am including a quote from the state appellate decision upon which the federal judge in the *Smith/Crews* case, above relied. This is from *Boatwright v. State*, 452 So. 2d 666, 668 (Fla. Dist. Ct. App. 1984):

> A second prosecutorial tactic also demands comment. During cross-examination of a key defense witness, the prosecutor skillfully established the differences between the witness's testimony and that of earlier state witnesses. Up to this point, the cross-examination was perfectly legitimate. Then, over defense objection, the prosecutor asked the witness whether each of the earlier witnesses had been lying. This effort to isolate and thereby discredit the witness is improper for a number of reasons. It is elemental in our system of jurisprudence that the jury is the sole arbiter of the credibility of witnesses. *Barnes v. State,* 93 So.2d 863 (Fla.1957). Thus, it is an invasion of the

> jury's exclusive province for one witness to offer his personal view on the credibility of a fellow witness. *Bowles v. State,* 381 So.2d 326 (Fla. 5th DCA 1980). Moreover, the fact that two witnesses disagree does not necessarily establish that one is lying. Lying is the making of a false statement with intent to deceive. Absent some evidence showing that the witness is privy to the thought processes of the other, the first witness is not competent to pass on the other's state of mind. Therefore, we hold that this part of the prosecutor's cross-examination was improper; the trial court erred in failing to sustain the defendant's objection.

The best approach a client can take is to decline invitations to comment on other witness' testimony. There is no basis for it. A client would not have an answer. It is not admissible. It might be reversible error to even attempt the admission of such a question an answer.

§11.06 [Impatiently] "What is your answer? It's a simple question."

Some lawyers seemingly attempt to conduct depositions of opposing witnesses at high speed. They ask questions at break-neck speed, and demand equally-swift answers. That usually isn't to save time. It is to create mental chaos for the witness.

I urge clients to pace their answers according to their need to evaluate questions before responding. Even seemingly simple questions may have nuances. Deponents get one chance to answer each question. They must get it right.

There is no bright-line rule about how long deponents should take, after a question is asked, before answering. Anecdotally, most seem to take between two and five seconds. You might practice a sample examination with your clients, using a stopwatch or app that displays seconds, to help them develop a pace that works for them.

This is not to teach them to slow festivities to a crawl. It is to teach them the value of paying close attention.

Some reflection is appropriate. Inaccurate sworn testimony has consequences. Clients must be told that answering questions quickly might seem impressive, but that is not the goal, and it is not desirable.

Fast answers are often wrong answers. Speed kills. Let them know it is okay to pause before responding. Tell them the opposing lawyer has no place telling them to answer questions more quickly. The opposing lawyer is entitled to ask questions and is entitled to straightforward complete answers. They are entitled to nothing else.

§11.07 "I don't care what you think. And I don't believe anything you're saying."

Commentary by an opposing lawyer on your client's testimony is clearly improper. And you should never tolerate an adversary who is aggressively disrespectful to your client.

Remember the core principle of Rule 30(c): "The examination and cross-examination of the deponent proceed as they would at trial..." While judges will allow an aggressive examination of a witness on the stand, they will not tolerate disrespect, taunts or insults toward the witness. There is a difference. Can you imagine a state or federal judge's reaction if a lawyer examining a witness during trial said that?

You will likely know the opposing lawyer, and his or her style of examination. In my specialized field, I generally run into the same twenty or thirty lawyers. I know who will conduct a respectful examination, who will be aggressive, and who will be disrespectful and demeaning. Where appropriate, I will talk to my client about the opposing lawyer's reputation and style, and the best way to deal with it.

I urge clients to remain professional and respectful but to speak up if they feel the opposing lawyer is treating them in a demeaning way. For my part, I will not tolerate more than a question or two that I feel is truly unprofessional before I have a dialogue with the lawyer. Whether I terminate the deposition or continue is situation-dependent, but I will not allow a deposition to proceed with a lawyer that continues to be abusive or disrespectful. Abuse affects outcomes.

Our clients can quickly become exhausted from exposure to degrading examination tactics, and it is our job to shield them and to seek court relief if it continues. While I am very slow to terminate depositions, I will do so if I feel an abusive environment is affecting the quality of the testimony. But I always engage the opposing lawyer in dialogue about their conduct before doing so.

§11.08 "I'm just here to find out what happened."

I've covered this elsewhere in the book. It is important during prep sessions to outline the roles of each deposition participant. Make sure your clients know lawyers are not neutral. They are the front-line warriors for their side, and they are there to do harm . I routinely explain the role of lawyers, judges, and juries to my clients. That way, they do not lower their guard when an opposing lawyer comes in, shakes their hand, smiles, and acts like their best friend. Even so, I have clients from time to time who buy into an opposing lawyer's charitable façade, at least until that charming lawyer starts to show his or her fangs So be sure your clients know why the opposing lawyers sit on the other side of the table. They are figuratively and literally opposite your client in every way.

§11.09 Questions Asserting Unprovable Facts

This section deals with cross-examinations about facts opposing lawyers cannot independently prove. They have a hunch that something is true (or need it to be true) but cannot establish it as a fact unless your client admits it.

Getting that admission usually depends on the lawyer's use of (a) a fast-paced examination and (b) a forceful tone of voice. Both are intended to short-circuit your client's thought process and result in swift agreement.

Some examples:

- To a deponent who did not receive a manual, "*You received a copy of this manual, correct?*"
- To a deponent never trained on reporting harassment, "*The supervisors trained you during orientation about how to report harassment, right?*"
- To a deponent never trained on heavy equipment, "*You were taught how to operate the front-end loader on soft soil, right?*"
- To an employee who never received the handbook, "*You know the handbook forbids that kind of conduct, true?*"
- To an employee never told about the ethics hotline, '*You were trained to call the ethics hotline if you believed there was a problem, right?*"

Often the questions involve ordinary matters that sure sound like they'd be true. But maybe they aren't *here*.

I mean, who isn't told about company hotlines? (Many employees.) Who doesn't get a handbook? (Quite a few.) Who isn't properly trained on everything the checklist says will be covered. (Same.) With the passage of time, though, we forget the mundane. Lawyers know that and will try to patch holes in your client's memory through the power of suggestion. Without your preparation, client recollections may very well be what should have happened, not what did happen.

So it's important to educate clients about this tactic.

Stress that lawyers don't always know if assumptions in their questions are true. The rules allow them to make assumptions and demand your client admit them, though, because (the reasoning goes) a deponent will not admit something that did not happen. Lawyers only need a good-faith foundation for making assumptions, and that foundation can be very thin. For example, a random manager might have said offhandedly, "Pretty much everyone gets the handbooks and training." That could provide the basis even if, upon further inquiry, the lawyer would have learned that the manager knew of lots of examples where employees did not receive either.

It is always up to your client to determine if assumptions in questions are true, and to answer accordingly. This is a point worth repeating during prep sessions.

Their skepticism should be dialed all the way up. They must use their own judgment in responding to questions based on assumed facts. If your clients are not cautious, there is genuine risk they will admit to plausible-sounding, but entirely fictitious, events.

This is another situation where a mock cross-examination session is invaluable. Test your client's fortitude by rapidly and forcefully making declarative statements like those above, and ending with words like " ....correct?" and "......isn't that true, ma'am?" See how often your client admits to things you know are untrue or never happened merely from the sheer force of your insistence and the seemingly-plausible nature of the assertion.

Tell clients the same thing judges tell juries: what lawyers say is not evidence. Your clients must learn to testify from their own knowledge and memory, and not from the facts your adversary is attempting to force-feed them.

§11.10 Influencing Testimony Through False Facts

Can a lawyer falsely represent (or imply) facts to your client - such as "There are tapes of that conversation, just so you know" - as a tactic to encourage the witness to be truthful? The short answer is that knowingly making false representations of material fact to a witness during a deposition might trigger serious disciplinary charges against the attorney.

On rare occasions, you may encounter lawyers who make a show of placing a carefully marked folder or binder in front of your client before beginning a line of examination. The item suggests the lawyer has evidence regarding the questions that come next. You have no reason to believe such items exist, but there they are – or seem to be - and your client takes note.

I know of only a few occasions when lawyers have gone as far as creating folders or other items to falsely imply to the deponent that certain evidence exists and that the deponent had better not lie.

In *Cincinnati Bar Assn. v. Statzer*, 800 N.E. 2d 1117 (Oh. Sup Ct 2003), a lawyer allegedly placed a bogus, and bogusly-labeled, stack of cassette tapes on the table in front of the deponent. The purpose was to suggest the witness shouldn't lie because there were actual recordings of conversations to prove otherwise. But there weren't.

The Ohio Supreme Court, in reviewing the bar's recommended discipline, looked at it as an integrity-of-proceedings issue. The lawyer argued there was a legitimate reason for the bluff. Here's a blurb and the court's response:

Here the Respondent, however, urges us to distinguish trial conduct from "discovery depositions," arguing that the latter require greater freedom of inquiry into matters that may be relevant but inadmissible. See Civ. R. 26(B)(1) (inadmissible evidence reasonably calculated to lead to the discovery of admissible evidence is also discoverable). This was particularly the case, respondent insists, in the deposition of the legal assistant. She argues that wide latitude was imperative during that proceeding to draw honest testimony from a theretofore untrustworthy witness and that use of the audio cassette tapes was merely a tactic intended to achieve this legitimate end. We recognize that the discovery process, particularly the pursuit of information through deposition, cannot be overly restricted if it is to remain effective. We must draw the line, however, when an attorney engages in subterfuge that intimidates a witness. While respondent's primary purpose during the legal assistant's deposition may have been to elicit the truth, her tactic also tricked the legal assistant into thinking that the revelation of embarrassing confidences was at stake.

"Throughout these proceedings, respondent has asserted that her "bluff" worked. Regardless, the success of her tactic is not at issue, and respondent can not, with any degree of certainty, assert that her witness would not have testified truthfully in the absence of her subterfuge. Further, while such deception may induce truthful testimony, it is just as likely to elicit lies if a witness believes that lies will offer security from the false threat.

> Respondent's deceitful tactic intimidated her witness by creating the false impression that respondent possessed compromising personal information that she could offer as evidence. For these reasons, we agree that respondent violated DR 1–102(A)(4) and 7–106(C)(1).

The lesson to be learned is that misrepresentations, verbal or demonstrative, are improper. It might be fine in a law enforcement interrogation, where bluffing can be taken to the extreme, but not in court proceedings. If you suspect the opposing counsel is using phony props during the deposition, raise the concern on the record, demand the lawyer preserve the items, consider photographing them as a precaution, and then seek court relief, either on the spot or immediately after the deposition ends.

§11.11 "We've only got another hour or so. I'm about to wrap up."

I once heard former Navy SEAL commander Jocko Willink say that one way instructors test the mental toughness of recruits is by falsely telling them they're going on a three-mile jog. At the three-mile mark, the recruits are told there was a mistake; it is actually a four-mile run. Many loud groans are heard. As recruits cross what they now think is the real finish line, they're immediately told another mistake has been made. This time, though, they're told to keep running. No promises of the end.

In fact, the real stopping point is just another half-mile -

far enough past the last false finish line to test the recruits' mental resolve. Some drop out at the false finish lines. They burned all their mental energy zeroing into phantom goal lines. As the expected end came and went, they couldn't reorient and muster more energy. They were done.

This kind of thing happens daily in many workplaces. For example, office workers may be told on a Friday at 9:00 AM that they can leave for the day as soon as they process a stack of forms. Everyone races through. The mood is super positive. At 11:00 AM, the stack is done and the cheering begins. Then, someone discovers more stacks on a back shelf. *Instantly,* the air is sucked out of the room. Defeatism rules. The mood is terrible and remains so even if the workers still leave by early afternoon. They were so fixated on a single endpoint that they couldn't adjust.

So tell your clients to plan on a very long day. Set the duration higher than the deposition could ever go. Caution them about false wrapping-up points. You might even tell them that lawyers often declare "I'm just about done" *four or five times* before it actually ends. With that knowledge, you're insulating your clients against those false goal lines.

§11.12 "This is like a regular conversation."

Depositions aren't anything like a regular conversation.

Sometimes lawyers tell deponents during preliminary instructions to think of the experience as a conversation. I'm sure many say this in good faith to help the deponent relax.

But it's important to let clients know that it is nothing like a regular conversation. Regular conversations are not under oath. Regular conversations do not involve high stakes. No one hires a lawyer to have a regular conversation. So I tell clients that while depositions have some elements of a conversation, they should not view it so informally. They should see it as a critical event.

§11.13 "Remember, you're under oath."

Some lawyers will repeatedly remind your clients they're under oath. I consider this a form of witness intimidation. It strongly implies the witness has lied, is lying, or is expected to lie, and that there are severe consequences for an incorrect answer. If it occurs more than twice, ask the examiner to refrain from further reminders. Your clients should not be laboring under a fear of being charged with perjury.

§11.14 "Okay. So what you're saying is...."

It is wise to caution clients about lawyers who summarize or rephrase their answers. The recasting is likely to be a less favorable variant of what your client just said.

Examples:

A: I was talking to my daughter about her outfit and had just dropped my bag when I turned around, looked up and saw your client run the red light.

Q: So what you're really saying is that you had an awful lot going on and you just happened to catch a glimpse of the intersection.

A: After I rejected my boss' advances, he would constantly complain about my timesheets, ignore me in meetings, and reject my suggestions.

Q: So what you're saying is that you disagree with his management style.

Summarized testimony becomes your client's testimony unless your client insists their answer remains the only answer. In the first example, the reworked summary suggests the witness' account is unreliable. In the second, it converts what might be a sexual harassment retaliation case into a non-actionable, ordinary disagreement between subordinate and supervisor.

Your clients may not realize what the lawyer is doing. One reason is that this is common in social conversations. Our family and friends often rephrase what we say, and we think nothing of it. Thus rephrasings in depositions are not likely to trigger alarm bells because it is an ordinary conversational experience.

Precisely because this tactic may seem innocent, you should educate clients about it. It may seem like the lawyer is trying to help. Stress that if the opposing lawyer restates what they say, they must firmly repeat their answer exactly as they gave it, or simply say that their answer is their answer, not what the lawyer just said.

§11.15 "I'm going to ask you again. Did you..."

Often an opposing lawyer will repeat questions previously asked and answered. It may be that the lawyer believes your client did not fully answer the question. Or it may be that the lawyer did not like the first answer and is angling for something more favorable. The solution is to listen carefully to the examination and to use your judgment in determining whether repetitious questions are improper.

There is no specific rule that forbids asking the same question more than once. The reason is that there are simply too many circumstances where asking a question more than once might be necessary to get a full and complete response. Here's what one court said about that:

> In passing, the court must note that it would not be appropriate for counsel examining a deponent to repeatedly and deliberately duplicate questions previously asked by other counsel. Such a practice, although not shown to have occurred in this instance, could support a motion to terminate a deposition under Rule 30(d), if employed to such an extent that bad faith or a motive to harass the deponent could properly be inferred.
>
> At the same time, however, an oral deposition is not merely a device to uncover and develop information. It also provides a legitimate and efficient means of testing a witness' knowledge, recollection and veracity. To these ends, counsel should be free to follow-up and explore the same subject matter covered during a previous

examination, especially where the deponent's earlier responses were evasive, equivocal, or inconsistent with other testimony or evidence.

Smith v. Logansport Cmty. Sch. Corp., 139 F.R.D. 637, 646 (N.D. Ind. 1991)

Note that instructing a deponent not to answer a question because it has already been asked is typically improper. Rule 30(d) informs that you may instruct a deponent not to answer only when necessary to preserve a privilege, to enforce a limitation ordered by the court, or to present a motion under Rule 30(d)(3). That rule authorizes you to terminate or limit the deposition on the ground that it is being conducted in bad faith or in a manner that unreasonably annoys, embarrasses, or oppresses the deponent or party.

Occasional repetitious questions, therefore, provide no basis for a Rule 30(d) instruction. *Gall v. St. Elizabeth Med. Ctr.*, 130 F.R.D. 85, 87 (S.D. Ohio 1990) ("The fact that a question is repetitive is not an appropriate ground for instructing a witness not to answer a question, since it does not involve a matter of privilege"); *Smith v. Logansport Cmty. Sch. Corp.*, 139 F.R.D. 637, 647 (N.D. Ind. 1991) ("The action of plaintiffs' counsel in directing Langley and Smith not to answer certain questions on the ground that they were repetitive was clearly inappropriate.")

On the other hand, if the repetition reaches the point where you believe the examination is abusive or harassing, you have the authority to orally move for a protective order on the record, suspend the deposition, and then immediately seek court relief under Rule 30(d)(3).

§11.16 "Have you ever used drugs or alcohol?"

There are situations where this is a legitimate question. But they are few and far between.

Depending on your case, the topic of past drug, alcohol or other substance use might be something you've already discussed with your client. If necessary, tell your clients that if the question is asked, they should pause to allow you to assert the proper objections. That could be to instruct them not to answer because the question serves no purpose but to annoy, embarrass or oppress them. Remember that if you do this, you must immediately file a motion for a protective order and seek a court ruling.

§11.17 "Did you record anything?"

I presume that in doing your own due diligence, you asked whether your client has video or audio recordings of conversations or other events. It's important because some states criminalize nonconsensual recordings depending on the circumstances.

For example, some states make it a felony to record conversations or calls unless at least one participant consents. So if I am in a conversation with others, and I am taping the call, I satisfy the one-party consent requirement because I am obviously one party to the call. Some states require the consent of all participants. There may be further twists. For example, when participants on a phone call are in multiple states, which state's law determines the legality of the recording?

These laws typically require proof the participants had a reasonable expectation of privacy in the conversation. This means recording conversations in a crowded restaurant isn't likely to result in charges, whereas doing the same thing in a private passenger car might.

And there may be other exceptions. Some courts hold that recordings of conversations in the workplace are not illegal, for example, because no one in a workplace can claim a reasonable expectation of privacy in their conversations.

Whether recordings expose your client to criminal liability depends on the facts. But you must ask during your preparation session (if you've not already inquired). So many people carry recording devices these days that it's a certainty that some clients have done so. Once you learn recordings were made, you must determine whether your client should seek criminal counsel and/or assert the Fifth Amendment privilege.

§11.18 "How much did your other cases settle for?"

Most settlement agreements contain confidentiality clauses. Those clauses usually impose penalties to punish unauthorized disclosures of their terms.

If your client has previously settled a judicial or administrative dispute, he or she needs to know the risks of revealing anything about the settlement. Many lawyers ask about prior case outcomes. You should advise your client in advance of the deposition how to handle this.

An instruction not to answer may be appropriate under Rule 30(c)(2) if, at the conclusion of the prior lawsuit, a court entered an order directing the parties to comply with the terms of the agreement. This is a good reason to ask courts to order parties to comply with the settlement agreement as a final ruling in a case. That becomes the foundation for seeing relief under Rule 30(d)(3) because doing so is to "enforce a limit ordered by the court," which is language straight from the rule broad enough to cover your situation.

You may also move to terminate or limit the deposition if the inquiry meets the test of bad faith, annoyance or harassment.

Unless I can conclusively determine that testimony about a prior settlement is permitted, I do not allow clients to discuss them. Further, the outcome of a prior lawsuit rarely informs issues in a subsequent, pending case.

In some states, settlements with government entities enjoy no such protection. Where that is the case, your client will have to answer the question. Florida, for example, passed a law forbidding confidentiality clauses in settlement agreements, on the ground that the public should know how their tax dollars are being used.

§11.19 "Have you ever filed for bankruptcy?"

A lawsuit is an asset just like a TV, watch or house. A person filing for bankruptcy must disclose their claim or case in their filings, if the claim was known at the time the petition was filed, or if the claim arose while the bankruptcy proceeding was pending. Failure to disclose it is deemed a act of fraud and results in judicial estoppel. This means the current lawsuit would be dismissed.

If you represent plaintiffs, this is a question to ask during the intake process. If you represent defendants, this is something to check using PACER and to ask at deposition.

Plaintiffs who fail to list the lawsuit as an asset can sometimes amend their petition to add it, even if the case is closed and all the debts were discharged. The bankruptcy trustee can be asked to reopen the bankruptcy estate to administer the lawsuit. Some trustees will do that. Some will not. If a petition cannot be amended, the odds are high that the current litigation will be dismissed on grounds of estoppel or judicial fraud.

§11.20 "Have you ever sought Social Security benefits?"

This is something else often asked of deponents. If the witness' health or ability to work are issues in play, the content of an application for Social Security retirement or disability - even the fact of an application - can be a goldmine for lawyers.

An application for retirement benefits is a clear sign that

the deponent decided to stop working on a part-time or full-time basis. That goes directly to the mitigation of damages.

As for disability benefits, and very generally, applicants for Social Security disability benefits (known by the acronyms SSDI and SSI) must generally attest in their application that they are unable to work in any capacity and should be granted federal disability benefits. Such representations, though, can limit or extinguish damages (e.g., lost wages) being sought by a plaintiff. If you represent plaintiffs, this is a must on your consultation checklist.

Note that in some situations, SSDI and SSI applicants do *not* have to claim an inability to work. The Social Security Administration automatically deems certain conditions as disabilities. These are known as "listed impairments." So it's important to know the basis for the application for disability benefits. If a person has a listed impairment, they are entitled to benefits whether they can work or not.

§11.21 "Did you take documents or materials from the workplace?"

Many people remove documents from the workplace when they intend to file a lawsuit. Sometimes these documents contain trade secrets, confidential customer information, or medical information. Removal of such material can expose them to serious civil and criminal liability.

It is important to ask clients during the intake process whether they taken documents, tangible items or electronically-stored information from the workplace. This includes physical documents, email forwards, photocopies or downloaded digital files. While the information can prove critical claims or defenses, the removal might place your clients in serious legal jeopardy.

§11.22 "Have you logged into computers or devices since your separation?"

It's not unusual for employees, contractors, vendors or others to access computer systems after their employment or business relationship ends. It's so easy to do, and so tempting to log in and grab whatever documents might seem useful. IT departments don't always block access as swiftly as they should.

But even if the person can still gain access, doing so is likely a crime under any of the myriad of state and federal computer-crime laws. And there is always a perfect audit trail of such access – where, when, from what IP address, and using what login and password. The audit trail will also show what the unauthorized user accessed, and what documents were copied, forwarded or downloaded.

Again, this is an essential topic to discuss in every deposition prep session, if not long before.

And it applies equally to individuals and organizations. Sometimes defendants capture employee usernames and passwords when they access personal accounts on company systems. I have been involved in cases where, after a termination, the employer accessed the employee's personal email accounts to see what the employee was saying. The ease of access and perception that "no one will know" is sometimes too tempting to resist, but can lead to serious criminal charges.

§11.23 "What did you tell your [lawyer] [accountant] [spouse] [doctor] [pastor]?"

Clients are usually unaware of testimonial privileges. As a result, they may reveal highly-confidential information unless you counsel them early.

The topic of testimonial privileges is always on my deposition prep list, as well as on my new-client checklist. I explain the reason why privileges exist, and I offer examples of the many types: attorney-client, doctor-patient, clergy-parishioner, accountant-client, and the spousal privilege.

I've found that giving them an overview helps them understand what privileges are intended to do - allow people to speak freely and candidly where the subject is likely of great importance. I make plain that all communications with me, my lawyers, and my staff are all covered.

Finally, I explain how privileges are waived. If I am representing more than one person or entity, I stress that communications between them may not be covered by a privilege, even if they are talking about our pending legal matter. Great harm can result from a breach of the privilege and so time devoted to its parameters is time well spent.

§11.24 "Do you have his number on your phone? Do you have those documents in your car?"

Unbeknownst to you, your client might have all sorts of evidence in their pocket, on their phone, or in their car on the day of the deposition. Sometimes you might not even notice that they are carrying a folder or notebook into the deposition room, loaded with additional items they grabbed the day before.

It is important to talk about what to bring, and what not to bring, on the day of your client's deposition. Absent guidance, you might have some unpleasant surprises as the opposing lawyer randomly asks about something and your clients volunteer that they happen to have relevant documents in the bag at their feet. This touches again on the crucial important of managing every facet of the deposition.

§11.25 "Well, what would you have done if……"

Hypothetical questions can be a legitimate form of inquiry, depending on the witness and depending on the question. Some courts hold they are improper if they seek to elicit opinion testimony from a non-expert, commonly citing FRE 602 (personal knowledge requirement), 701 (opinion testimony by lay witnesses), and 703 (opinion testimony by expert witnesses). There is no single rule, however, squarely addressing this issue. Courts sometimes disagree even as to what constitutes lay opinion testimony. Sec. *& Exch. Comm'n v. Sabhlok*, No. C-08-4238 EMC, 2010 WL 2944255, at *4 (N.D.

Cal. July 23, 2010) (addressing dispute whether testimony from auditors was lay opinion or disguised undisclosed expert testimony).

But what clients can be asked in a deposition, and what can be used at trial, are two different matters. So if a hypothetical question is asked in a deposition, your client must generally answer it. You cannot properly instruct clients not to answer a hypothetical question solely on the ground it is hypothetical.

Rule 30(c) makes plain that all objections made at the time of the examination shall be noted and that evidence objected to shall be taken subject to objections. Absent a claim of privilege or of a harassing examination, instructions not to answer questions at a deposition are almost always improper. Shapiro v. Freeman, 38 F.R.D. 308, 311 (S.D.N.Y. 1965) ("It is not the prerogative of counsel, but of the court, to rule on objections. Indeed, if counsel were to rule on the propriety of questions, oral examinations would be quickly reduced to an exasperating cycle of answerless inquiries and court orders.").

Further, Rule 26(b) says "parties may obtain discovery regarding any matter, not privileged, which is relevant to the subject matter involved.... It is not ground for objection that the information sought will be inadmissible at the trial if the information sought appears reasonably calculated to lead to the discovery of admissible evidence."

It's best to alert your client to the possibility of hypothetical questions, and to include them in your mock cross-examination. Many hypothetical questions are incomplete and may require your client to engage in pure speculation. Unless your clients are cautioned about hypothetical questions - what would you have done, what would you do, what should have been done - they may buy right into it. They may even feel that answering a hypothetical shows the depth and breadth of their knowledge.

Often the proper answer to a hypothetical question is, "That isn't what happened, and I have no way of knowing what I would have done." You can use illustrations during deposition prep to show your client how an innocent hypothetical can lead them astray.

§11.26 "You have other documents? Would you give them to your lawyer, so she can give them to me?"

There are occasions where the opposing lawyer realizes during the deposition that your client has information or evidence the lawyer did not previously request. Once this happens, the next question is typically something like "Would you be willing to provide a copy of that your lawyers? So they can provide it to me?"

This request seeks to short-circuit the discovery process, which requires the opposing lawyer to serve a request for production and wait thirty days or more to receive the documents.

I ordinarily object or ask the lawyer to serve a proper request for production. Informal requests to deponents or their counsel (during depositions or during breaks) to produce documents are generally not enforceable discovery requests. So said one federal judge in a 2018 Memorandum Opinion. *Troutman v. Louisville Metro Department of Corrections et al.* No. 3:16-CV-742-DJH, 2018 WL 3873588, at *3 (W.D. Ky. Aug. 15, 2018.)

This kind of mid-deposition ask is so common that I am quoting verbatim the somewhat lengthy commentary by the court. The bottom line: If you need something from a deponent, follow ordinary discovery procedures using document requests, interrogatories or subpoenas.

From the judge's order:

> "The common thread throughout Troutman's complained-of discovery requests is that they were all informally made. The informality of the requests serves as the primary basis for defendants' objections, with both defendants essentially stating that they tried to accommodate Troutman's requests as best they could. (DN 93, #644; 94-1, #652–53.) The informality of the requests is also the reason why Troutman's motion for sanctions based on them must be denied. Federal courts across the country have routinely denied motions to compel on the basis that the discovery requests were informally made. *See, e.g., Garrison v. Dutcher*, 2008 WL 938159, at *2 (W.D. Mich. April 7, 2008); *James v. Wash Depot Holdings, Inc.*, 240 F.R.D. 693, 695 (S.D. Fla. 2006). In *Sithon Maritime Co. v. Holiday Mansion*, 1998 WL 182785 (D. Kan. April 10, 1998), the District of Kansas explained why federal courts cannot grant motions to compel when the discovery requests are informal:

"The Federal Rules of Civil Procedure provide necessary boundaries and requirements for formal discovery. Parties must comply with such requirements in order to resort to the provisions of Fed. R. Civ. P. 37, governing motions to compel. Informal requests for production lie outside the boundaries of the discovery rules. Formal requests may be filed under some circumstances, not letter requests. Formal requests require certificates of conferring and service. Letters do not.

Formal requests certify representations of counsel under Fed. R. Civ. P. 11(b). Letters do not. To treat correspondence between counsel as formal requests for production under Rule 34 would create confusion and chaos in discovery." Id. at *2. See also *Studio & Partners, s.r.l. v. KI*, 2007 WL 896065, at *1 (E.D. Wisc. Mar. 22, 2007 (holding that an informal request for production for documents made at a deposition was not an appropriate discovery request under the federal rules) (citing *Roberts v. Americable Intern., Inc.*, 883 F.Supp. 499, 501 n. 2 (E.D. Cal. 1995)).

§11.27 "If you don't know, it's okay to say so."

Watch out. This is a trap laid by many lawyers, and it preys on your client's natural desire to avoid conflict and to get the deposition over with. Your clients do not appreciate that saying "I don't know" in deposition likely precludes them from offering a substantive answer at trial, or at minimum allows the adversary to impeach the client's newfound knowledge with the prior deposition testimony.

"I don't know" often closes a door that can't be reopened. With enough "I don't know's" in deposition, your client will be unable to rebut what opposing witnesses will say in court.

§11.28 "I'm going to stand beside you and go through these documents with you."

I occasionally see lawyers get out of their chair, walk over to my side of the table and stand next to my clients while they review documents. Sometimes, lawyers will point to various paragraphs in the document and inquire as they stand there.

I respectfully request that such lawyers return to their seat and resume the examination there. I never want adversaries standing over or next to my client during testimony. The risk of intimidation, intentional or otherwise, is too high.

§11.29 "Have you now told me everything that is important about your claims?"

Beware this type of question if the examiner has only superficially covered the claims or specific topics. It is rare, unless the examiner is unusually thorough, that your client will have revealed absolutely everything of significance.

Further, your client may not know all the facts that are important to the legal issues.

Thus some of my clients have responded along the following lines:

> I have fully answered your questions to the best of my ability and have not purposely withheld anything responsive to your questions. But if there are things you have not asked me about, then there may be things I have not told you. And I don't know what else the law says is important in this case.

It's essential to prep clients for this kind of question, because it's intended to make your clients look dishonest if they add anything more to their testimony at trial. It's an especially unfair tactic, too. Deponents only answer the questions asked. If the examiner does a poor job, the fault lies with the examiner, not with the deponent. The question ought to be turned back on the examiner: Have you now asked me about everything that is legally and factually important?

§11.30 "Have you and your partner ever separated? Have you ever been unfaithful in the relationship?"

On occasion, particularly in cases involving claims for emotional distress, there may be questions coming out of left field at your client. In one recent case – not mine - a defense lawyer asked the plaintiff whether her marriage had a history of infidelity.

The plaintiff's lawyer objected under FRE 412, which

addresses issues of sexual conduct. The defense lawyer responded that infidelity goes beyond mere sexual contact, which drew scoffs from the plaintiff's counsel. Eventually, dueling motions to compel and for a protective order were filed.

The problem, though, was that the plaintiff blurted out "Yes" before her counsel could instruct her not to respond.

Educate your clients about the possibility they may be asked surprise questions about deeply personal matters - about their sex life, divorces, relationships, marriages, children, mental disorders, criminal histories, chemical addictions - you name it. Tell them firmly they are not to answer those questions without a long pause, so that you may object and instruct them not to answer if needed.

Then be sure to drill your clients during your mock cross to see if they'll blurt answers out. Slip this kind of question in several places during the practice session. It will help get them ready if an adversary attempts to catch them off guard.

12

FRCP 30(B)(6) DEPOSITIONS

Covered in This Chapter:

- *§12.01 Overview and Purpose*
- *§12.02 Using 30(b)(6) Depositions To Help You Wisely Assess Remaining Deposition Needs*
- *§12.03 Limits on Multiple 30(b)(6) Depositions?*
- *§12.04 Binding the Organization*
- *§12.05 Preparing the List of Topics*
- *§12.06 Basic Questions to Cover*
- *§12.07 Questions Beyond the Listed Topics*
- *§12.08 Dealing with Multiple 30(b)(6) Designees*
- *§12.09 Percipient Witnesses*
- *§12.10 Setting the 30(b)(6) as Duces Tecum*
- *§12.11 Clarifying the Use of Audio & Video*
- *§12.12 Superior for Locating Evidence*
- *§12.13 Calling 30(b)(6) Witnesses at Trial*

- *§12.14 Sample Obligation-To-Prepare Warning*
- *§12.15 Defending the 30(b)(6) Deposition*
- *§12.16 Overly Burdensome 30(b)(6) Topic Lists*
- *§12.17 Taking Topic Lists Seriously*
- *§12.18 Lengthy Topic Lists*
- *§12.19 Mounting a Topic-List Challenge*
- *§12.20 Duty to Prepare 30(b)(6) Witnesses*
- *§12.21 "I Don't Know" & "I Don't Remember"*
- *§12.22 Preparing with Privileged Documents*
- *§12.23 Choosing the Right Designee*
- *§12.24 Submitting Prior Discovery in Lieu of Producing 30(b)(6) Witnesses*
- *§12.25 Re-Deposing Designees as Fact Witnesses*

In this section, I talk about one of the most underutilized tools in a litigator's arsenal: the designated-representative deposition.

This type of deposition is available when (a) your adversary is an organization and (b) you suspect individual fact witnesses will show up and claim they don't know or can't remember. Situations like that are the litigator's equivalent of "whack-a-mole," the child's game where hitting a toy mole that suddenly pops out of a hole on the board causes more to pop up elsewhere.

As an idiom, whack-a-mole refers to performing a repetitious and futile task, meaning that each time a specific job or task is completed, another one pops up. That's the concept when your corporate adversary has skillfully taught its witnesses to evade key questions.

Courts refer to this as "bandying" – essentially, the calculated plan of an adversary to have its individual witnesses each claim that someone else, not them, has the information needed.[1] This is a frustrating experience, especially when you've burned through your available number of depositions and still don't have clear answers.

Overview and Purpose

THE DESIGNATED-REPRESENTATIVE DEPOSITION, colloquially referred to as a "30(b)(6)," is designed to help you avoid that experience. In the 30(b)(6) deposition:

- You prepare a notice listing the topics you want the entity to address
- The entity must prepare and produce someone to fully testify about those topics
- Answers are deemed answers of the organization itself
- You generally get complete, detailed answers – rather than lots of "I don't knows" and "I don't remembers" - because severe penalties follow an organization's failure to properly prepare a designated representative.
- Even if the entity produces multiple witnesses, which it can, to testify about your topics (because a single person may not be able to absorb enough information to do so), it still counts as a single

deposition. So rather than deposing ten witnesses – the default in federal court - you can conduct a single (30(b)(6) deposition and still have nine slots left.
- You can in some jurisdictions take more than one 30(b)(6) deposition if needed.

If you regularly use this option, you know how useful it is. If you don't, your reaction might be, this is amazing. And that's the right reaction.

§12.02 Using 30(b)(6) Depositions To Help You Wisely Assess Remaining Deposition Needs

The majority of my cases are in federal court, so I generally start with a 30(b)(6) deposition.

This way, I can quickly gather key information and use just one deposition slot to do so. The federal rules impose a default limit of ten depositions per party. That compels lawyers to carefully evaluate their choice of deponents.

If you face a cap on the number of depositions you can take, you should give serious thought to using a designated-representative deposition for your first slot, with a second and third round of individual fact-witness depositions. You'll want time after the 30(b)(6) to ponder the import of the testimony, and to determine whether you need additional interrogatories or document requests before you begin deposing fact witnesses.

Put another way, it may be unwise to schedule a 30(b)(6)

at 9:00 AM on a given day and have fact witnesses lined up to start at 1:00 PM the same day. You will often learn a great deal in the 30(b)(6) that requires more paper discovery. That, in turn, may change your thinking about which witnesses should fill your remaining slots.

Further, scheduling a 30(b)(6) on a day by itself allows you the luxury of time to thoroughly explore every topic. You should not race through it. Your opponent's designated will have been prepared to answer detailed questions about each topic. It is essential to take the time you need to exhaust the entity's knowledge on them.

I also recommend, if you are permitted more than one 30(b)(6) deposition, that you set at least one more as your last deposition. This will allow you to wrap up any loose ends that remain.

§12.03 Limits on Multiple 30(b)(6) Depositions?

Note that some courts have held that you cannot take more than one 30(b)(6) deposition of the same entity. The reasoning is that, just as you cannot depose an individual more than once (without consent from the opposing party or court approval), you cannot repeatedly depose "the entity."

If your jurisdiction takes this position, you should make doubly sure that your 30(b)(6) notice lists all the topics you need the entity to address, and that you do not hold any back.[2]

I include the following lengthy quotation from a case holding that you are limited to one 30(b)(6) deposition per entity. My genuine apologies for the length, but the opinion contains the best complete analysis and reasoning for so limiting this type of deposition.

Thus it serves as both a warning that you may get only one and as a roadmap to the reasoning you'll need to argue around if you seek more. The discussion is from *State Farm Mut. Auto. Ins. Co. v. New Horizont, Inc.*, 254 F.R.D. 227, 234–36 (E.D. Pa. 2008) (and the "t" in "Horizont" is the correct spelling):

> A party need not normally obtain leave of court to take a deposition. Fed. R. Civ. P. 30(a)(1). The exceptions to this rule include the following:
>
> A party must obtain leave of court, and the court must grant leave to the extent consistent with Rule 26(b)(2):
>
> (A) if the parties have not stipulated to the deposition and:
>
> (i) the deposition would result in more than 10 depositions being taken under this rule ... by the plaintiffs, or by the defendants, or by the third-party defendants; [or] (ii) the deponent has already been deposed in the case; ... Fed. R. Civ. P. 30(a)(2).
>
> There is some disagreement as to whether the leave requirement in Rule 30(a)(2)(A)(ii) applies if a party seeks a second Rule 30(b) (6) deposition of a corporate party that has already been deposed. The text of the rule and the advisory committee notes are silent on the relationship between Rule 30(a)(2)(A)(ii) and 30(b)(6). In contrast, regarding the immediately previous subsection allowing

for a limit of 10 depositions without leave, the notes state: "A deposition under Rule 30(b)(6) should, for purposes of this limit, be treated as a single deposition even though more than one person may be designated to testify." Fed. R. Civ. P. 30(a)(2)(A) advisory committee's note (1993).

Reasoning from this note that "Rule 30(b)(6) depositions are different," at least one court has held that leave of court is not required when seeking a second Rule 30(b)(6) deposition of a corporate party who has already been deposed. *See Quality Aero Tech., Inc. v. Telemetrie Elektronik GmbH,* 212 F.R.D. 313, 319 (E.D.N.C. 2002); *see also Kimberly–Clark Corp. v. Tyco Healthcare Retail Group,* No. 05–985, 2007 WL 601837, at *3 n. 1 (granting leave but noting that "there is some question about whether leave of court is even required").

Other courts, however, have held to the contrary. *See Ameristar Jet Charter, Inc. v. Signal Composites, Inc.,* 244 F. 3d 189, 192 (1st Cir. 2001) (holding that it was not plainly wrong for the district court to quash a Rule 30(b)(6) subpoena when leave was not obtained); *In re Sulfuric Acid Antitrust Litig.,* No. 03–4576, 2005 WL 1994105, at *3–6 (N.D. Ill. Aug. 19, 2005) (following *Ameristar Jet,* rejecting *Quality Aero,* and citing 7 Moore's Federal Practice § 30.05(1)(c)). Among these courts is the only court in this circuit to address the issue. In *Sunny Isle Shopping Ctr., Inc. v. Xtra Super Food Cents. Inc.,* the Court noted in a footnote order that Rule 30(a)(2)(A)(ii) "has been held applicable to corporate depositions noticed pursuant to Rule 30(b)(6)." No. 98–

154, 2002 WL 32349792, at *1 (D. Vi. July 24, 2002) (following *Ameristar Jet*).

The latter view appears to be the better one. Neither the text of the rule nor the committee's note exempts Rule 30(b)(6) depositions from the leave requirement in the event of a second deposition of a party already deposed. Rather, the notes state only that a Rule 30(b)(6) deposition should be treated as one deposition, no matter how many designees testify, for purposes of the 10–deposition limit. This limitation has a readily discernable logic, as large corporations with voluminous and complex documents may require testimony from multiple officers and custodians to provide comprehensive testimony regarding all matters "known or reasonably available to the organization." Fed. R. Civ. P. 30(b) (6). Thus, a contrary rule would place an unfair constraint on the number of depositions allowed to parties needing to conduct Rule 30(b)(6) depositions.

The same cannot be said for Rule 30(a)(2)(A)(ii). The policy against permitting a second deposition of an already-deposed deponent is equally applicable to depositions of individuals and organizations. Taking serial depositions of a single corporation may be as costly and burdensome, if not more so, as serial depositions of an individual. In both cases, each new deposition requires the deponent to spend time preparing for the deposition, traveling to the deposition, and providing testimony. In addition, allowing for serial depositions, whether of an individual or organization, provides the deposing party with an unfair strategic advantage, offering it multiple bites at the apple, each time with better information than the last. In short, the unfairness that manifests under Rule 30(a)(2)(A)(i), justifying an exception to the 10–deposition limit, does not manifest under Rule 30(a)(2)(A) (ii).

Here, Defendants have not sought leave of court to conduct an additional deposition of State Farm; thus the May 20, 2008 notice of deposition was improper. Plaintiffs' motion for protective order with respect to the May 20, 2008 notice could be granted on that basis. In the interest of efficiency, however, and in order to turn the litigation back to the merits, the Court will address the appropriateness of the discovery requested as if Defendants had sought leave of court.

B. *Rule 26(b)(2)(C)*

The Court may only grant leave to conduct multiple depositions of a single organization "to the extent consistent with Rule 26(b)(2)." *See* Fed. R. Civ. P. 30(a)(2).

Rule 26(b)(2) provides:

On motion or on its own, the court must limit the frequency or extent of discovery otherwise allowed by these rules or by local rule if it determines that:

(i) the discovery sought is unreasonably cumulative or duplicative, or can be obtained from some other source that is more convenient, less burdensome, or less expensive;

(ii) the party seeking discovery has had ample opportunity to obtain the information by discovery in the action; or

(iii) the burden or expense of the proposed discovery outweighs its likely benefit, considering the needs of the case, the amount in controversy, the parties' resources, the importance of the issues at stake in the action, and the importance of the discovery in resolving the issues.

Fed. R. Civ. P. 26(b)(2)(C); *see also Melhorn v. N.J. Transit Rail Operations, Inc.*, 203 F.R.D. 176, 180 (E.D. Pa. 2001) ("Absent some showing of need or good reason for doing so, a deponent should not be required to appear for a second deposition.").

At the July 14, 2008 hearing, when asked why State Farm was not asked questions in connection with its non-fraud claims at the two prior Rule 30(b)(6) depositions, defense counsel responded as follows:

[T]his is a very complex matter. The way we decided to proceed is, *we decided to take the fraudulent issues which were related to the four counts of the complaint first, then see what happens* and then, you know, seek depositions on the other three counts of the complaints which are RICO conspiracy, unjust enrichment, and restitution which are side issues really. *We just simply decided to proceed in that manner.*

Hr'g Tr. 19:2–10, July 14, 2008.

The justification provided is insufficient. Defense counsel provides *no* reason, let alone a good reason, why the questions relating to State Farm's non-fraud claims were not noticed at the previous two Rule 30(b)(6) depositions; Defendants simply chose to proceed in such a manner. However, the Federal Rules do not contemplate

> the "wait-and-see" approach to discovery taken by Defendants. Such an idiosyncratic approach would permit Defendants, without having demonstrated any good cause for doing so, to avoid drafting a comprehensive notice of deposition and instead conduct depositions seriatim, thereby shifting costs to the opposing side, which would be forced to expend resources preparing for several Rule 30(b)(6) depositions, instead of one.
>
> Therefore, the Court cannot grant Defendants leave to conduct additional Rule 30(b)(6) depositions of State Farm, as "the party seeking discovery has had ample opportunity to obtain the information by discovery in the action," and has not provided a good reason for failing to do so. Fed. R. Civ. P. 26(b)(2)(C). Accordingly, Plaintiffs' motion for protective order (doc. no. 381) has been granted.

There you have it - the argument for listing all your topics in a single notice. Again, be sure to check your jurisdiction. You might be able to take more than one representative deposition. You might not.

Let's go over the basics for taking and defending this type of deposition.

§12.04 Binding the Organization

The basic purpose of a 30(b)(6) is to bind the organization and hold it accountable. The rule applies to any type of organization, including governmental entities. *FTC v. Vylah Tec LLC*, 2018 WL 7361111 (M.D. Fla. Dec. 18, 2018).

It differs from ordinary depositions of individuals because, in the typical deposition, you get little more than individual deponents' knowledge. Their testimony generally does not bind the organization. But an entity's 30(b)(6) designee *represents and is the voice of* the organization, just as individuals represent themselves. The designee ties down the entity's positions. Designees, then, will almost always testifying to matters beyond their personal experience.

§12.05 Preparing the List of Topics

The art in conducting this type of deposition is in the proper preparation of the topic list. The rule says you must describe the topics "with reasonable particularity." Courts say this means you must provide considerable detail and specificity.

Of course, the more specific you are, the more likely you end up with a long list of topics. It is a balance. As you gain experience drafting them, you will learn that a long, detailed list will draw complaints that your topics are excessive and burdensome. On the other hand, a shorter, broad-brush list will draw objections that your list is too vague and that the entity does not know how to prepare its designee.

I say again, it's a balance.

How many topics are too many? It depends on the type of case, the complexity of the issues, the number of parties, and other factors. There is no set limit. If you draw objections for one reason or the other, your judge will take a practical approach, balancing your interest in complete answers, the organization's burden in providing them, and the answers actually given.

But a long list of topics isn't automatically an inappropriate one. Sometimes, there are just many topics to cover.

To illustrate, Facebook and a virtual reality company – codefendants in a lawsuit - served 30(b)(6) notices to the plaintiff that contained 86 topics apiece, for a total of 172 topics.

The court said the number wasn't unreasonable given that the operative complaint was approximately 200 paragraphs, with multiple claims against multiple parties. *Zenimax Media, Inc. v. Oculus VR LLC*, 2016 WL 11476858 (N.D. Texas Jan. 27, 2017). It also approved the use of 30(b)(6) topics as legal contention inquiries (e.g., "Tell us any and all facts supporting your claims"), which is noteworthy because most courts do not allow legal contention questions in depositions. And in another case, the judge seemed unperturbed by a topic list with 52 topics, but did require the plaintiff to revise the list. The examples in the opinion are instructive. *Klopman-Baerselman v. Air & Liquid Systems Corp.*, 2019 WL 3717902 (W. D. Wash. 2019).

The bottom line? Drafting topic lists is a skill that grows with practice. You should strive to achieve balance in the length and complexity of your topics, so the responding entity can reasonably prepare its witnesses. The ideal list is specific enough to result in useful information, and general enough to allow you to drill down into the topics without triggering incessant objections that your questions are beyond the scope of the topic.

§12.06 Basic Questions to Cover

The substantive questions you ask the designee will depend on your case. But there are general background questions to ask all designees, about both their background and their relationship to the organization.

It's also important to confirm their understanding that they are the voice of the organization. You will occasionally encounter a designee with a deer-in-the-headlights look, as if to say they have no idea what you are talking about. That is never a good sign, but it's important to have that conversation to create a record if the witness was not properly prepared

Sample preliminary lines of inquiry include the following:

- Job history with, and relationship to, the entity; all positions held, pending or anticipated pay increases or position changes; disciplinary history
- Confirmation that witnesses understand they speak for organization; confirmation regarding topics that witness is/is not prepared to testify about

Next, before delving into the substantive designated topics, you should inquire about witness preparation efforts. Some suggested questions and topics for this segment:

- What did you do to prepare?

- Did you meet with anyone to prepare for your testimony?
- Identify each person by name and job title (including counsel)
- Dates of, and length of, each such meeting
- Documents reviewed and notes taken by anyone
- Identities of anyone else in the room or on the phone
- Contacts with former employees, third parties to prepare
- Notes taken at any point since designation; where and when
- Documents reviewed or provided
- Clarify which were provided and which were obtained or located by the deponent
- Did witness help respond to discovery generally in the case
- Review pleadings, discovery, deposition transcripts?
- Documents the witness reviewed.
- Documents supporting the witness' testimony; what they are and where they are located

§12.07 Questions Beyond the Listed Topics

Can you ask the designee questions that go beyond the topics you attached to the notice? Most courts say yes.

If your questions go beyond the list, then general deposition rules apply and the witness is no longer speaking for the entity. I recommend that when preparing your notice, you further state (as I do) that in addition to the listed topics, the representatives produced will be asked other questions outside the scope of the notice and based on their own personal knowledge. That will avoid unfounded arguments during the deposition about whether you can properly exceed the designated list of topics.

But if you do, I strongly recommend that you do so after finishing your questions to the designers-as-designee. Once you're done asking the witness to speak as the organization then announce or otherwise note for the record that you are now asking the witness questions from the witness' own personal knowledge. Why? To avoid confusion about which questions were answered as the entity and which were answered by the witness personally.

Here's an excellent overview of the issue from a Florida federal court in 2018, in the case *Fed. Trade Comm'n v. Vylah Tec LLC*, No. 2017-cv-228-FT-MPA-MRM, 2018 WL 7361111, at *5 (M.D. Fla. Dec. 18, 2018):

> Rule 30(b)(6) does not limit what can be asked at a deposition. *McMahon v. Presidential Airways, Inc.*, No. 6:05-cv-1002-Orl-28JGC, 2006 WL 5359797, at *4 (M.D. Fla. Jan. 18, 2006) ("The requirement that the party noticing the deposition 'describe with reasonable particularity the matters on which the examination is requested' does not limit the scope of the deposition to the contents of the notice."); *see also Bank of Am., N.A. v. Russo*, No. 6:11-cv-734-Orl-22GJK, 2013 WL

12158131, at *7 (M.D. Fla. Apr. 2, 2013); *King*, 161 F.R.D. at 476.

Rather, Rule 30(b)(6) simply defines a corporation's "duty to produce a representative who can answer questions that are both within the scope of the matters described in the notice and are 'known or reasonably available' to the corporation." *King*, 161 F.R.D. at 476.

Thus, "[i]f the examining party asks questions outside the scope of the matters described in the notice, the general deposition rules govern (*i.e.*, Fed. R. Civ. P. 26(b)(1)), so that relevant questions may be asked and no special protection is conferred on a deponent by virtue of the fact that the deposition was noticed under 30(b)(6)." *Id.* "[I]f the deponent does not know the answer to questions outside the scope of the matters described in the notice, then that is the examining party's problem." *Id.*

The Court finds that Plaintiff's counsel's instructions to Mr. Adler not to answer questions that fell outside the scope of the noticed deposition topics in his representative capacity were improper. (*See, e.g.*, 228:21-229:20; 235:1-236:3). The fact that Mr. Adler was permitted to answer the questions in his "personal" or "individual" capacity does not cure or ameliorate this impropriety. A Rule 30(b)(6) witness represents the collective knowledge of the entity and provides testimony that is binding on the *entity*, not the individual. *See QBE Ins. Corp.*, 277 F.R.D. at 688; *Continental Cas. Co. v. First Fin. Emp. Leasing, Inc.*, 716 F. Supp. 2d 1176, 1189 (M.D. Fla. 2010).

The Court finds that in the context of this deposition,

the instruction not to answer questions in a representative capacity was improper because the witness clearly had information responsive to the questions posed – as evinced by the fact that he answered them – and Plaintiff offers no explanation for why that factual information could not have been offered through the same witness in a representative capacity in the context of this particular Rule 30(b)(6) deposition.

In other words, if the witness knows the information in his individual capacity, then the entity also has that same information and should be able to offer it through the same witness testifying in a representative capacity even if the information falls outside one of the duly noticed deposition topics.

As noted above, no special protection is conferred on a deponent by virtue of the fact that the deposition was noticed under 30(b)(6). It would certainly be different if the witness sitting in a representative capacity was unable to answer the question fully or *at all* because the information sought fell outside the noticed deposition topics and the witness was not otherwise prepared or sufficiently knowledgeable to provide an answer on behalf of the entity.

But here, the questions were relevant, and the witness actually had answers. Accordingly, the Court finds that the instruction not to answer in a representative capacity was improper. The Court discusses the appropriate remedy for this conduct below.

§12.08 Dealing with Multiple 30(b)(6) Designees

The responding entity must designate a representative or representatives to address the topics. It is up to the organization, not you, to choose the representatives and decide whether one or more are needed to fully address the inquiries.

The designee(s) produced do not need personal knowledge about the topics. Remember they are speaking for the organization, not themselves. So lawyers must often sit down with the people chosen by the entity and ensure they've been spoon-fed enough information to answer your questions.

An organization cannot refuse to comply with your notice by asserting that there is no one that has the information you need. And if it appears they must prepare more than one person, they are obligated to do so. *Catalina Rental Apartments, Inc. v. Pac. Ins. Co.*, No. 06-20532 CIV, 2007 WL 917272, at *2 (S.D. Fla. Mar. 23, 2007) ("If it becomes obvious that one corporate designee is deficient, the corporation is obligated to provide a substitute or additional designees to comply with the corporation's obligations under Rule 30(b)(6).").

If the entity refuses to designate a witness or witnesses, the remedy is to seek an order compelling designation. *See Ortiz v. Cybex International, Inc., 2018 WL 2448130 (D. Puerto Rico May 30, 2018).*

§12.09 Percipient Witnesses

When your case revolves around events personally witnessed by individuals - such as an accident, fight, conversation or similar event - your interests are usually better served by deposing the eyewitness(es), rather than pursuing the information from a corporate designee. In legal parlance, eyewitnesses are referred to as "percipient witnesses" - those who personally perceived the events.

The question to ask in deciding whether to use FRCP 30(b)(6), or to just set individual depositions is this: Would a 30(b)(6) deponent be forced to interview eyewitnesses in detail and then simply recount (second-hand) the individualized observations of multiple people? Or is the topic one for which there is an institutional answer or position that could be better gathered by the organization and easily presented through a single witness, much like an interrogatory answer?

Where you can depose actual eyewitnesses, and where they may have differing individual perspectives, a judge upon receipt of a motion for protective order may prevent you from setting a 30(b)(6), if doing so would force the entity to conduct interviews and develop a singular account.

This issue was discussed in excellent detail in *Jones v. US Border Patrol Agent Gerardo Hernandez*, Case 3:16-CV-01986-W-WVG, Order On Discovery Dispute FRCP 30(b)(6) Deposition Notice (CM/ECF Doc. 84) (S.D. Ca., order filed Jan 23. 2018). This order is well worth reading if you face this issue.

§12.10 Setting the 30(b)(6) as Duces Tecum

Can you require designee witnesses to bring documents with them? Yes.

Just as with any other deposition, you can require designees to produce documents by noticing the deposition *duces tecum. Richardson v. Rock City Mech. Co., LLC*, No. CV 3-09-0092, 2010 WL 711830, at *4 (M.D. Tenn. Feb. 24, 2010) ("There is no reason to believe that a Rule 30(b)(6) deposition is not subject to Rule 30(b)(2).")

Just attach a list of the documents to the notice. What might you ask the designee to bring? Many lawyers require the production of all documents the designee used to prepare for the deposition, *e.g.*, "All documents the designee was provided or used to prepare to testify about topics 1 - 25."

When serving this on a party, you are effectively grafting a Rule 34 request for production of documents onto your deposition notice. Be mindful that, unless you have agreement otherwise, you must allow the full period for response to a request for production if you want the party designee to bring documents. In other words, you cannot short-circuit the time the opposing party would have to respond for a request for production by making the request within a 30(b)(6) notice.[3]

§12.11 Clarifying the Use of Audio, Video

If you plan to record the deposition using audio or video devices, be sure your deposition notice clearly says so. Your notice should also clearly say that it will be used for all permissible purposes, including discovery and trial.

§12.12 Superior for Locating Evidence

A 30(b)(6) deposition can be of great value in determining how an organization stores and retrieves information. It is particularly useful now that so much evidence is stored digitally. Thus one of your standard topics should be the manner in which information is stored, retrieved, archived and deleted on the entity's computer systems. In fact, you may not get straight answers to these questions unless you schedule a representative deposition.

To get you started, here is some sample language you might use in your notice on the topic of information storage and retrieval. You are welcome to use this language verbatim:

> Corporate representative, designated under Rule 30(b)(6) as knowledgeable about how [Entity] stores information on mail systems, archives, local drives, shared networks, portable devices, removable media and databases. Many devices require different search terms because they store and retrieve information differently and often use or require different search term characteristics (e.g., Boolean constructs, proximity searches, "stemming," and fielded searches, to name a few that come to mind. Each device and system may require different approaches to ensure all data is retrieved properly. Plaintiff will also examine the witness about the software programs used in the relevant

store by managers and supervisors in the store(s) where Plaintiff worked; how emails, memos, records and reports are stored, backed up and retrieved, including the format for storage and the methods including search terms for retrieval. Plaintiff will examine the witness about similar topics for market managers and HR personnel. Plaintiff will examine the witness about the witness' background, education and experience; position(s) held within [Entity]; how long information is stored, specific to emails, memos, counseling and coaching memos and evaluations; how coachings, counselings, suspensions, firings and similar adverse employment action is maintained and searched on [Entity] systems, including the steps needed to conduct specific searches, such as for all persons under a particular manager or in a particular store who have been disciplined, coached, suspended, been given decision days or fired for the same or similar offenses; how many times, and for what, a manager has imposed discipline, coachings or counselings, and related inquiries.

Adjust as you see fit to meet your circumstances.

§12.13 Calling 30(b)(6) Witnesses at Trial

Can you call the corporate designee who appeared for your 30(b)(6) deposition as a witness at trial - to speak for the company as they did in deposition? Courts vary, but the broad consensus seems to be yes.

Considering that the deponent comes speaking for the

entity, and that there is no distinction between the representative and the company, the testimony on behalf of the entity is a statement of a party opponent and not hearsay when offered by the adversary. *See Ortiz v. Cybex International, Inc., 2018 WL 2448130 (D. Puerto Rico May 30, 2018). citing Sprint Comm v. Theglobe.com, Inc 236 FRD 524.*

Be mindful of the possibility that your adversary may also attempt to call its 30(b)(6) witnesses at trial. On this note, *see* Rule 32(a)(2), and check out another excellent resource, *Is Live Trial Testimony Permissible? A Primer on 30(b)(6) Witnesses*, by Lauren Bragin, DRI for the Defense, 57 No. 4, DRI For Def. 26 (April 2015).

§12.14 Sample Obligation-To-Prepare Warning

You will occasionally encounter some lawyers who have not been on the receiving end of a 30(b)(6) deposition request. They will not appreciate the preparation required in producing a designee. So, depending on whether tactical considerations are best served by a fully-loaded designee or one shooting blanks, you may wish to add the following cautionary language at the back of the notice:

Notice Regarding Preparation of Fed. R. Civ. P. 30(b)(6) Designees

In response to this deposition notice pursuant to Rule 30(b)(6), which reasonably particularizes the subjects of the intended inquiry, the responding party has a duty "to make a conscientious, good-faith effort to designate knowledgeable persons for Rule 30(b)(6) depositions and to prepare them to fully and unevasively answer questions about the designated subject matter." *Starlight Int'l Inc. v. Herlihy*, 186 F.R.D. 626, 639 (D. Kan. 1999). "Not only must the organization designate a witness, but it is responsible also to prepare the witness to answer questions on the topics identified and present the organization's knowledge on those topics." Wright, Miller & Marcus, 8A FED. PRACTICE & PROCEDURE CIV. 2d § 2103. The 30(b)(6) deponent must not only testify about facts within the organization's knowledge, "but also its subjective beliefs and opinions...[to] provide its interpretation of documents and events." *United States v. Taylor*, 166 F.R.D. 365, 361 (M.D.N.C. 1996).

Under, Rule 30(b)(6) [I]f the persons designated by the corporation do not possess personal knowledge of the matters set out in the deposition notice, the corporation is obligated to prepare the designees so that they may give knowledgeable and binding answers for the corporation. Thus, the duty to present and prepare a Rule 30(b)(6) designee goes beyond matters personally known to that designee or to matters in which that designee was personally involved. *DHL Express (USA), Inc. v. Express Save Industries Inc.*, 2009 U.S. Dist. LEXIS 102981, 2009 WL 3418148 (S.D. Fla. Oct. 19, 2009) (internal quotations and citations omitted). *EEOC v. Winn-Dixie, Inc.*, 2010 U.S. Dist. LEXIS 53005 (S.D. Ala. May 28, 2010).

"The party responding to a 30(b)(6) deposition notice

'must prepare deponents by having them review prior fact witness deposition testimony as well as documents and depositions, exhibits.'" *Calzaturficio S.C.A.R.P.A. S.P.A. v. Fabiano Shoe Co.*, 201 F.R.D. 33, 37 (D. Mass. 2001), quoting *Prokosch v. Catalina Lighting, Inc.*, 193 F.R.D. 633, 639 (D. Minn. 2000), quoted in *Chick-Fil-A v. ExxonMobil Corp.*, 2009 U.S. Dist. LEXIS 109588 (S.D. Fla. Nov. 10, 2009). "The burden upon the responding party, to prepare a knowledgeable Rule 30(b)(6) witness, may be an onerous one, but we are not aware of any less onerous means of assuring that the position of a corporation that is involved in litigation, can be fully and fairly explored." Id. at 638. The corporation and its counsel have a duty to prepare the witness so that he or she is able to give "complete, knowledgeable and binding answers on behalf of the corporation." *Continental Cas. Co. v. Compass Bank*, 2006 U.S. Dist. LEXIS 12288, 2006 WL 533510 * 18 (S.D. Ala. March 3, 2006) citing, *Marker v. Union Fidelity Life Ins. Co.*, 125 F.R.D. 121, 126 (M.D.N.C. 1989). The person being deposed is required to testify about the knowledge of the corporation as an entity and not his or her own knowledge. Id. An individual identified as a Rule 30(b)(6) witness may be called on to answer questions known to the corporation but not to himself personally. The duty to prepare the Rule 30(b)(6) witness properly attaches to the deponent corporation. Calzaturficio, Inc., 201 F.R.D. at 37.

"Producing an unprepared witness is tantamount to a failure to appear at a deposition." *Starlight Int'l Inc. v. Herlihy*, 186 F.R.D. 626, 639 (D. Kan. 1999). In response to

Rule 30(b)(6) deposition notices, parties are required "to have persons testify on its behalf as to all matters known or reasonably available to it and, therefore implicitly require such persons to review all matters known or reasonably available to it in preparation for the Rule 30 (b)(6) deposition." Taylor, 166 F.R.D. at 362.

The 30(b)(6) deposition requires a party to present a properly prepared witness whose testimony is binding on the corporation. E.g., *Calzaturficio*, 201 F.R.D. at 37. The organization has an affirmative duty to prepare the designated deponents so they can give full, complete, and non-evasive answers to questions posed regarding the relevant subject matter. 7 MOORE'S FEDERAL PRACTICE, § 30.25[3] at 30.68 (emphasis added) [hereinafter "Moore's"]. See, *Prokosch v. Catalina Lighting, Inc.*, 193 F.R.D. 633, 638 (D. Minn. 2000). A party is free to designate anyone who consents to testify on its behalf, so long as the designated witness is prepared to testify on behalf of that party as to the matters upon which examination is requested in the notice.

The duties imposed by Rule 30(b)(6), therefore, are: (1) the deponent must be knowledgeable on the subject matter identified as the area of inquiry; (2) the designating party must designate more than one deponent if necessary in order to respond to the relevant areas of inquiry specified by the party requesting the deposition; (3) the designating party must prepare the witness to testify on matters not only known by the deponent, but those that should be known by the designating party; and (4) the

> designating party must substitute an appropriate deponent when it becomes apparent that the previous deponent is unable to respond to certain relevant areas of inquiry. Id. § 30.25[3] at 30-68 (emphasis added).

§12.15 Defending the 30(b)(6) Deposition

Now let's take a look at this kind of deposition from the perspective of the lawyer defending it. There are several considerations in responding to the list of topics, in choosing those who will appear, and in preparing them.

§12.16 Overly Burdensome 30(b)(6) Topic Lists

The chief problem you will encounter in defending designee depositions arises because many litigators are not accustomed to crafting 30(b)(6) topic lists. This will be immediately obvious.

In fact, the first several tries by an attorney to draft a topic list usually results in a list that seems to cover every claim, defense, and fact in the entire case.

You may also see language like "including but not limited to...." This is generally improper because you have no way to determine the outer limits of the examination. Deficient topic lists also often lack geographic and temporal limits.

Nonetheless, you must take the list of topics seriously because you are obligated to produce witnesses who can speak to them unless you negotiate something better with the opposing lawyer or seek court intervention.

§12.17 Taking Topic Lists Seriously

Remember that the testimony of your designees are the official, binding answers of the organization. And as I pointed out elsewhere in this book, answers of "I don't know" and "I don't remember" can bind your client and bar it from presenting substantive testimony on the topics to which your designee claims a lack of knowledge or recollection. Organizations are bound by their 30(b)(6) testimony. Just as individual witnesses cannot come into a courtroom with a suddenly-improved memory, nor can the entity. Some courts have held that if your designated representative cannot answer questions in the deposition, the entity cannot present witnesses to provide that information at trial. You could be stuck with the memory failures. At best, such answers could result in uncomfortable impeachment of your witnesses.

§12.18 Lengthy Topic Lists

Avoid undue fixation on the number of topics. Courts have approved deposition notices for dozens of topics. *E.g., Tamburri v. SunTrust Mortg. Inc.*, No. C-11-02899 JST DMR, 2013 WL 1616106, at *2 (N.D. Cal. Apr. 15, 2013) (approving fifty topics); *Krasney v. Nationwide Mut. Ins. Co.*, No. 3:06 CV 1164 JBA, 2007 WL 4365677, at *1 (D. Conn. Dec. 11, 2007) (approving 40 topics).

Focus instead on the topics phrasings, and look for deficiencies. Inappropriate phrases, and other flaws to look out for, include:

- "All defenses"
- "All claims"
- "Any and all"
- "Including but not limited to"
- "All allegations in the Complaint"
- "All facts supporting your claims/defenses"
- All denials and Affirmative Defendants
- The absence of a specific date range
- The absence of geographic limitations
- The absence of a limit to the department, office or other compartment at issue
- Language calling for privileged information

In essence, you are using the same analysis you would for an ordinary request for production of documents or set of interrogatories. The list of topics in a 30(b)(6) deposition is subject to the same general objections you make in response to any discovery request. But just as judges vary in ruling on discovery requests, they may also vary in deeming specific topics proper or not. However the topics are words, the key is deciding whether as written they are inappropriate.[4]

§12.19 Mounting a Topic-List Challenge

What is the proper procedure for opposing an objectionable 30(b)(6) topic list? Serve objections? Or seek a protective order? Courts differ, but the majority say you must seek a protective order.

Representative of courts that say merely serving objections is sufficient is the decision in *Kaplan v. Nautilus Insurance Company*, No. 17-CV-24453, 2018 WL 6445886, at *1 (S.D. Fla. Sept. 17, 2018), where the court said, "When a party objects to the scope of a 30(b)(6) deposition notice, courts have found that the proper means for raising the dispute is by timely serving those objections upon the opposing party in advance of the deposition, not by filing a motion for protective order seeking anticipatory review before the deposition."

Many courts are critical of this approach because it allows lawyers to serve objections at the last minute and thwart the effectiveness of 30(b)(6) depositions. Such courts say that if you are going to challenge the list, you must seek court intervention, and risk being sanctioned for doing so. The obligation to involve the court serves as a deterrent to obstructive objection tactics.

A federal judge in his 2018 Order Regarding Discovery Dispute on Plaintiff's Proposed Rule 30(b)(6) Deposition Topics said the recipient of an offending 30(b)(6) notice *must* seek a protective order before the scheduled deposition. *See Rutherford, et al v. Evans Hotels LLC, et al*, No. 18CV435-JLS(MSB), 2018 WL 6246516 at *3 (S.D. Cal. Nov. 29, 2018).

For other cases following this rule, see *Robinson v. Quicken Loans, Inc.*, No. 3:12–cv–00981, 2013 WL 1776100, at *3 (S.D. W. Va. Apr. 25, 2013); *New England Carpenters Health Benefits Fund v. First DataBank, Inc.*, 242 F.R.D. 164, 166 (D. Mass. 2007).). ("Put simply and clearly, absent agreement, a party who for one reason or another does not wish to comply with a notice of deposition must seek a protective order.")

These courts have held it insufficient to serve objections and then declare that a witness will only testify within the scope of its objections. One court said such objections ". . exhibit exactly the type of technical objection-crafting the Rules seek to deter and for which Rule 37 sanctions were created." *Beach Mart, Inc. v. L & L Wings, Inc.*, 302 F.R.D. 396, 406–07 (E.D.N.C. 2014) Another court similarly held objections improper. *Espy v. Mformation Techs., Inc.*, No. 08-2211-EFM-DWB, 2010 WL 1488555, at *3 (D. Kan. Apr. 13, 2010)

So which path to take? It depends on your particular jurisdiction. If I were in a jurisdiction where the law was not yet settled, I might do both - file a motion for a protective order, candidly admitting my uncertainty about which line of cases will be followed, and at the same time, file and serve written objections.

Corporate representative depositions can make or break a case because the witness is the voice of the entity. So I would not hesitate to take both paths at the same time to ensure that I did not leave my client unprotected by choosing one or the other.

§12.20 Duty to Prepare 30(b)(6) Witness(es)

While the rule may not require the designers to answer every conceivable question - it speaks of the obligation to attest to matters known or "reasonably available to the organization" - it does require a concerted good-faith effort on your part to collect information by reviewing documents and interviewing employees with personal knowledge, just as an entity does in answering interrogatories.

This will often require a lengthy and time-consuming effort on your part to choose and prepare the designee(s). You are free to designate current or former employees. But whoever your designate, your obligation is to ensure they can answer the topics thoroughly.

Basic preparation includes the following:

1. Explaining the deposition process thoroughly
2. Explaining the role of 30(b)(6) witnesses
3. Carefully reviewing the topic list
4. Conducting a mock deposition
5. Determining the extent of elaboration on answers
6. Addressing expressions of opinion or belief
7. Addressing the entity's stance on issues
8. Covering topics related to but beyond the topic list, as some courts consider the list to be the bare minimum that could be explored. *ChrMar Sys. Inc v. Cisco Sys, Inc.* 312 F.R.D. 560 (N.D. Cal. 2016) and *Fed. Deposit Ins. Corp. v. Giancola* 2015 WL 5559804 (N.D. Ill. Sep. 18, 2016)

§12.21 "I Don't Know" & "I Don't Remember"

There may be occasions where your designee says the entity lacks knowledge of a certain fact. It may simply not know, or it may simply have no answer. *Catalina Rental Apartments, Inc. v. Pac. Ins. Co.*, No. 06-20532 CIV, 2007 WL 917272, at *2 (S.D.

Fla. Mar. 23, 2007). But where this occurs, the adversary may be allowed to point to that inability to answer on summary judgment and at trial.

The adversary may also seek an order *in limine* flatly barring the entity from presenting evidence at trial on the topics it could not answer in the 30(b)(6) deposition. *See Kartagener v. Carnival Corporation,* 380 F. Supp. 3d 1290 (S. D. Fla. 2019) (*d*efendant precluded from taking position at trial —including introduction of testimony and exhibits—on 30(b)(6) topics which witnesses could not address; entity's inability to speak to topics in deposition will equally silence it at trial).

§12.22 Preparing with Privileged Documents

You may wish to exercise caution in preparing the witness or witnesses with privileged documents. Otherwise, the privilege may be waived as to those documents.

On the other hand, it is no answer to a 30(b)(6) deposition notice to claim that relevant documents or investigations are privileged and that therefore no knowledgeable witness can be produced. Similarly, the mere fact that you might prepare a witness or witnesses for a 30(b)(6) deposition would not create an attorney-client privilege as to the facts of the case that the attorney and the witness might discuss.

§12.23 Choosing the Right Designee

Where possible, my preference is to designate a single witness. This avoids the risks of confusion or conflicts where multiple designees are selected. It can also save you the possible nightmare of multiple seven-hour depositions under the federal rules, to the extent your jurisdiction considers each appearance by a separate designee as a new deposition.

My ideal designated representatives have certain testimony-friendly qualities. They:

1. are experienced litigation witnesses
2. are not easily flustered
3. have excellent memories
4. speak with clarity and precision
5. are patient
6. can tolerate lengthy or aggressive examinations

I avoid designees who are involved in legal strategy for the organization. While such individuals are otherwise perfect because they meet my basic criteria, they might also give testimony that could result in the inadvertent waiver of work-product or attorney-client privilege. This is because they might have problems mixing personal and corporate knowledge in this respect. That could allow the opposing lawyer to stray far beyond the listed topics.

§12.24 Submitting Prior Discovery in Lieu of Producing 30(b)(6) Witnesses

What if, after reviewing the list of topics, you conclude that other fact witnesses for the organization have already testified about those areas? Can you simply designate that deposition testimony in place of preparing and producing a live witness? I am not aware of the case that says this is inappropriate as a bright-line matter, but I would never recommend it.

First, fact witnesses do not speak for the entity. Second, an ordinary fact witness is not required to review all pertinent documents before appearing. A designated representative is. Third, it is unlikely that ordinary depositions of fact witnesses resulted in answers that are as thorough and complete as if the witness had been deposed under Rule 30(b)(6). Fourth, even if you have previously served interrogatory answers and documents on the same topics as the 30(b)(6) notice, you must still prepare and produce a representative if the adversary insists. *E.g., CRST Expedited, Inc. v. Swift Transportation Co. of Arizona, LLC*, No. 17-CV-25-CJW-KEM, 2019 WL 2714508, at *5 (N.D. Iowa Mar. 6, 2019) (producing documents and responding to written discovery is not a substitute for providing a thoroughly educated Rule 30(b)(6) deponent).

So, you risk sanctions if you represent an entity and fail to produce a properly-prepared representative witness. Remember that courts have said that the failure to present a properly-prepared witness is equivalent to failing to present any witness whatsoever at the deposition. Under Rule 37(d), your opponent can seek sanctions without first filing a motion to compel a better deposition. *E.g., Scott v Wabash National Corporation,* 2007 WL 9773389; *In re Brican Am. LLC Equip. Leave Litig.*, 2013 WL 5519980 (S.D. Fla. Oct. 1, 2013) (sanctions imposed against entity for merely designating prior fact witness depositions instead of presenting properly-informed representative for 30(b)(6) deposition); *see also Sciarretta v. Lincoln Nat. Life Ins. Co.,* 778 F. 3d 1205, 1211 (11th Cir. 2015) (affirming $850,000 in sanctions against party relating to failure to properly prepare designated representative under Rule 30(b)(6)).

§12.25 Re-Deposing Designees as Fact Witnesses

In some cases, your adversary may attempt to re-depose - as a fact witness - the same person you designated as your 30(b)(6) representative. Is this permissible? Should you object?

The clear answer is maybe. The question is whether the representative has substantial additional personal knowledge. Otherwise, a second deposition makes little sense.

This issue arose in *R.D. v. Shohola Camp Ground and Resort*, Case No. 3:16-CV-1056, 2017 WL 1550034 (M.D. Pa. May 1, 2017). There the plaintiff wanted to depose the witness, a records custodian, first under Fed. R. Civ. P. 30(b)(6) about corporate records and, separately, a second time as a fact witness. The defendant argued the witness should be forced to sit for deposition just once.

Note, as we progress here, that this plaintiff signaled in

advance his intention to depose the representative on an individual basis later. So the question of "one, or two?" arose before either deposition began, and was thus a hypothetical one at that point for the court.

The judge took the middle ground, ruling that he would only allow one deposition initially. But he permitted the plaintiff to seek a second deposition if there was a legitimate basis. The judge pointed out that discovery rulings were within his sound discretion, and it was not clear whether the deponent had sufficient personal knowledge to justify a second deposition.

In that case, combining the two kinds of depositions made sense because the 30(b)(6) piece was limited to some brief questions about records.

But conducting a combined 30(b)(6) and fact deposition of a single deponent poses risks to both plaintiff and defendant. For the defense, it leaves open the possibility that loose comments by the witness are deemed testimony of the company. For the plaintiff, it can make separating statements that bind the company and those that made individually a messy job. Plaintiffs need clean facts and testimony. Defendants need bright-line protection against liability. Combining corporate representative and fact witness depositions is risky business across the board.

13

EXPERT WITNESS DEPOSITIONS

Covered in This Chapter:

- *§13.01 A Word About Daubert and Frye*
- *§13.02 Daubert versus Frye*
- *§13.03 Timing the Daubert/Frye Challenge*
- *§13.04 The Reference Manual on Scientific Evidence*
- *§13.05 Scheduling Expert Depositions*
- *§13.06 Preparing the Expert Deposition Binder*
- *§13.07 Expert Deposition Objectives*
- *§13.08 Applicability of Privileges*
- *§13.09 Sample Expert Examination Topics*
- *§13.10 Defending the Expert Deposition*

Expert witness depositions, like 30(b)(6) depositions, require special preparation and thought. Both present considerable opportunities for the well-prepared litigator, and equally considerable risks.

In this section, I endeavor to cover as much as possible to get you on the right track. But keep in mind that the range of experts, and the range of issues in expert witness depositions, vary so widely depending on the nature of the case that it is simply impossible to cover everything.

§13.01 A Word About Daubert and Frye

I generally am not covering challenges to experts – known as a *Daubert* challenge in federal court, and as a *Frye* challenge in many state courts. The reason I opted not to address this in detail is that it depends heavily on the nature of your case and expert.

§13.02 Daubert versus Frye

In general terms, a *Daubert/Frye* challenge is an attack on the validity and admissibility of expert testimony. When such a motion is filed, the experts under siege must demonstrate that their methodology and reasoning are scientifically valid and can be applied to the facts of your case. This standard in the federal system comes from the Supreme Court case, Daubert v. Merrell Dow Pharmaceuticals, Inc., 509 U.S. 579 (1993).

Under the *Daubert* standard, the factors that may be considered in determining whether your expert's methodology is valid are: (1) whether the theory or technique in question can be and has been tested; (2) whether it has been subjected to peer review and publication; (3) its known or potential error rate; (4) the existence and maintenance of standards controlling its operation; and (5) whether it has attracted widespread acceptance within a relevant scientific community.

These may not be the exact elements your court uses, but they will be similar.

The *Frye* standard, originating in *Frye v. US*, 293 F. 1013 (D.C. Cir. 1923) is often referred to as the "general acceptance test." Under *Frye,* generally-accepted scientific methods are deemed admissible; anything else is not. This test carried great weight in both state and federal courts for many years. It is no longer used in the federal courts.

The chief distinction between a *Frye* analysis and one under *Daubert,* based on FRE 702, is that a *Daubert* analysis has multiple prongs of analysis and is more flexible. The thrust of most *Daubert* challenges is that the expert's testimony is unreliable or irrelevant. The attack may center on your expert's methods, qualifications or underlying scientific principles.

Attacks on methodology are the most common. This is because the methods used are the core of the resulting opinion. If the method is defective, the opinion likely fails.[1]

§13.03 Timing the Daubert/Frye Challenge

Many judges now require the filing of *Daubert* motions around the same time as dispositive motions. Absent a specific court-imposed or agreed deadline, though, the challenge can be raised later and in different contexts, such as within a dispositive motion, as a *motion in limine*, or even at trial. Most judges want such challenges raised as early as possible, because proper resolution can be time-consuming. So the longer you wait, however, the more problematic the challenge might become.

Some lawyers strategically time the challenge for assertion at trial. There are legitimate reasons for doing this, but at that point it is unlikely the judge can give the challenge the same in-depth consideration as if raised months before trial. Another downside in waiting, if you have a challenge to make, is that you will not know with certainty what evidence is going to be admitted until the court rules. This will affect how you prepare for trial.

Further, a successful *Daubert* challenge can gravely weaken an adversary's case and motivate them to engage in settlement talks. This benefit is foreclosed if your challenge isn't raised until the midst of trial.

It is best to become immersed in *Daubert* principles before you choose your expert. That will allow you to choose experts whose work is neatly tailored to *Daubert* concepts.

Finally, you may read about "*Daubert* hearings." Indeed, some sources speak of a *Daubert* hearing as always following the motion. This isn't so. Courts are not required to conduct actual hearings on the motion. The judge is required to thoroughly address the challenge and articulate the reasoning behind the grant or denial of the motion, but there is no rule or law that requires a separate hearing.

§13.04 The Reference Manual on Scientific Evidence

For an outstanding guide – the one federal judges use - on the admissibility of scientific evidence, visit the Federal Judicial Center at fjc.gov and search for The Reference Manual on Scientific Evidence, Third Edition. It assists judges in managing cases involving complex scientific and technical evidence by describing the basic tenets of key scientific fields from which legal evidence is typically derived and by providing examples of cases in which that evidence has been used.

First published in 1994 by the Federal Judicial Center, the *Reference Manual on Scientific Evidence* is used by judges, lawyers, and others for guidance on scientific and technical evidence, especially in the context of *Daubert* motions. You can download the entire 1,000-page manual for free, or buy a hard copy for around $75.00. If you routinely use experts, a hard copy is a wise investment.

§13.05 Scheduling Expert Depositions

Under the federal rules, you should generally wait for the opposing experts' mandatory reports before you depose them. Rule 26(a)(2)(B), (b)(4)(A).

The Initial Scheduling Order, issued by judges based on your joint report, will determine the dates for submission of expert reports. The expert disclosures should help you decide whether depositions of opposing experts is appropriate. *Krause v. Hawaiian Airlines, Inc.*, No. 2:18-CV-00928 JAM AC, 2019 WL 2598770, at *5 (E.D. Cal. June 25, 2019) ("An opposing party should be able (and be entitled) to read an expert disclosure, determine what, if any, adverse opinions are being proffered and make an informed decision as to whether it is necessary to take a deposition and whether a responding expert is needed," *citing Burreson v. BASF Corp.*, No. 2:13-cv-0066 TLN AC, 2014 WL 4195588 (E.D. Cal. Aug. 22, 2014).

While you will normally depose opposing experts, the decision should be the result of individualized, active analysis and not by default. In a handful of situations, deposing an opposing expert may deprive you of a tactical advantage. Sometimes they have made fatal flaws in their work, leaving them ripe for a *Daubert* or *Frye* challenge. If so, you may not want to depose the expert and give him or her a chance to timely correct the deficiencies. Alternatively, if you do decide a deposition is needed, you can set the deposition later in the case to minimize the possibility of correction within applicable deadlines.

Before you start the deposition, and apart from expert reports, you must conduct expert witness discovery through interrogatories, document requests, searches through specialized databases, and online searches.

Let's turn now to the development of a binder for your use in deposing the adversary's expert witnesses.

§13.06 Preparing the Expert Deposition Binder

A good binder on the opposing expert should include, at minimum, the following:

1. The expert's entire file and final report
2. Current resume
3. Photos and video in their possession
4. Transcripts of testimony relied on by the expert
5. Witness statements
6. The contents of publications or textbooks the expert relied upon
7. The expert's billing records for this case
8. Drafts of any reports
9. Fee arrangements with the expert
10. All communications between the expert and opposing counsel
11. The adversary's Rule 26 disclosure
12. Transcripts of prior testimony by the expert within applicable time frames
13. Publications by the expert within applicable time frames

This is the absolute minimum. Other additions to the binder will depend on the facts of your case. If you plan to hire your own expert, it is wise to do so before you depose the opposing experts so your expert can help formulate deposition questions.

§13.07 Expert Deposition Objectives

The goals for deposing an expert vary. You may be trying to determine the opinions and conclusions of the witness. You might hope to undermine or limit the impact of the opinions and conclusions. You may be using the deposition to develop your *Daubert* or *Frye* challenge, by determining whether the expert is qualified to give an opinion on the subject, has sufficient knowledge and understanding of the facts of the case, and is using a legitimate methodology.

You can also use the opportunity to determine whether the expert agrees with you on certain facts, or is relying on inadmissible evidence. Or you may simply be deposing the experts to lock the testimony down so that there are no surprises and undisclosed opinions later.

§13.08 Applicabilty of Privileges

The rules of attorney-client privilege generally don't apply here. Communications between the hiring attorney and expert are usually, if not always, discoverable. This is a point worth noting. You should always include a discovery request seeking communications between opposing lawyers and their experts.

Some lawyers misapprehend this. So it is critical to obtain everything available to you and to address privilege issues with the court if needed before the deposition begins. Once the expert deposition is underway, it is essential to ask questions about communications between the lawyer and the expert, the terms of hire, and the specific information the lawyer provided the expert in terms of facts and legal theories that the lawyer is asking the expert to adopt.

Make sure you also ask experts about their arrangement, how much was paid as a retainer, how much is being paid per hour out-of-court, and how much will be paid per hour in court.

If you are hiring an expert, be exceedingly careful about what you put in writing and what you share with the expert. Assume all the written communications, emails, letters, and documents are discoverable.

§13.09 Sample Expert Examination Topics

If you have not previously deposed an expert, the task can seem daunting. Your first thought might well be, how in the world do I challenge someone who is an expert in their field? How do I formulate inquiries for someone who has specialized expertise in an area about which I know nothing?

The answer is, you are probably far better qualified to challenge opposing experts than you might realize. The key to success in attacking an expert is breaking the challenge down into digestible pieces.

As you work through their background, training and experience, their sources, and their methodologies, you will begin to see flaws that will open doors to lines of attack.

More often than not, experts in litigation reach conclusions they were asked to reach. They are not talking about their work in general. They have in effect given puzzle pieces provided by a party and been asked to assemble them in a very specific way. What the puzzle looks like when fully assembled is, for the most part, a foregone conclusion.

In fact, experts sometimes reach conclusions that go far beyond their own prior research and that sometimes conflict even with their own published works. Remember this: What an expert chiefly offers is a subjective opinion. That is always ripe for challenge. If the topic were clearly established science, an expert might well be unnecessary.

The following suggested lines of inquiry and strategies should assist you in throughly exploring the expert's credentials, systems and methods:

1. Whether the expert agreed to serve as an expert before actually reviewing any documentation.
2. The information provided (e.g., pleadings, transcripts, articles, key documents).
3. Whether the opposing lawyers outlined their theory of the case.
4. If so, the theories suggested or requested.
5. The documents provided to support the theories.
6. Whether documents were provided but withdrawn.
7. Whether lawyers told the expert *not* to focus on or review certain documents once provided, even if not specifically withdrawn. Lawyers sometimes

stuff expert inboxes with all kinds of materials to create the impression the expert relied on all those sources, even if the expert did not.

8. The documents the expert obtained and reviewed on his or her own, and why.
9. What the expert requested from the lawyer, and why. What was important about the requested materials? What was the expert looking for?
10. Whether there was any information the expert was unable to obtain.
11. The methodology used by the expert, and conflicts in his or her line of work (or within the professional literature) over the expert's approach or theory.
12. Drafts of the expert report, and any notes taken.
13. Whether any documents have been destroyed, any notes discarded, or any evidence destroyed.
14. Whether prior versions of the report indicated that the expert saw a weakness in the case and thought it was necessary to revise the report.
15. Whether there are notes from the opposing lawyer or notes from the lawyer written on drafts of the report.
16. Whether any other evidence been discarded, destroyed or used up in testing.
17. Whether the expert consulted with any other experts or third parties.
18. The expert's qualifications. Under FRE 702, a party offering expert testimony must show the

expert is qualified to render an opinion relevant to the case. That includes a showing that the expert has sufficient specialized knowledge to inform the jurors.

19. The expert's knowledge, skill, training, experience, and education. It may be a matter of attacking the *actual* knowledge, skills, and experience as compared to the knowledge, skills and experience applicable to *your* specialized situation.
20. Don't waste time on generic questions.
21. Pin experts down on their exact qualifications and experience to show that they are not the same as the subject matter at hand. Example: A general surgeon with forty years' experience may be utterly incompetent to testify as an expert about a specific brain or spine surgery.
22. The expert's deposition preparation efforts.
23. Practice sessions in which the expert participated.
24. Review of videos or audio on being deposed.
25. The expert's education and employment history.
26. Prior specific experiences and expert in state and federal court.
27. Prior deposition experience in all cases.
28. How many times the expert has been qualified as an expert.
29. How many times the expert was rejected as an expert witness.
30. Suspensions and revocations of credentials.

31. Board certifications, including the need to repeat a board examination.
32. Prior lawsuits or disciplinary proceedings.
33. Amount of time spent testifying for plaintiffs versus defendants.
34. How many times the expert has testified for the lawyer's law firm.
35. The percentage of time the expert spends as an expert witness.
36. The exact nature of the claimed expertise. In other words, what field is the person an expert in?
37. All publications, and in any publication, on any topic, to determine how many times the expert has actually published in the claimed field, outside the field, and on non-scientific matters.
38. Seminars or presentations, the papers presented if any, and the topic of presentation.
39. Membership in professional societies and organizations.
40. Ask if the expert has formed an opinion.
41. If so, have the expert fully reveal it.
42. Ask for all bases of the opinion.
43. What specifically did they review, and who did they talk to that informed that specific opinion?
44. Did they perform any specific tests?
45. Inquire about the chain of custody as needed applicable to evidence tests?
46. Were any approaches or methodologies considered and rejected? The experts might have

rejected the best possible approach because it did not work for them. Address this fully.

47. Whether the expert's opinion would change if certain assumptions or information proved to be different?
48. If information relied on by the expert is untrue or unreliable, this is where you want to ask the expert to make assumptions based on the information *you* provide, and whether those assumptions would change the opinion of the expert.
49. If the expert agrees that your information would change their opinion, ask why.
50. Ask summarization questions.
51. Once you obtain all the bases for the opinion of the expert, it is wise to summarize them in a single question, e.g., "So you relied on the documents provided by the attorney for the defendant, you made the following assumptions, A, B, C, you made the following additional assumptions, D, E, F, and you did not take into account the possibility that there were other factors that you had not considered, correct?"
52. Conclude by asking whether the experts plan to undertake any additional work to refine their conclusions.
53. Ask if there are forthcoming discussions with counsel about additional documents.

54. Is there information provided by witnesses that has not yet been verified or explored?
55. Are there documents the expert has given thought to but not yet reviewed?
56. Does the expert have other current assignments that touch on the same issues?
57. Are there other current assignments of the expert with the opposing law firm or lawyer?

§13.10 Defending the Expert Deposition

The list above for deposing an expert has equal value for lawyers defending expert depositions. It is a checklist of the topics your expert needs to be prepared to address.

Basic preparatory steps include knowing just how well-versed your expert is in giving testimony. You need to ensure your chosen expert will be a strong witness. You must ensure your expert appreciates and understands the opposing expert's report and underlying credentials, documentation, and prior testimony. You must determine whether your expert has, since initial retention, offered opinions in other cases that might contradict your position.

In preparing experts, I generally assemble, for their use, the same materials my opposing lawyer will likely use in a deposition. This includes anything my expert relied on, background materials, retention agreements, and whatever else is likely to be the subject of attack. The closer your binder resembles that of the adversary, the more likely it is your expert will be unfazed by whatever the examiner raises.

The key is making your preparations as much like the actual deposition as possible.

Even if your expert has extensive experience in testifying, explain the process generally. Identify the likely lines of attack and the specific goals of the opposition. Point out weaknesses in your position and key points you feel the expert should emphasize.

When you feel you have thoroughly prepared your expert, conduct a full-on mock cross-examination. Cut no corners. Go after your expert. The more hardened your expert is on the facts and issues, the better prepared he or she will be. Softball preparation sessions have no value.

During the examination, for example, cut your expert mid-sentence. See how determined he or she is to finish her thoughts in the face of an obstructive opponent. Look skeptical. Question their credibility. Attack their profit motive. Go after every weakness you can think of. Teach your experts to watch out for overly broad questions – using words like always and never - and unfounded or confusing hypotheticals.

If you are interested in reviewing additional resources on expert witness depositions, there are many available. *E.g., No Second Chances: Best Practices for Expert Practice*, 38 Stetson L. Rev. 41 (2008); Howard Bruce Klein, *Expert Witness Depositions*, 19 No. 5 Prac. Litigator 9 (2008).

14

OBJECTIONS AND OBSTRUCTIONS

Covered in This Chapter:

This might be the most important chapter in this book. Everything matters, of course. But just as football is a game of inches, so is deposition practice. Many cases are won or lost solely because one side fought just a wee bit harder, stayed in the fight longer, paid attention to even the smallest details. If an opposing lawyer, through improper objections and obstructive behavior, prevents you from achieving your goals, you lose.

Objections and obstructions are what ruin most depositions.

I have provided my insights on many topics, and there are many important chapters. But, fundamentally, it is a deposition in progress that is the most critical moment in the case. That is where the most crucial evidence is generated. And it is where cases are won or lost, where cases stay on track or are derailed. Sometimes, even often, the derailment occurs because of the conduct of lawyers. That conduct surfaces in the form of objections, instructions not to answer, and physical, verbal or visual misconduct.

This section covers the general rules about lawyer behavior during depositions. The rules are not complicated. But you might think otherwise after seeing how some lawyers act. It is up to you, and no one else, to stop interference during your examination of witnesses, and, if you're defending the deposition, to stop abusive or harassing behavior of the deponent by the examining lawyer.

Remember that all depositions involve some measure of

annoyance, inconvenience and embarrassment. It's when such behaviors become unreasonably so that it's time to act. [1]

§14.01 Core Principles

The bedrock principle for lawyer conduct in depositions is spelled out in Rule 30(c)(1): "The examination and cross-examination of a deponent proceed as they would at trial under the Federal Rules of Evidence, except Rules 103 and 615." Rule 103 pertains to rulings you would otherwise get during the trial from the judge. Rule 615 relates to the exclusion or sequestration of witnesses.

It is worth repeating:

> *The examination and cross-examination of a deponent proceed as they would at trial.*

This means the examination and defense of depositions should resemble direct and cross-examination in a courtroom before a judge.

There are practical exceptions to this, of course. You might need to have conversations with opposing lawyers to resolve an issue about the testimony. You wouldn't do that in the courtroom. You might have very limited back and forth about an objection. You wouldn't do that in court, either. But the fundamental question about deposition conduct in general is this: Would this happen in front of a judge?

The 1993 Committee Notes to Rule 30(d) contain a variety of instructive comments. They are worth reading, and I open the section with important observations about deposition conduct:

> *Subdivision (d).* The first sentence of new paragraph (1) provides that any objections during a deposition must be made concisely and in a non-argumentative and non-suggestive manner. Depositions frequently have been unduly prolonged, if not unfairly frustrated, by lengthy objections and colloquy, often suggesting how the deponent should respond. While objections may, under the revised rule, be made during a deposition, they ordinarily should be limited to those that under Rule 32(d)(3) might be waived if not made at that time, *i.e.*, objections on grounds that might be immediately obviated, removed, or cured, such as to the form of a question or the responsiveness of an answer. Under Rule 32(b), other objections can, even without the so-called "usual stipulation" preserving objections, be raised for the first time at trial and therefore should be kept to a minimum during a deposition.
>
> Directions to a deponent not to answer a question can be even more disruptive than objections. The second sentence of new paragraph (1) prohibits such directions except in the three circumstances indicated: to claim a privilege or protection against disclosure (*e.g.*, as work product), to enforce a court directive limiting the scope or length of permissible discovery, or to suspend a deposition to enable presentation of a motion under paragraph (3).
>
> Paragraph (2) is added to this subdivision to dispel any

doubts regarding the power of the court by order or local rule to establish limits on the length of depositions. The rule also explicitly authorizes the court to impose the cost resulting from obstructive tactics that unreasonably prolong a deposition on the person engaged in such obstruction. This sanction may be imposed on a non-party witness as well as a party or attorney, but is otherwise congruent with Rule 26(g).

It is anticipated that limits on the length of depositions prescribed by local rules would be presumptive only, subject to modification by the court or by agreement of the parties. Such modifications typically should be discussed by the parties in their meeting under Rule 26(f) and included in the scheduling order required by Rule 16(b). Additional time, moreover, should be allowed under the revised rule when justified under the principles stated in Rule 26(b)(2). To reduce the number of special motions, local rules should ordinarily permit—and indeed encourage—the parties to agree to additional time, as when, during the taking of a deposition, it becomes clear that some additional examination is needed.

Paragraph (3) authorizes appropriate sanctions not only when a deposition is unreasonably prolonged, but also when an attorney engages in other practices that improperly frustrate the fair examination of the deponent, such as making improper objections or giving directions not to answer prohibited by paragraph (1). In general, counsel should not engage in any conduct during a deposition that would not be allowed in the presence of a judicial officer. The making of an excessive number of unnecessary objections may itself constitute sanctionable conduct, as may the refusal of an attorney to agree with other counsel on a fair apportionment of the time allowed for examination of a deponent or a refusal to agree to a reasonable request for some additional time to complete a deposition, when that is permitted by the local rule or order.

§14.02 Dealing with Objections

Courts have said that lawyers who are defending a deposition can do one of two things.

They can listen. And they can make objections. *Freedom's Path at Dayton v. Dayton Metropolitan Housing Authority* 2018 WL 2948021 (S.D. Ohio 2018); *Montiel v. Taylor,* No. 3:09-CV-489, 2011 WL 1532529, at *2 (E.D. Tenn. Apr. 21, 2011). This mirrors the role during trial of the non-examining lawyer. It also echoes the comment in the Note, above, that a lawyer should not engage in conduct during a deposition that he or she would not do in front of a judge.

So objections must be noted on the record, but the examination continues subject to the objection, unless one of the three grounds for instructing a witness not to answer is applicable.

§14.03 How to Express Objections

The rule explicitly says objections must be stated concisely in a non-argumentative and non-suggestive manner. Non-argumentative means no arguments. Commentary during objections is a common form of argument. Lawyers get confused about what "argumentative" means in this context. It does not necessarily mean you are quarreling with the opposing lawyer. It means you are adding commentary and viewpoint to the legal objection. "Foundation, he doesn't know that" is both a legal objection ("Foundation") and argument ("He doesn't know that").

Non-suggestive means no suggestions. "Foundation, he doesn't know that" is also a legal objection and suggestive. A witness who hears their attorney say "He doesn't know that" is likely to take that as a signal that he should not reveal information and, more often than not, the answer which follows is "I don't know that."

As one court put it, "[O]bjections that result in an incomplete answer or in the witness's adoption of counsel's statement are suggestive." In Re Ford Motor Co, etc., Case No. 2:18-cv-1893 AB (FFMx), No. 218ML02814ABFFMX, 2019 WL 3815721, at *4 (C.D. Cal. May 13, 2019), *citing Luangisa v. Interface Operations,* 2011 WL 6029880, at *11 (D. Nev. Dec. 5, 2011).

Is Just Saying "Form" Enough?

There is disagreement among courts where saying "Form," without citing the specific flaw in the question, is enough. In fact, one federal judge, noting this split, suggested that lawyers should reach agreement on the record whether saying "Form" alone preserves the objection. According to Chief Judge William C. Griesbach of the Eastern District of Wisconsin:

> When an attorney decides to assert such an objection, it is generally safest just to state "I object to the form of the question" or "objection–form," assuming opposing counsel is in agreement that by so limiting his objection, counsel is not waiving the more specific objection, such as "vague" or "leading." Asking for the agreement of opposing counsel is important because not all courts agree that merely objecting to the form of the question without stating the specific defect in the form is sufficient to preserve the issue. *Compare Cincinnati Ins. Co. v. Serrano*, No. 11-2075-JAR, 2012 WL 28071, at *5 (D. Kan. Jan. 5, 2012) ("But such an objection [to a vague question] to avoid a suggestive speaking objection should be limited to an objection 'to form,' unless opposing counsel requests further clarification of the objection."), *and Druck Corp. v. Macro Fund (U.S.) Ltd.*, No. 02 CIV.6164(RO)(DFE), 2005 WL 1949519, at *4 (S.D.N.Y. Aug. 12, 2005) ("Any 'objection as to form' must say only those four words, unless the questioner asks the objector to state a reason."), *with Sec. Nat'l Bank*, 299 F.R.D. at 602 ("Nothing about the text of Rules 30 or 32 suggests that a lawyer preserves the universe of 'form' objections simply by objecting to 'form.' "). Limiting one's objection to the form of the question,

when opposing counsel so requests, will avoid the risk of being accused of making so-called "speaking objections," which instruct the witness how to answer the question. *See Specht v. Google, Inc.*, 268 F.R.D. 596, 598 (N.D. Ill. 2010) ("Objections that are argumentative or that suggest an answer to a witness are called 'speaking objections' and are improper under Rule 30(c)(2)."). And it leaves to opposing counsel the choice of whether to ask for a more specific basis of the objection so that he can either cure the defect in the question or, if none exists, demonstrate the lack of any basis for the objection in the first place. Unless it is obvious the objection is baseless, opposing counsel should normally avail himself of the opportunity to ask for clarification. Indeed, without greater specificity, review by the court may be of little value, because "Unless an objector states with some specificity the nature of his objection, rather than mimicking the general language of the rule, i.e., "objection to the form of the question," it is impossible to determine, based upon the transcript of the deposition itself, whether the objection was proper when made or merely frivolous."

Otis v. Demarasse, No. 16-C-285, 2019 WL 1778955, at *5–6 (E.D. Wis. Apr. 23, 2019)

There is nothing wrong with stating the legal basis for the objection. Simply stating "Form," even with agreement of the examining lawyer, might still be treated by your judge as insufficient.

According to Miami federal judge William Matthewman, the proper objection must be "Objection, form, leading" because, he says in his 2017 ruling, "[a]n objection which merely states 'form' shall be deemed to be no objection and waived by the party making the objection."

In *Vargas v. Florida Crystals Corporation*, 2017 WL 1861775, Case No. 16:81399-CV-MARRA/MATTHEWMAN (S.D. Fla. filed 2016).Judge Matthewman looked at rulings from other states in his analysis, and concluded that nowhere in the federal rules does it say a lawyer cannot state the legal basis for the objection. He then ruled that a lawyer forfeits the objection if the specific ground is not stated.

His May 5, 2017 Order contains a summary of the federal rules and the proper way to make objections in depositions. It's worth a read.

My suggestion is that you state the legal basis of your objection. Asserting the specific ground basis can incentivize the examiner to ask better questions. "Form,"alone may be ignored, or may simply leave the examiner clueless as to the defect. Expressly voicing the specific legal objection, such as "Compound," is more likely to spur the lawyer to self-correct. That benefits everyone, if the alternative is a full day of objectionable, and therefore inadmissible, questions. It's a fact that some lawyers just don't know how to ask questions properly. Appropriate objections, respectfully asserted, can help fix that.

And you should make your objections even if opposing lawyers don't seem to care about the flaws in their questions.[2] You generally waive objections you do not make, unless you have agreed with the opposing lawyer that all objections except as to pure form are preserved. *See generally* Rule 32(d)(3); *see also Chapter 9, §9.32, supra, "The Usual Stipulations?" Huh?.*

§14.04 Instructions Not to Answer

In federal court, an instruction to a deponent not to answer the question is forbidden unless the basis falls into one of three narrow categories: (1) If it is necessary to preserve a privilege, (2) if it is to enforce a limitation ordered by court, or (3) if it is to present a motion under Rule 30(d)(3) ("At any time during a deposition, the deponent or a party may move to terminate or limit it on the ground that it is being conducted in bad faith or in a manner that unreasonably annoys, embarrasses, or oppresses the deponent or party.")

The first two categories are clear. The third is a catchall that allows you to instruct witnesses not to answer the question, and further to terminate the deposition, if needed to prevent bad-faith or harassing conduct. But be forewarned. You cannot instruct the witness not to answer and let it go. You will be sanctioned if you do not follow up and present a motion to the court.

Let's walk through specific objections and other forms of objectionable deposition conduct:

§14.05 Speaking Objections

A speaking objection generally is any commentary that goes beyond a statement of the specific legal basis. It can be argument, commentary, or a remark. Some examples:

1. 'If you know."
2. "If you can. *See Freedom's Path at Dayton v. Dayton Metropolitan Housing Authority* 2018 WL 2948021 (S.D. Ohio 2018); *see also In Re Epipen*, 2018 WL 6617105 (D. Kan. Dec. 14, 2018) ("Instructions to a witness they may answer a question "if they know" or "if they understand the question" are raw, unmitigated coaching and are never appropriate), citing *Cincinnati Insurance Company v. Serrano*, 2012 WL 28071, at *5 (D. Kan. Jan. 5, 2012)
3. "I don't think he/she is going to know that" *See Freedom's Path, above.*
4. "That question isn't clear."
5. "I'm going to keep you on a short leash about those topics" *In Re Epipen*, 2018 WL 6617105 (D. Kan. Dec. 14, 2018)
6. Extended commentary about the questions, the witness' knowledge, or the topic; *see also Continental Casualty Company v. Compass Bank* 2005 WL 8158672 (S.D. Ala. Aug. 8, 2005)
7. "He's not an expert." *See In Re Ford Motor Co. DP86 Powershift Transmission Products Liability Litigation,* Case 2:18-cv-1893 AB (FFMx), No.

218ML02814ABFFMX, 2019 WL 3815721, at *2 (C.D. Cal. May 13, 2019)

§14.06 Obstructive Conduct

Apart from speaking objections, other types of objectionable and disruptive behavior include the following:

1. Rushing the examiner to ask questions at a faster pace.
2. Interrupting to "clarify" a question for the witness
3. Crowding the witness, such as pulling a chair tightly against the deponent during testimony
4. Harassing and demeaning the witness and/or opposing lawyer
5. Calling the lawyer or witness "idiot" in stage whisper; calling the lawyer nicknames, such as "Egregious Steve;" asking if the lawyer washed his hands after using the bathroom; announcing that small words will be used so the opposing lawyer isn't confused, *see Lendus, LLC v. Goede,* 2018 WL 6498674 (Ct. Chan. Delaware Dec. 10, 2018)
6. Writing notes for the deponent to see. If this occurs, inquire immediately of both the witness and the opposing lawyer as to what the note says, and demand that a copy be attached as an exhibit in the deposition; *Ryan v. Astra Tech, Inc.*, 2014 LEXIS 21628 (1st Cir. 2014).
7. Taking breaks during pending questions, *see*

Horowitz v. Chen, 2018 WL 6498660 (C.D. Calif. Dec. 7, 2018)

8. Improper breaks to coach
9. Making contact by hand, arm or foot, or otherwise touching the deponent
10. Eye-rolling at the question or answer
11. Nodding as a visual cue to witness
12. Audible huffing in annoyance
13. Tapping hands, pencils, keys on the table
14. Disruptive note-passing between lawyer and client, such as the large scribbling of a note that says "LIAR!"

These are common forms of improper conduct by lawyers during a deposition. You should be on the lookout for anything taking place in the room that appears to be affecting the testimony or that would not otherwise be permitted in front of the judge.

An excellent overview of lawyer misconduct in depositions can be found in the Memorandum Opinion and Order on Sanctions, CM/ECF Doc. 205, *The Security National Bank of Sioux City, Iowa, As Conservator For.M.K., A Minor V. Abbott Laboratories*, No. C 11-4017-MWB (N.D. Iowa Western Div. July 28, 2014).

Another is the 47-page Order Granting Plaintiff's Motion for Sanctions [Doc. 103] in *La Jolla Spa MD, Inc. v. Avidas Pharmaceuticals, LLC,* 2019 WL 4141237, Case No. 3:17-cv-01124-MMA-WVG (S. D. Cal. Aug. 30, 2019).

Still another is the Order Granting Motion for Sanctions

in *In Re Ford Motor Co. DP86 Powershift Transmission Products Liability Litigation,* Case No. 2:18-cv-1893 AB (FFMx), No. 218ML02814ABFFMX, 2019 WL 3815721, at *2 (C.D. Cal. May 13, 2019). There, the judge excoriated the plaintiff's counsel for numerous, disruptive objections:

> As well, in approximately 60 instances, plaintiff's counsel interposed objections that implicitly instructed Mr. Hobart how to answer. Objections such as "Calls for speculation," "He is not qualified [to answer the question]," "To the best of your knowledge," "Don't guess," and "You can answer if you understand" evidently signaled to Mr. Hobart that he should claim ignorance or confusion, no matter how simple the question. For example:

Examples given by the court in its order include:

- "Objection; calls for speculation. He is not going to answer that question as to what he would have done. He is not here to answer hypothetical questions." (A speculative question is not a proper ground for instructing a deponent not to answer. See Fed. R. Civ. P. 30(c)(2)).
- (In response to a question asking the witness when he first hired a lawyer, which is usually not privileged): "You're trying to instruct me as to how I can make the record. So please let me make my record. I am advising my client not to answer the

question based on attorney-client privileged communications; based upon the confidential nature of the communication; relevancy and also violates his right to privacy. Advise him not to answer."

- "Let me object. Vague and ambiguous. If you understand the question, you can answer."
- "I'm going to object. Calls for expert opinion. You can answer if you understand the question."
- "Objection; you can answer if you understand it."
- "Objection; vague, ambiguous, overbroad. Calls for a legal conclusion and legal analysis. But to the extent that you're aware of anything, you can answer."
- "I don't want you to guess."
- "I'm going to object. It calls for expert testimony. He is not a mechanic. Foundation. However, you can describe it if you have an idea of where it thought it was, the general direction."

For still more resources, *see* C. Malcolm Cochran IV, "*But The Examination Still Proceeds": A Primer On Surviving The Difficult Deposition, ABA Section Of Litigation 2012 Section Annual Conference April 18-20 2012: Deposition Practice In Complex Cases: The Good, The Bad And The Ugly;* Eric B. Miller, *Lawyers Gone Wild: Are Deposition Still A "Civil" Procedure? 42 Connecticut Law Review No. 5 (July 2010).*

§14.07 Non-Lawyer Misconduct

The principles governing lawyer conduct in a deposition extend to others attending and observing the testimony. This includes representatives for the parties, lawyers for the witness (if independently represented), paralegals and staff, videographers, and court reporters.

In short, everyone in the room.

The most common misconduct I see from observers is eye-rolling, head shaking, audible sighs, or huffing. If the conduct is such that the deponent can see it, I voice my concerns immediately and memorialize the conduct for the record. Most of what occurs during a deposition is not captured by the reporter unless you verbalize it for the record. No court reporter will document eye-rolling or head-shaking by a paralegal or party representative. They capture the spoken word.

Everything else vanishes into the ether unless you memorialize it when it happens. Do not wait until a break or the end of the deposition to speak up

In one case a lawyer for the opposing party - but not the one conducting the examination - entered the room and sat at the opposite end, even behind the videographer. About ten minutes after the lawyer sat down, I noticed he was shaking and rolling his head in derision almost every time my client answered a question.

I could see him, and my client could see him. But neither the stenographer nor the videographer captured a bit of it. The misconduct was silent, and off the record - by design.

Had I said nothing, this calculated harassment could have gone on for hours, without a trace. The witness would have been deeply affected. She was disabled and had enough difficulty concentrating as it was. Worse, all a judge or jury would see on video is a person who seemed highly distracted. They would have assumed she suffered from ADHD or ADD. They would *not* assume this was the result of intentional harassment by a lawyer sitting off-screen.

After watching this for a few moments, and after making certain what I was seeing was a conscious act, I spoke up - vigorously, to say the least. I then stopped the deposition and immediately sought court relief, to bar anyone but the examining lawyer from being present for the balance of the deposition.

You must be sensitive to events in the room. Many deponents arrive already laboring under enough anxiety and fear to distract them. It takes very little additional effort to harm their testimony. You must pay constant attention to the behavior of everyone in the room while testimony is being taken.

§14.08 "Continuing" & "Standing" Objections

"A continuing objection is used to avoid repeated interruptions when a series of questions concerning the same arguably inadmissible evidence is anticipated."[3]

Some lawyers will offer to agree that you have a "standing" objection to particular inquiries, in order to tamp down the frequency of your interruption. But such offers are risky.

A "continuing" or "standing" objection has no value if you sit silent while improper questions are asked that go beyond the strict framework of the inquiries to which the purposed standing objection applies. A judge will not fault you for declining such an offer. *See Otis v. Demarasse*, No. 16-C-285, 2019 WL 1778955, at *5–6 (E.D. Wis. Apr. 23, 2019) (declining sanctions against defending lawyer who, in part, refused offer by examining attorney of a continuing objection).

§14.09 Objections to Deponent Answers

Just as you must make timely objections to defects in questions, you must also timely object to answers given by deponents if they contain irregularities. Rule 32(d)(3)(B)(i) deems defects in answers waived unless you timely objected while the deposition was in progress. This applies to defects that might have been corrected by the witness if you'd objected.

So if the witness offers an answer that is non-responsive, for example, it is critical that you speak up. Under Rule 32(d)(3) you must make the objection while the deposition is in progress and timely make it at the appropriate point in the deposition.

We all think of objections as something we do in response to questions, but Rule 32 makes clear that problematic answers must also draw timely objections, where the flaw might have been cured at the time. Failing that, the objection is waived.

§14.10 Objections to Other Irregularities

Rule 30 lays out basic deposition procedures for the lawyers, witnesses and court reporters. Included are a range of procedural requirements for the deposition, including, by example only, obligations of the reporter to identify everyone present, to properly administer an oath, and so on.

If there are defects in the manner in which the deposition was conducted, a party's conduct, or other matters that could have been corrected had a timely objection been made, you must timely object while the deposition is in progress or your objections are waived. *See* Rule 32(d)(3)(B)(i); *see also Delima v. Wal-Mart Stores Arkansas LLC,* 2018 WL 6729994 (W. D. Ark. Dec. 21, 2018) (applying Rule 32(d)(3)(B) to reject plaintiff's objections to alleged irregularities, where plaintiff failed to timely object during deposition).

15

POST-DEPOSITION CONSIDERATIONS

Covered in This Chapter:

- *§15.01 Errata Sheets - Overview*
- *§15.02 Transcript Changes Under Rule 30(e)(1)*
- *§15.03 Limits on the Use of Errata Sheets*
- *§15.04 Preserving Transcript Review Rights*
- *§15.05 Check Errata Sheets Before Quoting From the Transcript*
- *§15.06 Errata Sheet Challenges*
- *§15.07 Explaining Errata Sheets*
- *§15.08 Using Transcripts from Other Cases*
- *§15.09 Getting Transcripts from Other Cases*
- *§15.10 Authenticating Deposition Excerpts*
- *§15.11 Using Draft Transcripts*

Once the deposition is over, and assuming it went smoothly, the next step is to await. the transcript.

If you reserved the deponent's right to review the transcript before it is certified and sent out, it will typically be about two weeks before you receive it. From there, you will arrange for your deponent to review it, and then timely return it with properly-completed errata sheet.

Let's talk about this process.

§15.01 Errata Sheets - Overview

Errata sheets are the blank, lined pages at the back of the review copy of the transcript. The errata sheet is where your deponent notes changes to the transcript - misspellings, grammar and punctuation errors, places where words were omitted, and substantive changes in testimony.

There is great disagreement about the extent to which a deponent may correct or edit transcribed testimony. Some courts say changes on an errata sheet are limited to correcting incorrectly-transcribed answers. Others say the rules impose no such limit, and allow for whatever changes the witness deems appropriate.

§15.02 Transcript Changes Under Rule 30(e)(1)

Rule 30(e)(1) is the source code for correcting or editing deposition testimony:

> *Review; Statement of Changes.* On request by the deponent or a party before the deposition is completed, the deponent must be allowed 30 days after being notified by the officer that the transcript or recording is available in which:
>
> (A) to review the transcript or recording; and
>
> (B) if there are changes in form or substance, to sign a statement listing the changes and the reasons for making them.

The rule itself, as you can see from its text, expressly contemplates there may be changes to both form and substance. But courts differ sharply on the real meaning of the rule.

§15.03 Limits on the Use of Errata Sheets

But some courts read this language narrowly, representing the minority view. These courts hold that changes on an errata sheet may only be made where the transcript shows evidence of obvious confusion, where the contradiction is a result of court reporter error, or where the change does not materially alter testimony.

Other courts take a broad view. Under this more expansive and accepted interpretation, courts say, the plain language of Rule 30(e)(1) does not place limits on the types of changes a deponent can make. This broad, literal construction, advocates say, furthers the purpose of the discovery process by allowing parties to discover the true facts. It also tends to reduce surprises at trial.

An excellent overview of both viewpoints appears in *Metal Conversion Technologies LLC v. Environmental Integrity Company*, 2016 WL 11409555 (N.D. Georgia Aug. 25, 2016). This case contains some good citation to decisions supporting both interpretations. Another great case on errata sheets is *Ashcroft v. Welk Resort Group, et. al*, 2017 WL 5180421, Case No. 2:16-cv-02978-JAD-NJK (D. Nevada 2017).

Finally, there is the decision in the case involving the "Mother of All Errata Sheets," where the party made hundreds and hundreds of changes. That's *Norelus v. Denny's, Inc.* 628 F. 3d 1270, 1281, 1303-1308 (11th Cir. 2011).

My view? Put aside the debate about the extent to which you can make changes. *Even if permissible, extensive changes to the transcript pose considerable risk.* It invites court suspicion and scrutiny. It can also provide your opponents with a powerful basis to impeach a witness who has made meaningful changes to the transcript that go beyond grammar or obvious errors, or to reopen your clients' depositions if the changes "...make the deposition incomplete or useless without further testimony..." *Sanford v. CBS, Inc.*, 594 F. Supp. 713 (N. D. Ill. 1984).

My approach is to clear up problem testimony while the deposition is in progress. Put another way, I view the original transcript as my errata sheet. If I sense that my deponent has made a mistake, i clear it up through follow-up examination before the deposition ends.

§15.04 Preserving Transcript Review Rights

The right to correct a deposition transcript is not automatic. You must strictly comply with the requirements of Rule 30.

Here are the five steps for getting it right.

First, you must request the right to review before the deposition ends. Rule 30(e)(1).

Second, you must make the changes and return them to the reporter within thirty days after being notified that the transcript is ready for review. Rule 30(e)(1) and (2).

Third, the deponent must sign the errata sheet. Rule 30(e)(1)(B).

Fourth, the deponent must list the changes. Rule 30(e)(1)(B).

Fifth, the deponent must give the reasons for the changes. Rule 30(e)(1)(B).

These are five distinct traps. You only need to fall short on one to forfeit your deponent's right to note the changes.

While most reporters will, just before ending the deposition, ask "Read or Waive?", not all do. The rule expressly places the burden of preserving the right to review on you, not on the reporter. So if the reporter fails to inquire, and you say nothing, your right to have the witness review the transcript is foreclosed.

Similar traps lie for deponents who fail to review the transcript within thirty days after being notified, who don't sign the errata sheet, and who don't list *and explain* their reasons for the changes. It is not sufficient to simply list changes. Complete explanations must be given for each change.

The failure to check off each of these threshold items may allow the judge to disregard your changes. *Rios v. Bigler*, 67 F. 3d 1543, 1553 (10th Cir. 1995) (appellate court cited the appellant's inability to prove she requested the right to review, before the deposition ended, as a basis for refusing to overturn the trial court).

§15.05 Check Errata Sheets Before Quoting From the Transcript

And remember this important tip. When you are preparing dispositive motions and relying on deposition transcripts, be sure to check for errata sheets for each witness. Your court may roast you if a deponent made legitimate changes to the transcript that changed answers and your motion instead incorrectly cites the original transcript. In a September 22, 2016 order a defendant got called out for this precise problem - quoting inaccurate deposition testimony, in a summary judgment motion, that had been timely corrected in an errata sheet. So confirm the existence/absence of errata sheets before using deposition testimony in filings. The case is *Preayer v. Ryan*, 2016 US Dist. LEXIS 130472, Case No. CV 15-00069-PHX-DGC (DKD) (D. Ariz. Sept. 22, 2016)

§15.06 Errata Sheet Challenges

If you encounter a situation where deponents made substantial, material changes to the transcript, determine whether the witnesses met all five criteria for corrections. They often do not. And if they did, next check to see if you are in a jurisdiction that takes the narrower view, which provides an opening to seek an order striking the errata sheet.

Now, what if your clients want to make extensive changes?

First, caution them that making material changes could, at minimum, expose them to a second deposition about the modifications to the testimony. *See Unlimited Resources, Inc. v. Deployed Resources, LLC*, 75 Fed. Rules Serv. 3d 938 (M.D. Fla. 2010); *Dering v. Service Experts Alliance LLC*, 69 Fed. Rules Serv. 3d 939 (N.D. Ga. 2007).

Second, let them know that many judges take a dim view of changes and may not give them weight.

Third, emphasize that the opposing party may use these changes to make them look dishonest through impeachment at trial, by reading the original testimony and the changes in front of the jury. Point out that the original answers do not simply go away. Both the original version and the errata sheets are preserved. In fact, some judges may <u>require</u> the reading of both versions of the testimony, even without a request from counsel. *Unlimited Resources, Inc. v. Deployed Resources, LLC*, 75 Fed. Rules Serv. 3d 938 (M.D. Fla. 2010) (court permitted both substantive and corrective changes, but permitted both versions of transcript to be read at trial);

see also Zimmer Technology, Inc. v. Howmedica Osteonics Corp., 2009 WL 10721285 (N.D. Ind. 2009) (denying motion to strike errata sheet with multiple changes allegedly at odds with deposition testimony, but allowing both the errata sheet and original deposition testimony to be presented to jury as credibility issue).

§15.07 Explaining Errata Sheets

Some lawyers, perhaps to be helpful, open depositions by telling witnesses they have the ability to review the transcript and make changes on an errata sheet. This creates risk where none should exist. Why? It may encourage the witness to be less precise. If I am a deponent and am told I can correct or update the transcript later, why should I worry how accurate I am today?

I take a different approach. I tell witnesses the difference between ordinary conversations and sworn testimony is that sworn testimony demands complete accuracy. I say nothing about errata sheets. I say nothing about corrections. I stress that the order of the day is extreme precision. I say nothing to suggest carelessness today can be replaced by precision later.

A 2018 ruling by a California federal judge is a useful lesson about discussing errata sheets. You might skip such discussions altogether after reading this, if you address errata sheets at all.

In *Moriarity v. American General Life Insurance Company*, 2018 WL 4628365, Case No. 2017-CA-1709-BTM-WVG,

CM/ECF Doc. 96 (S.D. Cal. Sept. 27, 2018), the defense lawyer told the plaintiff in a casual, friendly way that she could make substantive changes to her testimony on the errata sheet, but that she might be impeached later if she did. This is an explanation many lawyers give, and I doubt they give it much thought.

Predictably, the plaintiff made many changes to her transcript and - here's the kicker - claimed the defense lawyer's explanation amounted to *a stipulation* that she could change whatever she wanted. The judge saved the lawyer by ruling that an actual stipulation would have been more formal, and that the instruction was not intended in that manner. He then granted the defendant's motion to strike the errata sheet.

The order contains useful citations to the law on errata sheets and an evaluation of arguments made by the plaintiff that are common in errata sheet fights. The order is well worth the read, and I've given information in the case cite to help you find it on PACER.

Here's the actual discussion from that case between the lawyer and the witness:

- Counsel: You understand - - just the last thing I'll say. You understand that once - - when the deposition is concluded, you will get a booklet. I assume you got a booklet of your deposition testimony in the county case. Is that right?
- Plaintiff: I did not.
- Counsel: Okay. Well, in this case, you will. You'll

get a booklet, it will be a script, a word by word of everything that was said today. You will have a chance to review your testimony, to make any changes that you feel are necessary to your testimony.

- Plaintiff: Okay.
- Counsel: You can change the spelling of a word, alter the grammar, whatever you want to do to the transcript. The only thing I want to caution you is, that if you make a substantive change - - for example, if I asked you was the light green or red and you said green in your deposition and then said red when you read your transcript, that would be the kind of substantive change that I or another lawyer could comment upon should the case go to trial to suggest that your testimony today wasn't truthful. It's a long way of saying that it's important for you to give us your best testimony today and that you understand that. Are you with me?

Sound familiar? I hope not.

The lesson here is simple. If you tell deponents about errata sheets - and there is nothing requiring you to do so - use caution. The judge here gave cover to the defense lawyer, but other judges may not. They might rule that if you told deponents they can make substantive changes, you've waived the right to complain.

§15.08 Using Transcripts from Other Cases

Can you use deposition testimony from other cases where your current opponent was a party? Usually, yes, as long as the issues were similar and your opponent had a motive to develop testimony in a way that would be relevant to the pending litigation.

This strategy can save tremendous time and resources for everyone. There's little point in redeposing witnesses just to hear them say the same thing. And judges are often receptive to efforts intended to avoid wasteful duplication of effort.

Here are two excellent blurbs from a defense memo in *Guarantee Insurance Company v. Heffernan Insurance Brokers*, 2015 WL 7422096, Case No. 13-CV-23881-CIV-Martinez/Goodman (S.D. Fla. Sep. 29, 2015):

> Whether to admit a deposition from a prior lawsuit is vested in the court's sound discretion. *Nationwide Mut. Fire Ins. Co. v. Kaloust Fin., LLC*, 2013 U.S. Dist. LEXIS 50933 (M.D. Fla. Apr. 9, 2013). As the court noted in *Hub v. Sun Valley Co.*, 682 F. 2d 776, 777-778 (9th Cir. 1982): "Depositions can save the time, effort and money of litigants, and help expedite trials. Because the underlying objective is efficiency at trial without jeopardizing accurate fact-finding, the district court is usually in the best position to decide whether a prior deposition should be admitted.

And:

While Rule 32 requires that the earlier action be between the "same parties," the circuit courts have not applied this provision literally, preferring instead to allow a party to offer a deposition against a party to the earlier action, even if the party attempting to use the deposition was not a party to the earlier action. See C. Wright & A. Miller, 8A Fed. Prac. & Proc. Civ. § 2150 (3rd ed.). See *Wallace v. City of Tarpon Springs*, 2007 U.S. Dist. LEXIS 2775, *9-10 (M.D. Fla. Jan. 12, 2007) (stating that courts have found that the requirement that the parties be the same in both actions is not controlling in determining admissibility under Rule 32(a) and that the main questions as to the admissibility of a deposition under Rule 32(a) are whether the underlying issues are the same and whether the party opposing the deposition's admission had adequate motive and opportunity to develop the witness' testimony as relevant to the case at hand); see e.g., *May v. Frisbie*, 2009 WL 792084 (S.D. Ind. Mar. 23, 2009) *5-6 (finding that deposition testimony should be admitted despite different plaintiff from prior deposition taken in criminal case); *Shirley v. Safeco Ins. Co. of IL.*, 2009 WL 765887 (M.D. Fla. Mar. 20, 2009) *1 (finding that 11th Circuit reads Rule 32(a)(8) in conjunction with Fed. R. Evid. 804 to "permit the use of deposition testimony taken in a different proceeding as long as the party against whom the testimony is offered 'was provided an opportunity to examine the deponent').

The same principle applies in bankruptcy proceedings, because Rule 32 has been adopted verbatim by the federal bankruptcy rules of procedure. *Re Maxus Energy Corp.*, No. 16-11501, 2019 WL 2581609, at *2 (Bktcy. D. Del. June 24, 2019). *See also Kravitz v. United States Dep't of Commerce*, 382 F. Supp. 3d 393, 402 (D. Md. 2019) (seemingly expanding scope of permissible circumstances for using depositions in subsequent cases even where parties in pending case were not parties in prior case, citing *Horne v. Owens-Corning-Fiberglas Corp.*, 4 F.3d 276, 283 (4th Cir. 1993) for notion that "privity is not the gravamen" of Rule 804(b)(1)).").

§15.09 Getting Transcripts from Other Cases

Now you know you can use transcripts (or videotaped deposition testimony) from other cases.

But how do you get them if you weren't a party? Perhaps a key fact witness in your case gave testimony in other, similar cases and you'd like to review it.

There are a few ways to do it.

One is to ask the parties to the other case. They may be willing to provide or obtain copies for you. Consent beats a battle every time. Unless the case and testimony involved confidential issues, this may be the shortest path to success. Even then, you can negotiate for appropriate redaction of extraneous matter.

Failing that, you might check the court files to see if the transcripts or video were filed. They often are.

You can also try asking the reporting agency to provide you copies upon payment of their ordinary charges. But be prepared for a swift rejection. Many agencies will not produce anything without the consent of all the parties to the other case.

If none of these approaches work, your only remaining option may be to issue a Rule 45 subpoena on the court reporter. There is nothing magic about it. Transcripts and video are well within the notion of "documents" under state and federal discovery rules. And the procedure is the same as for any non-party subpoena. Once you serve the subpoena, the reporter may serve objections and force you to seek an order compelling production (always upon payment of the ordinary costs of the transcript and video).

That's how events unfolded in my one my cases, *Magee v. Florida A & M University*, Case No. 6:19-MC-00038-RBD-DCI (M. D. Fla. July 11 2019). I was counsel in a federal lawsuit in the Northern District of Florida and needed a transcript and video of my client's prior testimony in an unrelated lawsuit three years earlier. I started by checking the court files. Some transcripts had been filed, but not the ones I needed.

Next, I asked the reporting agency. Their response? I could have them if all the parties consented or if a court ordered their release. I contacted all three parties. One consented. The other two ignored me.

On to federal court.

I initiated an ancillary action in the Middle District of Florida, for the whopping filing fee of $45, seeking an order compelling the agency to turn over the transcript and video. To its credit, the agency did not file an aggressive response. It merely said it considered the items confidential, and had declined to produce them without consent or an order. The judge quickly ordered the items produced upon payment of the reporter's typical fees.

Incidentally, the reporter had to transcribe my client's testimony because his transcript in the prior case had not been ordered by anyone. I paid for that and for the cost of the video.

§15.10 Authenticating Deposition Excerpts

How to use an excerpt of the deposition when filing dispositive or other motions? The key is authenticating the extract, which you do by ensuring that the deposition extract is accompanied by the cover page, the reporter's certification that the transcript is a true record of the testimony, and the reporter's signature. *See* Fed. R. Evid. 901(b); Rule 56(e) & 30(f)(1); *Beyene,* 854 F.2d at 1182; *Pavone v. Citicorp Credit Servs., Inc.,* 60 F.Supp.2d 1040, 1045 (S.D. Cal. 1997) (excluding a deposition for failure to submit a signed certification from the reporter); *Marketquest Group v. BIC Corporation* 2018 WL 2933518 (S.D. Cal. 2018).

Courts have deemed insufficient the submission, without more, of an affidavit from counsel identifying the names of the deponent, the reporter, and the action, and stating that the deposition is a "true and correct copy." *See Beyene, infra,* 854 F. 2d at 1182. Such an affidavit lacks foundation even if the affiant-counsel were present at the deposition. *See id.; Pavone,* 60 F.Supp.2d at 1045; *Orr v. Bank of Am., NT & SA,* 285 F. 3d 764, 774 (9th Cir. 2002) (cover page, reporter's certification); *Kelsey LLC v. Francis* 2009 WL 909530 (D. Ore. 2009) (same).

I recommend you include a bit more, specifically, the cover pages, interior pages up to the point where witnesses identify themselves, and the back pages, including the last page of testimony through the reporter's certificate (plus, of course, the interior pages containing your desired substantive content).

§15.11 Using Draft Transcripts

What if you don't have the final transcript - just a rough draft? My recommendation is to file it and to inform the court that the final is coming, assuming that is the case.

In *Delima v. Wal-Mart Stores Arkansas, LLC, Case No. 5:17-cv-5244-TLB (W.D. Ark. Dec. 21, 2018) (Memorandum Opinion and Order at ECF Doc. 77)*, delays and scheduling conflicts caused by the plaintiff prevented the court reporter from having more than an uncertified rough-draft transcript by the time summary judgment motions were due.

So that is what the defendant used in support of its motion. It did amend the motion and file the finalized transcript as soon as it was received, and the court deemed the situation resolved. No harm, no foul. So if that is all you have, go with it, and explain to the court the circumstances and the date by which you anticipate having a final, certified transcript. You can then file the proper version and ask the court to permit substitution.

AFTERWORD

We hope you found this book useful. We are genuinely grateful to you for purchasing it. Jim Garrity is widely considered the nation's leading expert on deposition procedure, and this book contains best thinking about deposition practice.

A few final thoughts.

Jim Garrity invites input. If you have tactics or strategies that you find effective in taking or defending depositions, Jim would love to hear about them, and possibly include them in the next revision of this book. You can communicate with him directly at Jim@JimGarrityLaw.com. (And if you have questions about specific deposition problems you're encountering, email him about those as well. He often responds directly, and may (with your prior express approval) post a generalized, non-identifiable response on the book's Facebook page to alert others to the problems and to his solutions.

Like and follow the Facebook page. Be sure to stop by the free companion Facebook page to this book. That's where Garrity regularly posts new tactics, strategies, and cases on depositions. Like and follow at www.Facebook/TenThousandDepositionsBook to receive his posts in your news feed.

Let us add you to our limited mailing list. A few times each year, Jim Garrity sends updates about new strategies and cases to a free, subscription-email group of litigators who've signed up to receive them. These come out before they appear on the Facebook page or in the next edition of the book. We'd love to add you to the list. He sends no more than four per year, and, typically, it's half that because he respects your time. Please email Josh Siskind, Director of Marketing, at JoshSiskind@RossAndRubin.com with "Please add me to the private email group mailing list" in the subject line. That's it. It's completely free.

Ask for a seminar. Jim Garrity regularly conducts live, full-day deposition seminars around the country. These programs receive rave reviews because they allow for direct interaction between Jim and litigators interested in sharpening their deposition skills. They also feature discussions of his newest insights and of cases released since the publication of this book. Interested? Reach out to Josh Siskind, our marketing director, at JoshSiskind@RossAndRubin.com for details.

Thank you again.

NOTES

1. Chief Functions Of The Deposition

1. One of Kahneman's favorite ways to show how easily people make cognitive errors is the bat and ball problem: "A bat and a ball cost $1.10 in total. The bat costs $1.00 more than the ball. How much does the ball cost?" If you went with the obvious, intuitive answer, you got it wrong. In fact, Kahneman posed this problem to students at elite US universities, and even those students got the answer wrong more often than not. The problem illustrates how we often rely on our own gut instincts to our detriment. You can find the correct answer online.

2. Tools for Capturing Testimony

1. Be mindful that, under certain circumstances, disclosures of work-product-protected materials could result in waiver., although disclosure in mediation may enjoy the benefit of a mediation privilege. *BouSamra v. Excela Health*, 210 A.3d 967, 978 (Pa. 2019) ("[W]e hold that the work product doctrine is waived when the work product is shared with an adversary, or disclosed in a manner which significantly increases the likelihood that an adversary or anticipated adversary will obtain it").
2. Order Barring Untimely Depositions, *Miller v. Department of Transportation*, Doc. 60, Case No. 4:08-CV-00356-RH-WCS (N. D. Fla. July 2, 2009).

3. Deposition Scheduling Issues

1. Note that once you properly notice a deposition, your opponent cannot unilaterally ignore it and/or wait until the last minute to seek a protective order. Such conduct is sanctionable. To illustrate, a Connecticut federal judge in July 2019 affirmed sanctions against a plaintiff for unilaterally deciding not to attend a properly-noticed deposition. The

plaintiff waited until a week before the deposition, then filed a motion for protective order. By waiting until the last minute, the plaintiff – who would have had to travel from Wisconsin to Connecticut – effectively thwarted the deposition from taking place as noticed. Said the judge: "There is nothing in the Federal Rules of Civil Procedure that permits a party to unilaterally withhold discovery as a self-help remedy.... [citations omitted].... As an experienced litigator, plaintiff's counsel undoubtedly knew that to obtain relief from the deposition notice the appropriate course of action was to file a motion for a protective order. ... Magistrate Judge Merriam properly determined that such manipulation of the Court and the discovery process cannot be countenanced by the Court." The case is *Christina Othon v. Wesleyan University*, No. 3:18-CV-00958 (KAD), 2019 WL 3051327 (D. Conn. July 12, 2019).

The key to the *Othon* outcome seems to be the judge's belief that the plaintiff purposely delayed filing the motion. Other courts say that filing a motion for protective order does excuse attendance at the deposition, even if the motion has not yet been ruled on. *Trident Atlanta, LLC, et al. v. Charlie Graingers Franchising, LLC, et al.*, No. 7:18-CV-00010-BO, 2019 WL 3162428, at *1 (E.D.N.C. July 15, 2019) (party's failure to appear is excused if party has pending motion for protective order under Rule 26(c), saying the rules require only that a motion be pending for the noticed party's absence to be excused, citing Rule 37(d)(2)).

2. *Evan v. Griffin*, __ F.3d __, 2019 WL 3720917 (7th Cir. Aug. 7, 2019) (citing a case where one day was held sufficient notice of a deposition because all counsel and parties were in the same city and already taking other depositions).
3. *See Leamon v. KBR, Inc., et al.*, 2011 WL 13340583, at *1 (S.D. Tex. Nov. 1, 2011) (general rule is that a plaintiff must make herself available for deposition in forum where action is brought, but court can issue protective order plaintiff be deposed in more convenient location than suit forum if plaintiff seeks protective order and provides evidence that traveling forum is unduly burdensome)

4. Subpoenas

1. EEOC v. CHIPOTLE MEXICAN GRILL, INC., et al., No. 17CV05382BLFSVK, 2019 WL 3842004, at *3 (N.D. Cal. Aug. 15, 2019) ("Rule 45(g) states that the court for the district where compliance with

a subpoena is required "may hold in contempt a person who, having been served, fails without adequate excuse to obey the subpoena or an order related to it." "[W]hen a non-party does not comply with a subpoena and does not appear for deposition, the most appropriate procedural step is to file an application for an order to show cause, not a motion to compel." Martinez v. City of Pittsburg, No. C 11-1017 SBA (LB), 2012 WL 699462, at *4 (N.D. Cal. Mar. 1, 2012) (citations omitted); see also AngioScore, Inc. v. TriReme Med., Inc., No. 12-CV-03393-YGR(JSC), 2014 WL 6706898, at *1 (N.D. Cal. Nov. 25, 2014) ("Under Federal Rule of Civil Procedure 37, a party may move for an order compelling discovery or a disclosure; ordinarily, however, subpoena related motions are filed under Federal Rule of Civil Procedure 45.")."

2. See also *Wells Fargo Bank NA v. Wyo Tech Inv. Grp. LLC, et al.*, No. CV-17-04140-PHX-DWL, 2019 WL 4101338, at *7 (D. Ariz. Aug. 29, 2019) ("As noted in an earlier order (Doc. 119 at 12 & n.3), the test for "relevance," in the context of a Rule 45 subpoena to a non-party, is no different than the test under Rules 26 and 34. *See, e.g., Transcor, Inc. v. Furney Charters, Inc.*, 212 F.R.D. 588, 591 (D. Kan. 2003) ("It is well settled...that the scope of discovery under a subpoena is the same as the scope of discovery under Rule 26(b) and Rule 34. Thus, the court must examine whether a request contained in a subpoena duces tecum is overly broad or seeking irrelevant information under the same standards set forth in Rule 26(b) and as applied to Rule 34 requests for production."); Fed. R. Civ. P. 45, advisory committee notes to 1970 amendment ("[T]he scope of discovery is the same as that applicable to Rule 34 and the other discovery rules."); S. Gensler, 1 Federal Rules of Civil Procedure, Rules and Commentary, Rule 45, at 1189 (2018) ("The scope of information that may be sought via subpoena is the same as the scope of discovery generally under Rule 26(b)."). Under Rule 26(b)(1), "[p]arties may obtain discovery regarding any nonprivileged matter that is relevant to any party's claim or defense and proportional to the needs of the case." Fed. R. Civ. P. 26(b)(1). Relevance "has been construed broadly to encompass any matter that bears on, or that reasonably could lead to other matter that could bear on, any issue that is or may be in the case." *Oppenheimer Fund, Inc. v. Sanders*, 437 U.S. 340, 351 (1978). However, non-parties are entitled to special consideration in the Rule 45 context when "weigh[ing] the burden to the subpoenaed party against the value of the information to the serving party." *Soto v. Castlerock Farming & Transport, Inc.*, 282 F.R.D. 492, 504 (E.D. Cal. 2012)."

5. Audiotaping and Videotaping

1. If you often take video depositions, ask a video production company what they offer and charge. You are not limited to court reporter-provided videographers, who are rarely trained in camera shooting techniques, cinematography and set lighting. Far better is available, at the same or lesser cost.
2. Some reporters have begun offering videographers who have earned "certifications" to use a video camera in depositions. Call me cynical, but I suspect such certifications were created solely to provide a better response to your question "So do you know how you do this?" than "Why, yes! I'm holding this camera!" Now the response will be, "Why yes! I'm *certified* to hold this camera!"

6. Court Reporters

1. As the court reporting industry consolidates through the acquisition of smaller agencies by larger national ones, I am increasingly seeing exorbitant charges for transcripts and related services, including wildly excessive per-page rates, photocopy charges, after-hours deposition charges, and "shipping fees" even when transcripts are delivered by email alone. I am not aware of current statutory or other legal ceilings on reporter fees, and so for now, lawyers are largely at the mercy of such practices. Perhaps the reckoning will come when courts refuse to award costs for exorbitant reporter charges, which in turn will motivate lawyers in large numbers to refuse to use agencies unless they adjust their rates.
2. *Choy v. Comcast Cable Commc'ns, Inc.*, No. CV 08-4092(RBK), 2015 WL 12835103, at *2 (D.N.J. Mar. 31, 2015), citing *Smith v. U.S. District Court Officers*, 203 F.3d 440, 442 (7th Cir. 2000) (where audiotape merely backs up reporter's stenographic record, that recording is not part of judicial record subject to inspection "unless some reason is shown to distrust the accuracy of the stenographic transcript." *See also In re Pratt*, 511 F.3d 483, 485 (5th Cir. 2007); *YHWHnewBN v. Bd. of Educ.*, 173 Fed.Appx. 518, 520 (7th Cir. 2006); *U.S. v. Kopp*, No. 00–CR–189A, 2007 WL 1461326, at *1 (W.D.N.Y. May 16, 2007); *see also Karakozova v. Trs. of Univ. of Pennsylvania*, No. 09–02564, 2011 WL 238711, at *3 (E.D. Pa. Jan. 21, 2011) (request

for back-up audio recording of deposition denied where plaintiff cannot establish a reason to distrust the accuracy of the transcript).

7. Witness Capacity & Characteristics

1. In a somewhat unique situation, a judge allowed the plaintiffs' deposition testimony to be admitted against the deceased defendant because the depositions were taken while the defendant was still alive. Thus the statutory incompetency imposed by the Pennsylvania Dead Man's statute did not apply because competency – legal or otherwise – is measured at the time the testimony is taken. *Hart. V. Friedman*, 29 F.R.D. 2 (1961).
2. If you represent a litigant who truly cannot afford to pay a large fee to depose the opposing expert, consider Rule 26(b)(4)€, which allows the judge to relieve a party of the obligation to do so if manifest injustice would result. For a discussion of the "manifest injustice" standard, and some nuances associated with expert cost-shifting, see *Reed v. Binder*, 165 F.R.D. 424 (D.N.J. 1996), where the court relieved the 'impoverished' plaintiffs in a medical malpractice case of the cost of paying six defense experts for their testimony at deposition. The court's analysis acknowledges the fuzziness of the "manifest injustice" standard and the fact that plaintiffs, in particular, are not always obligated to pay costs under their fee agreements with counsel. On that note, see *Morales-Arcadio v. Shannon Produce Farm, Inc.*, 2007 WL 9709805, at *2 (S.D. Ga. Nov. 14, 2007) (cost-avoidance disallowed where migrant field laborers were represented for free by legal services organization and had no obligation to bear case-related costs).
3. *Colonial Capital Co. v. Gen. Motors Corp.*, 29 F.R.D. 514, 517 (D. Conn. 1961) (affidavits submitted); *Mulvey v. Chrysler Corp.*, 106 F.R.D. 364, 365 (D.R.I. 1985) (affidavits submitted).

9. Taking Depositions

1. As an aside, the only thing I do that seems to inexplicably irk opposing lawyers more than audiorecording depositions with the Zoom H5 is placing my Canon Pixma ip110 printer on the table. Not *in their way*. Just *somewhere* on the table. (It occupies a space equal to a sheet of 8 ½"

x 11" paper.) As best I can tell, placing the printer on the table sends the message to opposing lawyers that this is my deposition, too, and that I'm using revelations from their questions to craft highly-specific discovery requests. One lawyer, ordinarily a complete gentleman, asked me in total exasperation not to bring a printer to his depositions again. I meant no disrespect, but I suspect he could tell from when he'd hear bursts of typing that I was using specific questions as guides for my next round of discovery.

2. A thorough understanding of the many types of cognitive biases is essential for trial lawyers. A cognitive bias, put simply, is a lens through which we tend to view and process information. Appreciation for this phenomenon will help you better understand how witnesses, judges and jurors might see a situation depending on the witness' own experiences. That, in turn, will likely cause you to rethink how you might pose questions to certain witnesses, how you argue matters to your judge, and how you present to a jury. A good overview of dozens of cognitive biases can be found on Wikipedia by searching for "List of Cognitive Biases."
3. A lawyer's objection tactics in depositions sometimes remind me of the child's game "Hot or Cold," where an object is hidden and one child is chosen to hunt for it. As the hunter moves away from the object, others shout "cold!", "colder!", or "freezing!" to tell the hunter she is moving in the wrong direction. When the hunter is moving closer, the shouts turn to "hot!", "hotter!", "burning!" or "scorching!".

   Sometimes objections resemble this. The closer you get to your hidden objective, the more aggressive and frequent your adversary's objections, which can tell you all you need to know.
4. Note that Rule 32(d)(3)(B)(i) expressly applies to both questions and answers. In other words, objections to defects in answers to questions, such as where an answer is non-responsive or is speculative, are also waived unless made at the time of the deposition or unless agreement to preserve such objections were made. *See Rosary-Take One Production Company Limited Partnership v. New Line Distribution, Inc., 1996 WL 79328 at *2 (S. D. N. Y. Feb. 23, 1996) (discussing application of Rule 32's waiver provisions to answers as well as questions).*

11. Creating Invincible Deponents - Part 2

1. I appreciate that these are approximations of the standards, but they make the point well enough with clients.

12. FRCP 30(b)(6) Depositions

1. A useful case on the topic of bandying is *Updike v. Clackamas County*, No. 3:15-CV-723-SI, 2016 U.S. Dist. LEXIS 2783 at *4-5 (D. Or. Jan 11. 2016). You can find the specific Opinion and Order on PACER at Document 40.
2. As a practice note, you could prepare a notice with the full list of topics, send it to opposing counsel, and then negotiate agreement to cover half the topics in one deposition and half in a subsequent deposition.
3. Note that production of documents, before, during or after a Rule 30(b)(6) deposition, is not a substitute for the deposition itself. Some entities have argued that they should not have to prepare a witness for a 30(b)(6) deposition if they've produced documents or served interrogatory answers that address the topics. Most courts reject this argument out of hand. *E.g., CRST Expedited, Inc. v. Swift Transportation Co. of Arizona, LLC*, No. 17-CV-25-CJW-KEM, 2019 WL 2714508, at *5 (N.D. Iowa Mar. 6, 2019) (producing documents and responding to written discovery is not a substitute for providing a thoroughly educated Rule 30(b)(6) deponent).
4. Sometimes the language may seem overbroad even if it isn't. For example in *Lessert v. BNSF Railway Company*, 2019 WL 3431282 (D. South Dakota July 30, 2019), the plaintiff used the phrases "in any form" and "any tangible things" in his topics. The defendant objected. The court ruled that, when these terms were read in context, they were limited by the information being sought, and thus were not overbroad and did not impose an undue burden.

13. Expert Witness Depositions

1. And courts routinely reject purported expert testimony where it isn't up to snuff. *Eberli v. Cirrus Design Corp.*, 615 F. Supp. 2d 1357, 1367 (S.D. Fla.

2009) (order rejecting expert, saying, "[t]his opinion is exactly the type of speculation that the Rules of Evidence attempt to preclude.). So buyer beware when hiring experts.

14. Objections and Obstructions

1. *Golato v. Gillespie,* 70 Pa. D. & C.2d 15, 20 (Pa. Com. Pl. 1975) ("The mere existence of some annoyance, embarrassment or oppression, or the mere imposition of some expense is not ground to forbid discovery or inspection. See Mackowain v. Gulf Oil Corp., 13 Monroe 109 (1951), appeal dismissed as premature, 369 Pa. 581, 87 A. 2d 314 (1952); Dorfman v. Phila. Transportation Co., 79 Pa. D. & C. 380 (1952), c.f. Fed. R. Civ. P. 30(d); Canuso v. City of Niagara Falls, 7 F.R.D. 159 (W.D.N.Y. 1945); Application of Zenith Radio Corp., 1 F.R.D. 627 (E.D. Pa. 1941); Goldberg v. Raleigh Manufacturers, Inc., 28 F. Supp. 975 (D. Mass. 1939).).
2. Otis v. Demarasse2019 WL 1778955 (E.D. Wis. Apr .23, 2019) ("The fact that Plaintiff's counsel didn't know or care whether the form of his question was improper is not a reason for the witness' attorney to refrain from objecting").
3. Otis v. Demarasse, No. 16-C-285, 2019 WL 1778955, at *5–6 (E.D. Wis. Apr. 23, 2019).

Made in the USA
Columbia, SC
12 August 2020